JN411232

An Interdisciplinary Introduction to German Law

An Interdisciplinary Introduction to

German Law

Judith Janna Märtens & Ulf Märtens

Korea University Press
145, Anam-ro, Seongbuk-gu, Seoul, 02841 Republic of Korea

ISBN: 978-89-7641-833-3 93360

Printed in Republic of Korea

For Robin Friedrich

Foreword

As a professor of law and former president of the Korea University, I have always been conscious about the relevance of German Law in academia and in legal practice in Korea.

In my own university career, I completed my Dr. iur. in law at the University of Tübingen with a scholarship of the German Academic Exchange Service (DAAD) and the Konard-Adenauer Foundation, and until today, it is my pleasure to be intensively involved in the Korean-German relationships.

Hence, I am familiar with the authors. Mrs. Dr. Judith Märtens is DAAD-lecturer for law in Korea and Professor at Korea University and Mr. Ulf Märtens is Professor for German Studies at Korea University Sejong Campus. Both authors represent German academia in the very best way in Korea since years. This book is their latest contribution on this mission.

With its interdisciplinary approach to German law, culture and history, the book covers a wide range of academic content, addressing itself to students of various disciplines. It can be considered as a basic textbook for students, professors and also legal practitioners dealing with the topic of German law, German legal culture and Germany in general.

hon. Professor Dr. Dr. h.c. mult. Ki-Su Lee
17th President Emeritus, Korea University.
Chairperson & CEO, Korean Arbitrators Association, Inc.

Geleitwort

Aufgrund der Intensivierung wechselseitiger Beziehungen zwischen den Staaten der heutigen Zeit, entwickelt sich die Welt durch immer zunehmenden wirtschaftlichen, kulturellen und institutionellen Austausch zu einer echten Völkergemeinschaft. Es ist daher eine Aufforderung unserer Zeit, die Geschichte, Kultur und Rechtsinstitute anderer Länder kennenzulernen und richtig zu verstehen.

Das vorligende Lehrbuch von Frau Professorin Dr. Judith Märtens und Herrn Professor Ulf Märtens stellt für mich ein gelungenes Werk zur Einführung in das deutsche Recht dar. Es kann nicht nur für die Studenten in juristischer Ausbildung, sondern auch für die Juristen in der Praxis sehr nützlich sein, zumal das koreanische Recht durch die Rezeption der deutschen Rechtswissenschaft nach dem kontinental-europäischen System aufgebaut worden ist.

Dieses Buch erläutert vorerst, im Gegensatz zu anderen juristischen Büchern, die Carakteristika der deutschen Kultur und Geschichte, überblickt dann die deutschen Rechtsinstitute im Ganzen, und stellt die wesentlichen Inhalte des öffentlichen Rechts (Verfassungs- und Verwaltungsrecht), des Zivilrechts (Grundprinzipien, Vertrags- und Deliktsrecht), des Strafrechts, des Arbeitsrechts (Kündigungsschutz, bezahlter Urlaub, Betriebsverfassung), und wichtige Arten des Prozessrechts sehr taktvoll und originell dar. Zum Schluß behandelt es das EU-Recht und die europäischen Menschenrechte im Zusammenhang der Supranationalisierung des Rechts und weist auf die Zukunft des Verhältnisses zwischen der EU und deren Mitgliedsstaaten hin, was uns in Korea auch viele Anregungen bietet.

Dieses Buch ist zwar eine Einführung im Umfang von ca. 200 Seiten, enthält aber systematische und inhaltsreiche Informationen mit neuen Aspekten. Es ist daher als eine zeitgemäße Einführung in das deutsche Recht sehr empfehlenswert.

Korea Universität Law School
Prof. em. Dr. Hyung-Bae Kim

Preface

The idea of this textbook grounds in the concept of the lecture "German Culture and Germany Law" at Korea University created and held by Professor Dr. Judith Janna Märtens. The aim of both the lecture and the book is to provide students, practitioners and scholars basic information on German law explained in a systematic manner. Moreover, the concept refers to an interdisciplinary approach to law which is done by culture. This is based on the perfection that the understanding of a foreign legal system is interconnected to particular cultural conditions of that country. Readers don't have to bring any previous knowledge of law studies. For readers who are also interested in learning German, selected terms are provided in German language.

Both authors are fully qualified lawyers with the qualification of a judge in Germany. Professor Dr. Judith Janna Märtens is Lecturer for Law of the German Academic Exchange Service (DAAD) and Professor at Korea University, first at Law School and then at the College for Public Administration at Korea University Sejong Campus. Professor Ulf Märtens is Professor for German Studies at the College of Global Business at Korea University Sejong Campus. Besides law, he also obtained a Masters-degree in history. He gained several practical experiences as an attorney in Berlin, specialized in employment law and criminal law.

The textbook is conceptualized as a systematic approach to the different fields of law by putting a focus on codified law. Due to the broad topic, the textbook can merely refer to basic and selected aspects without demanding to provide all-embracing information. Finally, we would like to thank Professor Dr. Judith Janna Märtens teaching assistant, Mr. Joonwoo Lee, for reviewing the whole book such as Mr. Jerry Bordeleau and Mr. Michael Langenohl for critical comments on the history chapter.

Seoul
Judith Janna Märtens & Ulf Märtens
March 2021

Contents

Chapter 4 Public Law

Chapter 5 Private Law

Chapter 6 Criminal Law

Chapter 7 Employment Law

Chapter 8 Law Procedure

Chapter 9 The European Union and European Human Rights

Chapter 1

Selected Aspects on German Culture

I. Introduction — the Interconnectedness of Culture and Law

To begin with, the word "culture" is recognized as a very broad term as it refers to plenty of aspects that describe the behavior and values of people in certain societies. In this context, firstly, culture comprises history, religion, domestic traditions and culture in a narrow sense which is related to art, literature and other cultural traditions practiced in society. Secondly, culture refers to the organization of the state and the political powers such as values in society including religion. This includes the question of legitimation of state power and democracy such as politics. Finally, culture is connected to law and justice since cultural values are the basis for legal interpretation and the "motor" for new legislation. Moreover, jurisprudence is bringing the law into force and has, therefore, a strong impact on society and standards of freedoms such as public security. Hence, there is an interconnectedness of Culture and Law.[1]

The interdisciplinary approach to law is shaped by this interconnectedness of Culture and Law. In order to become even more precious, the term culture should focus on its aspects of "legal culture" (*Rechtskultur*).[2] Instead of a holistic approach to the broad field of culture, the more specific approach to legal culture will refer to cultural developments and phenomena setting values which have influenced the law and jurisprudence. These aspects are explained in the context of German history in chapter one and selected aspects of German culture in chapter two of this book.

Vice versa, relevant issues of German law and jurisprudence will draw a picture of cultural developments. The basic structure of the German legal system will show the wide range of rights German citizens have and how

---

1) For further information *see* Julian Krüper(ed.), *Grundlagen des Rechts*, 2017, pp. 279–291.

2) *See* Ingo von Münch, *NJW* 1993, p. 1637.

these rights developed during the decades. Besides, the jurisprudence of German courts will reveal the meaning of certain rights. This will illustrate both the importance of individual rights and the meaning of other liberal values within German society. Therefore, the legal system is also able to mirror the legal culture.

II. Basic Facts — Area Studies of Germany

As for its geography, Germany is in the centre of Europe between the 6th and 15th degree of longitude east and the 47th and 55th degree of latitude north. Germany has two shores, one in the north-west to the North Sea and one the north-east to the Baltic Sea. By its topography, the north of Germany appears as a flat landscape, partly even hills are rarely seen. This area is called the North-German Lowlands, as a part of a landscape, which starts in Flanders/ Belgium and ranges until Russia. The middle of Germany exists mostly by low-mountain ranges, also ranging from the western border to the eastern borders of Germany. Going south, the landscape mounts high up to the peaks of the Alps with its permanent snow.

The weather in Germany is determined by four seasons and can be very different depending on the region. Located in the centre of Europe, the west of Germany has an oceanic climate, the east of Germany is of a continental climate. All-over the climate in Germany is mild. The highest average temperatures are in July with 21,8 degree Celsius, the lowest average temperatures are in January around minus 2,8 degree Celsius.[3] These average temperatures can contain days in summer with temperatures of more than 35 degrees Celsius as days in winter with less than minus 15 degrees Celsius. Snow can fall between the months of October and April. The sunniest regions of Germany are at the German northeast at the Baltic Sea coast on the islands of Usedom and Rügen, as well as in the southwest of Germany with 1,805 sunny hours in 2017. Other regions such as German northwest, where the clouds come from the North Sea, have shorter periods of sunshine (1,410–1,500 sun hours in 2017) and higher amounts of rainfall.[4]

The highest mountains of Germany are the Zugspitze with 2,962 meters, its neighbour peak Schneefernerkopf (2,875 meters), the Hochwanner (2,744 meters) and the Watzmann (2,713 meters). All of these mountains are located in the Bavarian Alps near the border to Austria in the German southwest.

The longest river through Germany is the River Rhine (*Rhein*). 865 kilo-

3) https://www.tatsachen-ueber-deutschland.de/de/rubriken/auf-einen-blick/geografie-klima. (15.07.2018).

4) https://de.statista.com/statistik/daten/studie/249925/umfrage/sonnenstunden-im-jahr-nach-bundeslaendern/ (15.07.2018).

metres of its total length of 1,233 kilometres flows through the western part of Germany from south to north. The second-longest river of Europe, the River Danube (*Donau*), has its spring in the town Furtwangen, in the southwest of Germany. 647 kilometres of its total length of 2,857 kilometres are running through the German south from west to east. Other big rivers are the River Weser and its headwater streams River Werra and River Fulda with 750 kilometres in the German northwest, the River Elbe running from the Czech-German border in the southeast to the North Sea in the north with a length of 727 kilometres in Germany, the River Main with 569 kilometres in Middle-west-Germany and the River Havel with 560 kilometres in East-Germany. The largest lakes are the Lake Constance (*Bodensee*) in the south of Germany at the borders of Switzerland and Austria with 536 km^2 and the Lake Müritz in Northeast-Germany with 117km^2. When checking water quality in 2017, out of 2.287 bathing waters, almost 93% were assessed of excellent water quality.[5] While the drinking water quality was assessed mostly as very good in the past, it has been criticised for being contaminated in small amounts with nitrate by agriculture at last.[6] All-in-all, more than 2% of Germany exists by waters.[7]

Germany is also typical for its forests; Germany is one of the most densely wooded countries in Europe. With more than 11.4 million hectare and around 90 billion trees, almost a third of its area exists by forests.[8] The biggest part of these forests is planted and used for forestry operations.[9] Only 1% of the German forests are untouched primeval forests. 56% of the forests in Germany are conifers, 44% are deciduous woodlands. The most existing tree species are spruce (25%), pine (23%), beech (15%) and oak (10%).[10] As a result of global warming, spruces are disappearing massively from German forests and are replaced by trees which are able to stand warmer temperatures.

Germany is a country of high biological diversity with around 48,000 domestic animal species and 24,000 domestic plant species.[11] Among the big-

5) https://www.umweltbundesamt.de/wasserqualitaet-in-badegewaessern (12.09.2020).

6) https://www.umweltbundesamt.de/themen/fakten-zur-nitratbelastung in grund trinkwasser (12.09.2020).

7) https://www.tatsachen-ueber-deutschland.de/de/rubriken/auf-einen-blick/geografie-klima (12.09.2020).

8) https://www.bundeswaldinventur.de/index.php?id=665 (Bundesministerium für Ernährung und Landwirtschaft) (15.07.2018).

9) https://www.bundeswaldinventur.de/index.php?id=710 (Bundesministerium für Ernährung und Landwirtschaft) (15.07.2018).

10) Waldbericht der Bundesregierung 2017, https://www.bmel-statistik.de/fileadmin/user_upload/monatsberichte/FHB-0320126-2017.pdf, (Bundesministerium für Ernährung und Landwirtschaft) (21.08.2018).

11) https://www.bfn.de/fileadmin/BfN/presse/2015/Dokumente/Artenschutzreport_Download.pdf, Bundesamt für Naturschutz, Artenschutzreport 2015 – Tiere und Pflanzen in Deutschland, S. 13; URL (12.09.2020).

ger animals, cows and also horses can be easily observed in the agricultural areas of Germany. The German forests are home for roughly 140 vertebrate species.[12] Since the fall-down of the border fences to the Eastern European states also wolves and lynxes have returned to the forests of Germany.

In fact, the current external borders of Germany were drawn after the end of World War 2 in 1945. On the whole, Germany got common borders to nine other European nations, which are Denmark, the Netherlands, Belgium, Luxemburg, France, Switzerland, Austria, the Czech Republic and Poland. These borders are partly natural borders as there is the North Sea in the northwest, the Baltic Sea (*Ostsee*) in the northeast, the eastern border by the rivers Oder and Neisse (Oder-Neisse-line), the Alps and the Lake Constance in the south and the Upper-Rhine in the southwest. The other parts of the borders are political borders.

The Federal Republic of Germany is a member of the European Union and also of the system of the protection of European Human Rights (see, European Convention on Human Rights). Moreover, Germany is a member of the United Nations, NATO, G7 (formally G8), G20 and the OECD. As a federal republic, Germany exists by 16 federal states, which differ in 13 area states and 3 city states. The area states are always first the english name in straight letters, then in brackets the german names in italic letters: *Schleswig-Holstein*, Lower Saxony (*Niedersachsen*), North-Rhine-Westphalia (*Nordrhein-Westfalen*), Hesse (*Hessen*), Rhineland-Palatinate (*Rheinland-Pfalz*), *Saarland*, *Baden-Württemberg*, Bavaria (*Bayern*), Mecklenburg-West Pomerania (*Mecklenburg-Vorpommern*), *Brandenburg*, Saxony-Anhalt (*Sachsen-Anhalt*), Thuringia (*Thüringen*) and Sachsen (*Sachsen*). The city states are Berlin, Bremen and Hamburg.

Germany's capital is Berlin, which is also the largest city in the country with around 3.6 million inhabitants. Other important mayor cities are Hamburg, which is home to the biggest seaport of Germany, with 1.8 million inhabitants, Munich (*München*), the capitol of the state of Bavaria (*Bayern*), with a population of 1.5 million, Cologne (*Köln*), famous for its cathedral, with around 1.1 million inhabitants, and Frankfurt (*Frankfurt am Main*), the financial capitol of Germany and the European Union, with 736,000 inhabitants. Other big cities are Bremen, Hannover, Düsseldorf, Dortmund, Bonn, Stuttgart, Karlsruhe, Leipzig and Dresden.

82.6 million people live in Germany today.[13] More than 20% of these peo-

---

12) https://www.waldkulturerbe.de/fileadmin/Publikationen/UnserWald_WEB_doppelseitige_Ansicht.pdf, Bundesministerium für Ernährung und Landwirtschaft, Unser Wald – Natur aus Försterhand, p. 45 (21.08.2018).

13) https://www.tatsachen-ueber-deutschland.de/de/rubriken/gesellschaft/bereichernde-vielfalt (12.09.2020).

ple have a migration background,[14] which means that they or at least one of their parents have not been born in Germany.[15] Around 77% of Germany's population is living in cities or metropolitan areas, while around 15% is living in villages, which means settlements with less than 5,000 inhabitants.[16]

III. The German State

The structure of the German state is regulated in the German constitution Basic Law (*Grundgesetz*) in Article 20 Basic Law:

> (1) The Federal Republic of Germany is a democratic and social federal state.
> (2) All state authority is derived from the people. It shall be exercised by the people through elections and other votes and through specific legislative, executive and judicial bodies.
> (3) The legislature shall be bound by the constitutional order, the executive and the judiciary by law and justice.
> (4) All Germans shall have the right to resist any person seeking to abolish this constitutional order, if no other remedy is available.

From this as also by other regulations of the constitution as e.g. Article 20a Basic Law [Protection of the natural foundations of life and animals] descend the principles of the temporary German state.

1. The Federal State

Article 20 para. 1 Basic Law defines the German state as a federal republic. Due to this provision, federalism (*Föderalismus*) determines the state structure and organization as state power in Germany is practiced on different levels. First of all, Germany consists of sixteen constituent states (*Bundesländer*), which are secondly, further subdivided into districts (*Kreise*) and cities (*kreisfreie Städte*) and finally communities (*Gemeinden*) on the lowest level.

In fact, federalism refers to the mixed or compound mode of government

14) https://www.tatsachen-ueber-deutschland.de/de/jugend/offene-gesellschaft/offen-fuer-neue-buerger (12.09.2020).

15) https://www.bamf.de/DE/Service/Left/Glossary/_function/glossar.html?lv3=3198544 (27.10.2018).

16) https://www.deutschland.de/de/topic/leben/stadt-und-land-fakten-zu-urbanisierung-und-landflucht (12.09.2020).

by combining a general government on the federal level with the regional governments in one system. Both the national government and the smaller political subdivisions have the legal power to make laws and both have a certain level of autonomy from each other. Especially the organisation of the public administration is characterized by the federal structure of Germany and also by the autonomy of the lower subdivisions.[17] For reasons of decentralisation and participation, as much power and competence as possible are transferred from the federal level to the respective lower level of the federal states. Federalism in Germany is actually characterised by its cooperation between the states and the federal level.[18]

Compared to other states, as for example the United States of America, this kind of a federal state structure is quite unique. One important aspect is that living conditions are not supposed to be too different between countryside and cities. The achievement of equal living conditions (*Gleichwertigkeit der Lebensverhältnisse*) is even one aim of the German policies as mentioned in the constitution. As stated in Article 72 para. 2 Basic Law:

> The Federation shall have the right to legislate on matters (...) if and to the extent that the establishment of equivalent living conditions throughout the federal territory or the maintenance of legal or economic unity renders federal regulation necessary in the national interest.

2. The Democratic State

Germany is a democratic country as it is determined in Article 20 para. 1 Basic Law. The term democracy is meant as a parliamentarian democracy, in which political parties can be elected for representing the will of the people in a parliament.

Thus, the political system of the Federal Republic of Germany is based on free elections, which are held since the beginning in 1949. Due to its' importance for the democratic society, free elections are guaranteed by article 38 Basic Law and even the political parties have their right as important institutions within the German state which is guaranteed und der Article 21 Basic Law.[19] Both aspects will be explained in more details later since they are important aspects of German public law. The political parties transmit and bundle the different wills and interests in society and form a political will, which

17) *See also* Richard Haase and Rolf Keller, *Grundlagen und Grundformen des Rechts*, 2003, pp. 352–353.

18) Heinz Laufer and Ursula Münch, *Das föderative System der Bundesrepublik Deutschland*, 2006, p. 247.

19) For further information *see* Chapter 4.

can be presented and forced on political and parliamentary stage.[20] Insofar, parties are the core element of modern parliamentarianism.[21] Reaching the 5% of all the votes in an election, a party can enter the German Parliament.[22]

In the legal context, a political party is defined as an association of citizens who aim at influencing the political views of the public and participating in the representation of the German people in the parliament or in a state legislature for a long or indefinite period of time.[23] According to article 39 para. 1 Basic Law, the election of the federal German parliament is held every fourth year. Basically, the structure of political parties in Germany is self-financing, which means that parties rely on membership fees and donations. Moreover, to a certain extend a public financial support is possible (*Parteienfinanzierung*) in order to provide especially smaller parties realising their political work. The public financial support of political parties started in the 1960s and became even more comprehensive than in other established democracies by concerning several aspects as a fair and transparent concept of support.[24] As a result, the goal to establish a democratic structure with a variety of political opinions worked out successfully.

The major political parties in Germany, usually represented in the parliaments, are the Social-Democratic Party of Germany (*Sozialdemokratische Partei Deutschlands, SPD*), the conservative Christian Democratic Union (*Christlich-Demokratische Union, CDU*), and its even more conservative sister party in Bavaria (*Christlich-Soziale Union, CSU*), the neoliberal Free Democratic Party (*Freie Demokratische Partei, FDP*) such as the party The Left (*Die Linke*), the ecologically-orientated Alliance 90/The Greens (*Bündnis 90/Die Grünen*) and recently the right-winged orientated party Alternative for Germany (*Alternative für Deutschland, AfD*).

3. The Social State

As stated in article 20 para. 1 Basic Law, the Federal Republic of Germany is a democratic and *social* federal state. Moreover, article 28 para. 1 Basic Law points out explicitly that it is a social constitutional state under the rule of law (*sozialer Rechtsstaat*). The guarantee of this principle of the social state (*Sozialstaatsprinzip*) is also quite unique compared to other democratic states since it is the aim of the state, codified on the constitutional level. In conjunc-

20) *See* Gerhard Robbers, *German Law*, 2017, p. 62.
21) Stefan Marschall, *Parlamentarismus*, 2016, p. 62.
22) For further information *see* Chapter 4.
23) Gerhard Robbers, *German Law*, 2017, pp. 62–63.
24) Martin Morlok, "Spenden – Rechenschaft – Sanktionen, Aktuelle Rechtsfragen der Parteienfinanzierung," *NJW* 2000, p. 761.

tion with the order to respect and protect human dignity, the principle of the social state obliges all state organs to provide for social conditions that are compatible with human dignity.[25] The concept of the social state is actually closely connected with the idea of a welfare state (*Wohlfahrtsstaat*). Under a broad and common definition, a welfare state involves state responsibility for securing some basic modicum of welfare for its citizens.[26]

In fact, the concept of the social state has a long tradition in German history since the first welfare system was already introduced by the Prussian statesman Otto von Bismarck (1815–1898) by bringing up a system of social security insurances (*Sozialversicherungen*).[27] The costs of these insurances were distributed on the workers as well as on the employers. At first this welfare system focused merely on special situations and matters of health and invalidity. However, this concept later developed in a comprehensive welfare and social system which now also aims to establish equal social standards and social security for all citizens within the German state.[28] Today, the principle of the social state is realized by several regulations and provisions based on federal statute laws (*Sozialgesetzgebung*), which provide a minimum standard of living under acceptable conditions (*Existenzminimum*) such as several forms of social security. The right to social security is not only provided for the weakest in society but rather for everybody including the working middle class. The concept of social security in Germany is based on the idea of a society, including every citizen, as a community of solidarity (*Solidargemeinscheinschaft*). The various types of social insurances are codified in several books of German Social Codes (*Sozialgesetzbücher, SGB*) that guarantee health insurance (*SGB V*), pension insurance for elderly people (*SGB VI*), invalidity insurance (*SGB VII* and *IX*), child support (*SGB VIII*), social care (*SGB XI*) and finally unemployment insurance and public employment agencies (*SGB II* and *III*).

4. The Green State

In fact, environmental policies and laws have a strong tradition in the Federal Republic of Germany, which finds its roots in the so-called green movement of German citizens decades ago. The early beginnings of this movement were in the 70's and 80's of the last century when the anti-nuclear protest movement commenced by massive protests of German citizens who were

---

25) Gerhard Robbers, *German Law*, 2017, p. 51.

26) Costa Esping-Andersen, *The three worlds of welfare capitalism*, 1998, p. 19.

27) Manfred. G. Schmidt, *Der Deutsche Sozialstaat – Geschichte und Gegenwart*, 2012, pp. 10–11.

28) Andreas Voßkuhle and Thomas Wischmeyer, "Grundwissen – Öffentliches Recht: Das Sozialstaatsprinzip," *JuS* 2015, p. 693.

demonstrating in Wackersdorf and nationwide after the catastrophe of Chernobyl in 1986. This was also the time when the political Green Party (Bündnis 90/Die Grünen) was founded and became more and more powerful during the last decades. Today, green policies are an important issue in public life in Germany. After the nuclear catastrophe in Fukushima in Japan in 2011, Germany started the nuclear power phase-out (*Atomausstieg*) and focuses on renewable energies. By the end of 2022, Germany will shut down all nuclear power reactors in the country. This is also part of the energy transition (*Energiewende*) that works on a long-term structural change to use sustainable energy instead of producing energy nuclear power, coal and oil. This change is part of the agenda to protect from the global climate change (*Klimawandel*) and especially from global warming (*Erderwärmung*).

Environmental law (*Umweltrecht*) and protection of animals (*Tierschutz*) is one important part of the public law within the German legal system and, moreover, an aspect which is characteristic to German legal culture. While the environmental law and the protection of animals generally belongs to specific administrative law such as partly to criminal law, there are many relevant regulations on the level of European Union Law. Therefore, especially the environmental law is recognized as a field of law consisting of a framework of regulations and a law influenced by many changes and recent developments.

Regarding the law, firstly, the importance of Germany's green policies is illustrated in the German Constitution under Article 20a Basic Law [Protection of the natural foundations of life and animals] by expressing explicitly the protection of nature as an aim of the German state:

> Mindful also of its responsibility toward future generations, the state shall protect the natural foundations of life and animals by legislation and, in accordance with law and justice, by executive and judicial action, all within the framework of the constitutional order.

The protection of the natural foundations of life and animal protection under the German constitution which came into force in 1994 is quite unique compared to other countries.[29] This goal is concretised in several codified laws on the level of ordinary law in the field of public law which are partly extremely specified. However, some of the laws concerning the protection of nature and environment are even older than the green movement of the last century.

To give a few examples of statute laws, the regulation of Water Usage (*Wasserhaushaltsgesetz; WHG*) such as the law on Soil Protection (*Bundes-*

---

29) *See also* Dilling Köck, "Was bleibt? Deutsches Umweltrecht in vergleichender Perspektive," *DÖV* 2018, p. 594.

bodenschutzgesetz; BBSchG) should be mentioned since those laws built up the basis for the protection of elementary natural resources. Another important statute law on a federal level is, for example, the Closed Substance Cycle and Waste Management Act *(Kreislaufwirtschafts- und Abfallgesetz), enacted in 1996,* which concentrates on a closed cycle economy and the responsibility manufacturers bear for their products. Referring to the responsibility of manufacturers, the Environmental Liability Act *(Umwelthaftungsgesetz)* from 1990 also has to be mentioned since it introduced several regulations concerning the legal responsibility for damages caused by the environmental impacts of certain high-risk installations.

Environmental law is a part of public administrative law. However, while in administrative law, in which usually the individual must allege the violation of own subjective rights (*Klagebefugnis*) in order to bring an action to court,[30] this is different in environmental law. In fact, there is some exemption from this general rule administrative law procedure since it is possible for associations to bring up a case in certain situations (*Verbandsklage*).[31] There are some special regulations for recognized environmental associations. A strong development of extending the protection of environment, nature and animals can be recognized. The state of Bremen, for example, is very progressive by having a specific law, legitimating animal protection associations to bring up actions (*Gesetz über das Verbandsklagerecht für Tierschutzheime*). Furthermore, scholars even argue to recognize subjective rights of animals that would legitimate to put the ground of argumentation in a claim on the violation of rights of a specific animal, like it was practiced in the case of seals in Hamburg ("*Hamburger Robben-Klage*").[32]

Environmental issues today are still shaped by the peoples' intensive green movements. One of the most powerful projects of green activists these days is the protest against uprooting of Hambacher Forst which has been a vast 12.000 years old forest in Western Germany. In fact, the forest was bought by RWE, a giant energy company in Germany, decades ago to expand lignite mining (*Abbau von Braunkohle*) in that area. RWE already started with uprooting the trees but in the summer of 2018 massive protests began after the company announced their plans for uprooting the forest in further dimensions to make a way for mine enlargement. The protests were shaped by huge demonstrations of citizens and protest camps in the wood were treehouses having been built by the activists within the previous six years. By autumn 2018, the protest and the fight between the people and the police had become violent. In society, the Hambacher Forest turned out to be a symbol of the struggle between the greed of industry and the citizens' fight against

---

30) *See* Richard Haase and Rolf Keller, *Grundlagen und Grundformen des Rechts*, 2003, p. 489.
31) Hans-Joachim Koch, "Die Verbandsklage im Umweltrecht," *NVwZ* 2007, p. 369.
32) Andreas Fischer-Lescano, "Natur als Rechtsperson," *ZUR* 2018, p. 205.

climate change.

5. The Liberal State — German Legal Culture

Although most of the Western and especially the European states share common values on democracy and freedom, the jurisdictions between the different states differ in many aspects. This is due to the fact that a legal system is always determined by national values and these values mostly find their roots in historical traditions and experiences. Depending on the historical legal traditions, especially the lines of jurisdiction (*Rechtsprechungslinien*) are shaped and influenced by different factors in each state.

a. Regulations Resulting from History

In Germany, both the law and the jurisdiction are strongly influenced by the terrible experience of the Nazi-Regime (*Herrschaft der Nationalsozialisten*) and World War 2 (*Zweiter Weltkrieg*). First of all, the German constitution contains many elements that illustrate that the German law seriously intents any thread of a fascist ditatorship coming to power again. Therefore, the protection of human dignity (*Menschenwürde*) is regarded to be the first article of the German constitution, indicating that the importance of this guarantee and its influence on the whole legal system. According to that, the guarantee of basic rights following this article such as the basic principles under Article 20 Basic Law securing the democratic structure of the state, partly explained above, are special and unique protection. This is the result of the guarantee of eternity (*Ewigkeitsgarantie*) article 79 para 3 basic law. Under this regulation, certain fundamental positions cannot be changed at all. Naturally, article 79 para 3 basic law itself cannot be abolished. Moreover, the principle of the rule of law (*Rechtsstaatsprinzip*) under Article 20 para. 3 Basic Law, which means that all state power is bound by law and justice.

Referring to the experiences under the Nazi-regime, the German Criminal Code intents to prohibit certain kinds of expression, especially if this is in a manner that is capable of disturbing the public peace including racist agitation and antisemitism under section 130 German Criminal Code.[33] Compared to other legal systems worldwide, this regulation is quite unique.

b. Values and Jurisprudence in a Social and Liberal State

As mentioned above, the principle of the social state and all regulations resulting from that characterize the legal culture in Germany. By that, a modern and socially secure society developed. Closely related to that, there is the

33) For more information *see* Chapter 6.

German labour and employment law (*Arbeitsrecht*), which is famous for its high protection standard for workers and employees.[34] Then, anti-discrimination law and policies also play a great role in German society. Referring to German labour and employment law, the General Equal Treatment Act (*Allgemeines Gleichbehandlungsgesetz, AGG*) on anti-discrimination, which was enacted in 2006 is of high significance for the job-market since discriminations on the ground of personal features like, for example, religion, confession, race, age and gender are prohibited. This corresponds with the special equality right guaranteed in the German constitution under Article 3 para. 3 Basic Right which aims to prevent from any kind of discrimination.

Article 3 para. 1 Basic Law, as the main equality right, firstly guarantees very generally equality before the law between all citizens. This idea has been shaping the German society since decades. However, Article 3 para. 2 Basic Law gets more precious because it states equality between men and women. In order to concretise this provision, the regulation explicitly states that the state shall promote the actual implementation of equal rights for women and men and take steps to eliminate disadvantages that now exist. This instruction is practiced seriously. As a result, more high positions in public offices have been filled with female employees.

Gender policies and rights became a relevant topic in Germany during the last decades. By now, the focus also turned to LGBTQ (lesbian, gay, bisexual, transgender, queer) people and their rights. In October 2017, the so-called same sex marriage (*Ehe für alle*)[35] was accepted by law on the ground of the new wording of section 1353 para. 1 sentence 1 German Civil Code which now legally defines marriage between persons and not necessarily between man and woman.[36] However, it has to be clarified that even before, lesbians and gays were not without rights. From 2001 until September 2017, these couples had the possibility to live in a registered partnership, which was regulated in the corresponding law (*Lebenspartnerschaftsgesetz, LPartG*). The newly accepted same sex marriage however, provides a wider scope of rights including the right to adopt children, and can be seen as the ground for equal acceptance in society.

The liberal attitude regarding gender in German society, politics and public life can also be seen by the acceptance of the third gender as stated by the German Federal Constitutional Court in October 2017. In its decision named "Third Gender Decision" the court firstly accepted that there is a third gender between man and woman and secondly, stated that the legislator is obliged to create a third gender category, especially in the public birth register, for people who do not identify as either male or female or were born with ambig-

34) For further information *see* the Chapter 7.

35) Martina Knoop, "Die Ehe für alle," *NJW-Spezial* 2017, p. 580.

36) Hanns Engelhardt, "Die 'Ehe für alle' und ihre Kinder," *NZRam* 2017, p. 1042.

uous sexual traits.[37] In society, this very progressive decision has been controversially discussed and also criticized,[38] however due to the constitutional courts' ruling, the category of the third gender will be accepted by law.

The German society has a very liberal and tolerant handling of religion. Historically, Germany is shaped by the Christian belief, both protestant and catholic. However, under article 4 Basic Law religious freedom is guaranteed for every person (*Religionsfreiheit*). Para. 1 guarantees that freedom of faith and of conscience, and freedom to profess a religious or philosophical creed, shall be inviolable. Then, para. 2 states that undisturbed practice of religion shall be guaranteed. During the last years, the Muslim belief increased in Germany as an effect of the rising number of immigrants and refugees from Muslim countries coming to Germany. Although the broad guarantee of religious freedom positively includes the freedom to change a religion or belief, to manifest a religion or belief in worship, teaching, practice and observance, it also gives negatively the right not to have any kind of religion or believe. Religious freedom and practice are related to the citizens' private life. In contrast to that, women are partly not allowed to wear burqas and niqabs in some professions in the public sector (*Kopftuchverbot*). This is recognized for teachers, judiciary, military and several parts of civil service.[39]

Finally, democratic freedoms like freedom of speech and freedom of assembly enjoy a high standard of protection in Germany, both in society and under the law. Since its early jurisprudence, the German Federal Constitutional Court emphasized the strong protection of these rights as a pillar of a democratic society.[40] In German society, discussions are held openly and controversial opinions are welcome. This refers to the idea of the so-called marketplace of ideas in which the most convincing argument will accomplish the outcome of the discourse.

Individual freedom rights have always been important values of the German society.

With the Corona-pandemic, the German legal culture experienced its strongest tension test after World War II since the state enacted several measures (Maßnahmen) limiting freedom rights in order to prevent the spread of Covid-19. German lawyers discussed carefully in what extend these policies can be justified under German constitutional Law. Primarily, since these measures cannot be enacted by executive bodies, the specific law section 28a of the German Infectious Diseases Protection Act (Infektionsschutzgesetz)

---

37) Bundesverfassungsgericht, Decision 10.10.2017 – 1 BvR 2019/16, *NJW* 2017, p. 3643 – *Das dritte Geschlecht*.

38) Critical towards the decision *see* Klaus Märker, "Drittes Geschlecht? – Quo vadis Bundesverfassungsgericht," *NZFam* 2018, p. 1.

39) Bundesverfassungsgericht, Decision from 27.6.2017 – 2 BvR 1333/17, *NJW* 2017, p. 2333 – *Kopftuchverbot für Rechtsreferendarinnen in Hessen*.

40) Just *see* Bundesverfassungsgericht Decision from 15.01.1958, *BVerfGE* 7, S. 198 – *Lüth*.

was enacted as an adequate legal basis for various administrative policies. Then, under German constitutional law all these measures have to be proportional regarding the limitation of freedom rights in every concrete case.

Chapter 2

German History at a Glance

I. Germanics, Celts and Romans

Around the middle of the first century BC, Roman soldiers, called Legionnaires, under the command of the Roman General *Gaius Julius Cesar* (100 BC-44 BC), arrived at the western side of the River Rhine. The Romans defeated and colonised the Celtic tribes, who lived mainly on the western side of the Rhine, and founded many cities commonly known in present-day Germany, for example Cologne (*Köln,* latin: Colonia Claudia Ara Agrippinensium), Koblenz (lat.: Castellum apud Confluentes) and Trier (lat.: Augusta Trevorum) in Western Germany, also Regensburg (lat.: Castra Regina) and Augsburg (lat.: Augusta Vindelicorum) in Southern Germany.

Beginning as a fort for Roman soldiers, often built close to already existing settlements of the Celtic or Germanic natives, these places grew by the accrual of the families of the Roman legionnaires and the thereby developing infrastructure. As cities, they became centres of administration for governing the colonised territories for the emperor of Rome. Under the Emperor *Konstantin I* (the Great), Trier even became capital of the Western Roman Empire in the 4th century AD. In Trier, the heritage of the Roman era is still visible by the remains of Roman architecture. The city's north-gate Porta Nigra, the Roman arena and the Roman imperial thermal bath are the most evident. The Romans also brought their culture to these regions of Germany and thus it became part of the culture of those regions, e.g. the viniculture on the Rivers Rhine and Mosel, as well as the Christian religion, which came with the legionaries to the Roman-Germanic colonies.

The borders of the Roman Empire in present-day Germany were roughly the Rivers Rhine and Danube. Aside those natural borders, the Romans built a fortified border wall, the Limes. The Limes was less of a line of defence as more than an infrastructure of controlling migration and trade and also serving as an alarm system for raids by people who lived on the other side of the border, the Germanics.

Germanic is a term brought up by the Romans. Historically, it is not certain where the term originated from. One explanation is that the term is made up by the two words, *Ger,* as the name of the long lance or the dart, which was a characteristic armament of the Germanic warriors, and *man* for "man" or "human". Another explanation claims the term originated from the Celtic language meaning "neighbour". The Germanics were not a homogenous nation. Moreover, the term described a conglomerate of tribes of people living in the territory between the Rivers Rhine, Danube and Vistula. Even when seeing themselves not as a unit and being in conflict which each other constantly, they had several aspects of a common culture such as a similar language, a common religion, which was based on polytheism around 100 BC containing a pantheon possibly originated from the Grecian religion, and a common social system.

Written record has permitted to learn and understand about Roman society and civilisation, but this important source of historiography does not exist for Germanic civilisation. The Germanics around the year zero BC were a civilisation without script. Decades later, with the first evidence dating circa 160 AD, they developed a script called "Futhark", named after the first six letters of its alphabet (*f-u-th-a-r-k*). But Roman historians wrote about the Germanics, so information about their society has been recorded, for example by the Roman historian *Publius Cornelius Tacitus* (58 AD–120 AD) in his magnum opus "Germania". Tacitus wrote about the Germanics that they were living in small settlements with no more than 20 houses in the form of longhouses and a maximum population of 200–300 people, which is confirmed by archaeological excavations. The biggest part of such village population, around two-thirds, is assumed to be children as it is ascertained by archaeological excavations of Germanic cemeteries. Tacitus reports about the social order of the Germanics that the Germanic society was not an absolutistic society with a king deciding on its own but moreover a kind of oligarchic system with democratic elements. On a *Thing*-assembly all "free men" were coming together to discuss issues of public interest as well as legal cases. The Thing-assembly also carried out the election of a head of a tribe, a chieftain, through a voting system, which was still valid in a similar form in later ages during the time of the Holy Roman Empire of the German Nation. On rule of law, they took what they thought was the best for settling affairs the right way. Therefore, it was a kind of common law system.

Circa 0 AD, the Roman Empire undertook the attempt of expanding its borders over the River Rhine westward to the shores of the River Weser in contemporary Centre-Northwest Germany. This operation was executed for a period of 20 years including the founding of model cities to promote

Roman culture to the "barbarians" and fortified camps for military control. But in the second half of the year 9 AD, a Roman military campaign ended in a heavy defeat for the Roman colonisers. The Roman Legions XVII, XVIII and XIX, under the command of Senator and General *Publius Quinctilius Varus* (46 BC-9 AD),were almost eradicated by Germanic warriors under the command of the Germanic Prince *Arminius* (17 BC-21 AD), who had been a high-ranking officer in the Roman army and a confidant of General Varus before. Trapped in the Germanic forests and attacked in ambush for four days, the final battle took place close to the present-day city of Osnabrück in Northwestern Germany. Numbering up to 20,000 Roman soldiers, not too many had survived. For the Roman Empire, which viewed itself as the superior civilization in contrast to the 'barbaric' Germanics, this defeat was an absolute shock. Years thereafter, several Roman military actions still took place on the Germanic Eastern side of the Rhine River, but there were no more attempts made to colonise the Germanic territories, ensuring the survival of Germanic civilisation.

II. The Barbarian Invasion and Period of Migration

In the second half of the 4th century, the Huns migrated from Asia to Europe. Because of their military supremacy, this invasion was almost unstoppable. The Germanic nations had no means to resist the invaders and advanced westward into the Roman Empire. As a memory of this period *Attila*, King of the Huns, appears as King Etzel in "The Song of the Nibelungs" ("*Nibelungenlied*"), which dates back to this period and served in the 19th century as inspiration for *Richard Wagner's* opera "The Ring of Nibelung" ("*Der Ring des Nibelungen*").

In the first half of the 4th Century AD, warriors belonging to the tribes of the Saxons, Angles, Frisians and Jutes from present-day North and Northwest Germany and Denmark went to England. Coming to England to serve the Romano-British nobility as military protection against the invasions of the Picts from present-day Scotland, they took power over England. Aside from their Germanic language, which consists a significant part of the modern English language, the names of the Germanic gods of the Anglo-Saxons live on in the names of the English language weekdays:

- Tuesday is the day of the god Tyr, who gave his right hand in order to capture the demonic wolf Fenrir.
- Wednesday is the day of Wotan, the Father of the Gods.
- Thursday is the day of Thor (germ.: *Donar*), the God of War, who rides over the skies in stormy nights, bringing thunder and lightning by

beating his war hammer Mjölnir against the clouds.
- Friday is the day of the goddess Frigg, the wife of Wotan. Other interpretations go to the goddess Freya, the Goddess of Love.

In the 4th century, the west-Germanic nation of the Franks also assumed power in the former Roman territory of the present border triangle of Belgium, the Netherlands, Luxembourg, Western Germany and France. With this unfolding of events, the age of the Roman Empire in Western Europe came to its end. After the Fall of Rome, the Franks inherited huge aspects of Roman culture as well as their religion, their legal system and large parts of their language, meaning that Roman Culture thereby lived on among its successors.

III. The German Middle Ages

1. Karl der Große and the Founding of the Holy Roman Empire of the German Nation

In the second half of the 8th century, *Karl der Große* (engl.: Charlemagne, 748-814) became King of the Franks. Under his reign, he expanded the Frankish Empire over a territory of the size of present-day France, Switzerland, Northern Italy, Luxembourg, Belgium, the Netherlands and Western Germany all the way to Elbe River. One of the most difficult phases of this expansion was the Saxon Wars, which took place in present-day Northwestern Germany. The resistance of the Saxons, who were still living within their traditional Germanic social system and believing in the Germanic gods, against the Christian Frankish-Roman conquerors was fierce and caused bloodshed on both sides. So, the legend says that 4,500 Saxons who refused to submit under the Frankish rule and to convert to the Christian religion were massacred by the soldiers of Karl near the present-day city of Verden in Lower Saxonia of Northwestern Germany in 782. The leader of the Saxon resistance in this area, *Widukind* (Germanic: “Child of the Woods”, wolf), surrendered to Karl in 785 through a peace treaty: Karl and Widukind agreed on peace, on submission of the Saxons under the Frankish rule and on the conversion of the Saxon nobles to the Christianity. But the Saxon nobility remained in their elite position of society in their Saxon homeland. After the conclusion of the contract, Karl gave Widukind a white horse as a sign for his good will and respect. This white horse is still observable in the coat of arms of the German federal states of Lower Saxony and North Rhine-Westphalia.

In 800, Karl was crowned Emperor by *Pope Leo III*. Thereby Charlemagne was the founder of the Holy Roman Empire, which is also known as the Holy Roman Empire of the German Nation (*Heiliges Römisches Reich deutscher Nation*). Karl died in 814 in the city of Aachen, Western Germany, where he was buried in the Palatine Chapel. The grandchildren of Karl divided his empire into three dominions. In later times, the western dominion became France, while the eastern part became Germany.

The reign of the Frankish monarchs in the eastern part ended when *Heinrich I.* (*"Herr Heinrich"*), of Saxon noble lineage, became king of the Eastern Frankish Empire in 919 by using the weakness of the Carolingian Frankish nobility during the Hungarians' invasion campaigns and a clever policy in common. Heinrich's son, *Otto I.*, vanquished the Hungarians finally and set an end to their invasions in 955. After defeating the Slavs, followed by their conversion to Christianity, Otto was crowned emperor in 962. With his coronation, Otto and his successors took up the Carolingian idea of a continuation of the Roman Empire by the German kings, which also meant a continuation of the idea of a Holy (Christian) Roman Empire of the German Nation. From the 13th century forward, the emperor of this Empire, which was more of a confederation than a central state, was elected by the prince-electors (*Kurfürsten*). This habit of electing the emperor instead of determining him by birth right appears as a traditional Germanic one, which can be found in the descriptions of the *Thing*-assemblies by Tacitus. The Holy Roman Empire of the German Nation existed until 1806, when Napoleon Bonaparte conquered Germany and terminated the political entity of the Empire.

2. The Social Structure of Medieval Society

a. The Countryside

The social system of Germany in the middle ages (circa 600 until 1500) was a feudalistic society and thereby it was highly hierarchical. At the very top of the society was the emperor. Beneath the emperor came the high nobility and the church, followed by the knights. The lowest class and the foundation of this society were the farmers, among whom many were bondmen.

The high nobility was a socially, legally and politically privileged class. The only way to become a nobleman was by birthright. They were the owners of a large land or the land was given to them by the emperor as a fief (*Lehen*), which means that the land was given to them for farming or other economic purposes. The nobility could also leave the land to nobles of lower ranks or farmers for feudal duties.

Lower ranking nobles were, for example, the Knights (*Ritter*). From the times of Karl der Große to this point, knights were armour-equipped soldiers on horses. They made up the strongest wing within an army. Because this equipment was expensive, only the rich and this meant only noble people could become a knight. Due to their importance for every sovereign, the knights formed their own class of warriors, which often caused problems to medieval society by having feuds (*Fehden*) among each other and thereby raiding each other's territories, being a thread to the people.

The lowest and also biggest class of the medieval era was that of the farmers. Except for a selected few, most of them lived under impoverished conditions, exploited by their liege lords, having no access to education or health care at all. Many of them were bondmen, which means that they were unfree, not allowed to leave the land of their landlord.

b. Monks and Monasteries

Next to this secular rural structure lived the monks in the monasteries. The monasteries were not only religious places, but also places of production, e.g. for wine or beer. For example, "ora et labora" (engl.: pray and work) was the motto of the lives of the Benedictine monks. In fact, the monasteries were also centres of the collection of knowledge. The monks, who were able to read and write, copied the existing books by writing them down word by word and adding little colourful pictures often showing their own life before collecting the books in the monastery's library.

c. Cities and Citizens

From the Medieval era forth, a structure, which vanished after the Roman era, redeveloped: Cities with townsmen, the citizens. While cities like Cologne were almost abandoned after the fall of the Roman Empire, the cities grew again while the medieval era was advancing. The citizens of a city were free of control from their former landlords so they were not bondmen anymore like the people in the countryside. Hence, the sons of many farmers fled to the cities and after living there for one year, they were free men. The story of "the Bremen Town Musicians" reminds us of this time by bringing up the slogan: "Let us go to the city of Bremen and let's become musicians. Something better than death we will find anywhere."

The cities were governed by a city council, whose members were mostly *Patrizier*, rich citizens who became richer by trade business like the nobles in the countryside ever were. An individual worth noting in this context is *Jakob Fugger* (1459–1525), a businessman and banker from Augsburg, who became so rich that he could be even hardly compared with a multi-billionaire in our time. Craftsmen, who made up the cities' middle class, also lived in the cities, which made up of approximately 40,000 inhabitants as Cologne had around in the year 1200. Other inhabitants included day labourers and beggars.

Excursus: The Hanse

Having Become rich by trade and governed by rich citizens, whose powers in the cities were not as limited by the nobility as they were in the countryside, northern German cities such as Bremen, Hamburg, Lübeck and Rostock associated from the 12th century on in the Hanseatic League (*Hanse*), a commercial and defensive confederation of traders. The Hanse dominated the trade especially in the Baltic Sea for more than 400 years, guaranteeing their member cities wealth and independence. Today, cities like Bremen, Hamburg, Rostock, Lübeck and others call themselves proudly Hanseatic cities (*Hansestädte*) still, showing a "H" on their car license plate (as an example for a car license plate: "HB-WJ 325": "HB" = Hansestadt Bremen; "HH" = Hansestadt Hamburg; "HRO" = Hansestadt Rostock etc.).

Typical of the Hanse was a type of ship called *Kogge*, a mix of a cargo vessel and a war vessel, having a structure at its back and sometimes also at its front, which reminds in its form to a small tower. The Kogge was in use in the 14th century during a time when many pirates made maritime trade dangerous in the Baltic Sea and North Sea. The most famous pirate figure from this age is *Klaus Störtebeker*, a man of two metres in height with red hair, who is still admired as the German Robin Hood especially in Hamburg. Factually speaking, it is not certain whether Störtebeker really existed or if he is only the product of fantasy of people aching for a self-determined life organised in fair structures. The legend says that in 1401, in front of the isle of Helgoland, the war vessels of the Hanse found Störtebeker and his crew of 150 men. After a heavy battle, most of Störtebeker's men were dead, the rest of them including Störtebeker were brought to Hamburg where they were executed by beheading. Having many different variations, one myth tells the story of Störtebeker being asked for his last wish and said that he asked for freedom for every one of his comrades so he could walk by after his head was decollated. The legend ends with Klaus passing all his remaining eleven comrades without head and liberating them thereby before the mayor of Hamburg stopped him by throwing a stone in front of his feet. Even though it is doubtable whether it is true or not, the story shows the sympathy people share with a rebellious figure, one which survived throughout the centuries.

d. The Jews

The Jews lived inside the cities, however, outside the urban society. The lives of the Jews in the medieval era were very restricted. They were discriminated against by the medieval ideology, one that blamed them collectively for the execution of Jesus Christ. It was forbidden for Jews to work as farmers or craftsmen so they earned their living as creditors, a business which was forbidden for Christians until the late medieval era. Jews were only permitted to live in special parts of town, like in the Jew's Lane (*Judengasse*) in Frankfurt for example, and had to wear special clothing including a special hat, which would complicate contact to Christians as a tool of social control. Pogroms, which means riots including murder and plundering against Jews, happened, often caused by religious fanatics and especially in times of crises such as the Black Death epidemic in the middle of the 14th century.[1] In addition, some people also used pogroms as an instrument of "debt cancellation" by murdering their creditors.

e. Cathedrals and Universities

Becoming a centre of trade and thereby of wealth, Christian citizens were donating large amounts of money to the church in order to ensure a safe passage to heaven in the afterlife. This enabled huge building projects in the form of cathedrals as they still can be seen in every old German city. The construction of these cathedrals often took many centuries. For example, it took nearly 600 years to build the Cologne Cathedral. Aside financial bottlenecks, wars and other political disturbances gave reasons for long construction periods. When finally a cathedral was completed, it was an advantage for everyone; the Church had a new place of power representation, the citizens in common had a respectful place of worship and the city's demonstration had grown. The lower classes in the city also had benefits out of the construction period, as there were jobs for the day labourers, even though working conditions were very poor in this age, and beggars were profiting from higher numbers of people due to attendants' donation to beggars in front of the cathedral's gates.

The schools of the cathedrals as well as the schools of monasteries in the cities, where scholars as *Albertus Magnus* (ca. 1200–1280) in Cologne were reading, became the originating ground for universities. Universities were founded in Germany from the end of the 14th century on, which was somewhat more than 100 years later than it happened in Italy, France or England. The first German university cities were Erfurt (1379), Heidelberg (1385) and Köln (1388). Thereby the cities got the chance to become new centres of knowledge by not only collecting but also developing science.

3. The Knights of the Teutonic Order

An important role of the later formation of Germany had the Teutonic Order

1) From the age of the pest epidemic called "Black Death," which took place in Germany between 1346–1351 and took the life of around one-third of the population comes the habit of saying "Gesundheit!" (engl.: "health"; in England: "Bless you!") if somebody sneezes. The first symptoms of Black Death were like symptoms of a cold, so wishing the sneezing person good health meant wishing him not to be infected by the pest.

(*Deutscher Orden* or also *Deutschritterorden*). Founded by crusaders as the "Order of Brothers of the German House of Saint Mary in Jerusalem" in Acre, Kingdom of Jerusalem (present-day Israel), the knights continued their crusade military campaigns in Eastern Europe from the beginning of the 13th century on, especially in the Baltic region. After conquering a large region in present-day Poland and the Baltics and ruling these lands for centuries as a result, the order was decisively defeated in the battle of Grunwald in 1410 by a Polish-Lithuanian army. The order's Grandmaster *Albrecht von Brandenburg-Ansbach* (1490-1568) finally converted to Protestantism and transformed the order's territory to the Duchy of Prussia (*Preußen*), becoming a vassal of the King of Poland. Thereby the order did not lose all of its land. Later, Prussia would become the core of the German Empire in the 19th century.

Remains of the Teutonic Order are still to be found in their colours and coat of arms, which shows a black cross against a white background. The Duchy and the later Kingdom of *Prussia* took it over as their national colours, and when the German national football team (*Deutsche Fußballnationalmannschaft*) was playing for the first time in 1908, the colours of this prevailing German state were assigned to this team. The black cross against the white ground is also the coat of arms of the Armed Forces of the Federal Republic of Germany, the *Bundeswehr,* today.

4. The Legal System of the Medieval Era

To better understand the legal system of medieval Germany, it is important to know that the one state authority, which we are used to today, did not exist. Moreover, there were two authorities governing the land and the people, which were the emperor as the secular ruler and the church as the divine ruler (Doctrine of the two Swords, *Zwei-Schwerter-Lehre*). Both, emperor and church, saw themselves as successors of the Roman Empire, thus Roman law was practised in case of legal disputes between the two powers. The two legal circles of emperor and church stood in addition to other legal circles as there were the rule of law of the kings, of the cities, of the village communities and much more.

Much of the rule of law in medieval Germany was common law, while the jurisdiction was practised by laypersons. An important legal source from the German medieval era is the *Sachsenspiegel*, a record of customary law, written in Germanic language instead of Latin, which was in use in some jurisdictions in Germany until 1900. Another important legal source, although written in 1532 and thereby a little after the medieval era ended, was the *Constitutio Criminalis Carolina*, the first embodiment of German criminal law. Aside from substantive criminal law, including punishments such as hanging, burning, premature burial and others, it contained the rules of criminal law proceedings.

IV. The Early Modern Period in Germany

During the 15th century, medieval society in Germany began to change. This change was basically how to observe humans and the world, followed by the challenging of the prevailing ideology. Amongst others, this change became visible in the paintings of *Albrecht Dürer* (1471–1528). A common feature of Dürer's paintings is his close look on the object of his paintings that is accurate in every detail and can be seen in his painting "*Feldhase*" from 1502. While persons before are not individuals but moreover representatives of their positions, as the king is always the king on paintings, Dürer analyses how things really were and not how they were supposed to be. One of his most provocative works in this context is his self-portrait from 1500, where he painted himself most accurately in a way, which reminds the observer of how Jesus Christ was pictured in this era – almost an act of blasphemy in a time when heretics were burnt at the stake by the Roman Catholic Church-supported Inquisition.

A turning point of the era was the invention of the printing press with moveable letters by *Johannes Gutenberg* (1400–1468) in 1450. Thus, information including all kinds of ideas could be duplicated in large numbers during a short period and then spread everywhere. Gutenberg's invention became a big advantage for *Martin Luther* (1483–1546). Luther was a monk before he began to criticise the Roman Catholic Church for its commercial and decadent orientation in his time, in which he considered a turn away from the true Christian belief in God. Also, his opinion of the Roman Catholic Church was that it was wrong when preaching to the people about an angry God, who would condemn them to hell for their sins in case of disobedience to his representatives, the Roman-Catholic Church itself. In Luther's opinion, God was not an angry and punitive, but a merciful and loving God. Only the Holy Bible would have theological authority, and not the representatives of the Catholic Church. Thus, Luther drew the conclusion that those and other grave theological fallacies of the Roman Catholic Church had to be corrected by establishing a new and pure kind of church as a reformation of the Christian belief. Holding the view that the Holy Bible would support his opinions, Luther wanted to translate the Bible from Latin into German in order to achieve captivation of the people as his audience. But he had one big problem to solve; a common German language did not exist at that time. Moreover, different kinds of German dialects were spoken, so different that a person from Northern Germany could hardly communicate with a person from Southern Germany. Luther found a solution by striking a balance between the different dialects and thereby creating a uniform German language, which was comprehensible all over Germany. In the following, his translated version of the Bible and many others of his theological scripts were printed in huge numbers and spread throughout the entire Holy Roman Empire. Thereby not only Luther's theological ideas of a reformed Protestant Church became popular in all of Germany, but also his new version of a common German language. People began to use this new version of the language as a more standard form of communication throughout Germany. Therefore, it became the major root for the standard German language of today.

Luther's criticism of the prevailing ideology upset medieval Germany. The ancient ideology, in which church and nobles were ruling the world by God's will, had lost authority over the people's minds and blended together with the economic misery many people lived in. As a result, the oppressed and exploited farmers, the foundation of medieval society, began to revolt against their masters at the beginning of the 16th century. The revolt which would be known as the Peasant Wars (*Bauernkriege*) began in South-western Germany and quickly rushed throughout the land. The historian *Lorenz Fries* (1489–1550) wrote in his book "History of the Peasant Wars in Eastern Franconia" about this time:

> From Augsburg to the Lake Constance, peasants and underlings of all authorities were in disturbance and outrage.

Led by men like the Reverend *Thomas Müntzer* (1489–1525) in Thuringia or the bondmen's son *Joß Fritz* (1470–1525) in present-day Baden-Württemberg, the peasants were successful at first by driving out the Church and nobility from their lands and establishing their own kind of social order in the liberated territories, which can be described as an early form of communism. But the old authorities only needed time to reorganise by deploying modern armed mercenary armies. Not being united as one large organisation, but being divided in small poorly armed groups, so-called "*Haufen*" (engl.: mobs, bunches), the revolution was smashed by the old masters, who took merciless revenge by killing up to hundreds of thousands of peasants. For centuries since then, the class of the German peasants endured and remained doomed to an unfree life of misery.

Another result of Luther's theology of reformism was that many noblemen converted to Protestantism, not only for religious but also for political reasons as they aimed at detaching from the rule of the Roman Catholic emperor. The emerging religious suspensions within the Holy Roman Empire of the German Nation could be calmed down by the Peace of Augsburg in 1555, by which the nobility compromised a co-existence between Catholic and Protestant regions within the Empire.

Later, the religious and political tensions between the nobilities of the two confessions were one reason for the Thirty Years War (*Dreißigjähriger Krieg*) from 1618–1648. Beginning as an inner-German conflict, it elevated to a full-scale European war of dynastic conflicts of interests, in which big parts of the Empire were completely devastated and around 30% of the population, amounting up to 6 Million people in total, were killed. But none of the rivalling parties could win the war by military means. Moreover, the war ended by exhaustion. Finally, representatives of the waring powers ended military action through the Peace of Westphalia in 1648. This settlement secured peace within the Empire for decades, but domestic wise, the Empire stopped existing by guaranteeing complete sovereignty to the regional sovereigns, diminishing the centralised authority of the Emperor. While losing territories, particularly in the west to France, it took almost a century within the Empire to fully recover from the aftermath of the worst war Germany ever faced. In the following decades it was Prussia, which ascended as a strong central European power by raising a powerful army and a massive and effective bureaucracy. This was most noticeable under the reign of *Friedrich II.* (*Frederick the Great*, 1712–1786), when Prussia could expand its territories to the east. A typical absolutistic ruler in his foreign policy, Friedrich was inspired by the upcoming ideology of the Enlightenment. Indeed, Jews and Catholics did not have equal rights in protestant Prussia, but they had more rights than in other protestant countries. Also, he allowed minorities from other nations to settle in his empire just as his predecessors on the throne of Prussia did with the Huguenots, who were protestant refugees expelled from France for their confession. To this day, names of places like *Französisch-Buchholz* near Berlin remind us of this settlement policy.

V. The Age of Enlightenment in Germany

1. The Enlightenment in Prussia

In the 18th century the ideology of Absolutism went into an ethical and intellectual crisis, which led to the rise of the Age of Enlightenment. The German philosopher *Immanuel Kant* (1724–1804) characterised this upcoming ideology in his script "What is Enlightenment?" ("*Was ist Aufklärung*?") as follows:

> Enlightenment is man's release from his self-incurred tutelage. Tutelage is man's inability to make use of his understanding without direction

> from another. Self-incurred is this tutelage when its cause lies not in lack of reason but in lack of resolution and courage to use it without direction from another. Sapere aude! 'Have courage to use your own reason!'- that is the motto of enlightenment.

While in France the main reason for the success of this new ideology was a lack of justice by despotism and bad governance, which led to the impoverishment of large segments of the population, in Prussia, however, the rise of the Enlightenment took a different path, as the Prussian King Friedrich II promoted it to become the prevailing philosophy and the main formative principle. Thereby, rationalism was ruling Prussian society, from the king as "the first servant of the state" downwards to the bureaucracy, the military, and even in the schools. The General State Laws for the Prussian States (*Allgemeine Landrecht für die Preußischen Staaten,* abbr. *ALR*) from 1794, derived its reforms to form the purpose of the state and society to live by the ideas of the Enlightenment. Moreover, society began to change from the 1750s on, not only in Prussia but also in other German states, such as in Sachsen-Weimar, where the poet *Johann Wolfgang von Goethe* (1749–1832) was director of a theatre in Weimar (1776–1817). A bourgeois culture came into existence, in which the merchants in the bigger cities were assuming more important social positions while acting inside their business relatively independent and having the possibility of alternative decisions. Because of this, they were in the need of information, which led to an increase of newspapers and magazines. Reading became popular and thereby public libraries came into existence in large numbers. Art and literature were no longer a privilege of the nobility and became commonly accessible to the masses. Meanwhile in France, a bourgeois revolution in the spirit of the Enlightenment took place in 1789. Many representatives of the German intellectual life (*Geistesleben*) such as the poet *Friedrich Schiller* (1759–1805) or the philosopher *Georg Friedrich Wilhelm Hegel* (1770–1831) supported the French Revolution at first but turned away from it because of its radical excesses.

2. Napoleon Bonaparte in Germany — the French Occupation

In 1806, *Napoleon Bonaparte* (1769–1821), "Emperor of the French People," conquered Germany, including Prussia. Thus, the old Holy Roman Empire of the German Nation finally ceased to exist. This political and also by reparations economic disaster forced the Prussian King *Friedrich Wilhelm III.* (1770-1840) into reforms. The public officer *Karl vom und zum Stein* (1751–1831) enacted reforms, which should have replaced the rule from above into self-government. These reforms were not only aiming to create a more effective administration, but also on creating a positive emotional relationship with the German people to develop a strong resistance against French domination, which was not too strong until then. Moreover, when Napoleon came to Germany, first to the Rhineland in 1804, many Germans supported Napoleon for their hopes that this would mean the end of the absolutistic Ancien Régime, the feudal system of the nobles, in Germany and the beginning of a better, fairer time for ordinary people. In the beginning, these hopes seemed to be justified, namely when Napoleon introduced the *Code Civil* in 1804 to Germany, which included amongst others equality before the law, liberty for all citizens and the separation of church and state, remaining in force until 1900. Soon thereafter, Napoleon began to appear to the Germans as just another tyrant who pressed countrymen into his army and plundered the land for financing his wars. After the disastrous end of Napoleon's Russian campaign from 1812–1813, Prussia ended the forced alliance with France and started to recruit soldiers for a campaign aiming to achieve the final defeat of Napoleon. Here, a German volunteer corps called *Freikorps Lützow* was formed. The Freikorps Lützow was rather unsuccessful from a militaristic point of view but had significant propagandistic effect as "fearless freedom fighters" to the German population. The members of the Freikorps kept on wearing their black uniforms with red collar borders and golden buttons when they returned to university in the city of Jena, where they founded the students league *Urburschenschaft*. Choosing their uniform colours black-red-gold as the colours for their then progressive students' league, these colours quickly became a symbol for a united and democratic Germany.

3. Germany and Europe after Napoleon — the Vormärz (1815–1848)

During the Liberation Wars against Napoleon, a new political consciousness was spreading in Germany. On the one hand, it was a sense of national consciousness. For the first time, people in the different German territories saw themselves as one, united German people. But in contrast to France, this new national sense of consciousness was not of only including, but also excluding character as its roots were not settled in a revolution against its own authority but in a resistance against an alien occupation. Thus, from the very beginning, this new German national consciousness had an aggressive nationalistic and exclusive touch. On the other hand, this new consciousness was a liberal democratic one in tone, one longing for civil liberties. After the victory against Napoleon, many Germans thought that a new era would make their hopes come true by forming a united liberal Germany. But instead, Germany was divided into 39 states with dictatorial, anti-liberal governments at the Congress of Vienna in 1814–1815, although hopes for reforms were answered with restoration from above. However, the German nationalist movement continued with its struggle for a united Germany and civil rights. Important political manifestations from this age were the *Wartburgfest* in 1817, a gathering of students at the castle where Martin Luther translated the Holy Bible from Latin into German, and the *Hambacher Fest* in 1832, an impressive political festival of the democrats with more than 30,000 participants under flags showing the colours black-red-gold. Furthermore, militant actions took place at the *Frankfurter Wachensturm* in 1833, the failed attempt by mostly students but also by workers and officers took its action for calling out a bourgeois revolution in Germany by attacking police stations in Frankfurt. Intellectual support came from poets like the democrat *Heinrich Heine* (1797–1856), who attacked the authorities with biting mockery, while the nationalist liberal *Hoffmann von Fallersleben* (1798–1874) later wrote the German national anthem *"Das Lied der Deutschen"* in 1841, on the at that time English isle of Helgoland. The absolutistic authorities reacted adamantly on those activities. Police and secret police took their action against every person who was known for standing in opposition to the regime. Censorship prohibited every book and script, that was deemed suspicious because of revolutionary tendencies. Many liberal activists were arrested, exiled, or banned from their professions. Scared by the terror of the state, many Germans went into some kind of inner exile by a lifestyle known as *Biedermeier* in this time, by focussing on domestic life and avoiding any conflict with the organs of the state, acting as "apolitical" in their own opinions.

4. The Revolution of 1848–1849

Despite all the repression having been executed by the state apparatus, however, the terror of the absolutistic states could not hold down the desire of the masses for political change. The uprisings in February 1848 in Paris and a few weeks later in Vienna against the absolutistic regimes were successful and eventually the revolutionary wave swept to Germany. Especially in Western Germany, namely in Baden, Palatinate, and Rhineland, the public demands for freedom of the press, universal franchise, a pan-German parliament and national unity grew louder and stronger. In the beginning of March 1848, public meetings were held by artisans, workers, students and young merchants in Berlin. On the evening of 13th March 1848, clashes between demonstrators and military arose, resulting in barricade and street fights causing many casualties, with the tensions only escalating in the following days. On the 19th of March, the Prussian king *Friedrich Wilhelm IV.* (1795-1861) began to set a pathway for a Prussian national assembly, which would elaborate a constitution for a united and liberal Germany. Having the Holy Roman Empire in mind, the Prussian king would be the Emperor of this constitutional monarchy. On the 18th of May 1848, the Frankfurt Parliament *(Frankfurter Nationalversammlung)* convened in the St. Paul's Church *(Paulskirche)* in Frankfurt and on the 28th of March 1849, the Prussian king was elected emperor by delegates. In the meantime, however, the conservative elites of the monarchy, nobility, military and bureaucracy had recovered from the revolutionary uprisings and reorganised well, in contrast to the revolutionaries who were not able to organise the masses of the cities and the countryside, as well as the petit-bourgeoisie, into one. So, when the *Nationalversammlung* offered the crown to the Prussian king, he rejected the offer by saying, that he would not accept being an emperor elected by representatives but only by the will of God. Thereby, the revolutionaries' plans were nullified. Many of them resigned as members of parliament. On the 30th of May 1849, the *Nationalversammlung* moved to the city of Stuttgart, where it was dissolved by the Wuerttemberg army a few weeks later.

VI. The Industrial Revolution, the Labour Movement and Karl Marx

Despite the failure of the Revolution of 1848–1849, it was another development, which permitted the bourgeoisie to enforce their liberal interests, namely the Industrial Revolution. From the beginning of the second half of the 18th century, but especially in the first half of the 19th century, the use of machines concentrated in factories increased. The demand for steel and iron products also grew. Therefore, the consumption of hard coal rose rapidly in Germany from the 1850s onward. The production of goods in large numbers also led to more rapid means of transport and communication. Society changed quickly and radically as never before seen in human history. The rise of this new industry demanded manpower. The former farmworkers left the countryside and moved to the regions of industrial production. New industrial centres as in the Ruhr region *(Ruhrgebiet)* grew rapidly. The former agricultural society disappeared and transformed into a new industrial society.

For the workers in the new industrial centres, the living conditions were extremely miserable, as *Friedrich Engels* (1829–1895) described it in his script "The Condition of the Working Class in England" ("*Die Lage der arbeitenden Klasse in England*", which were comparable to those in Germany) from 1845. Worker rebellions, aimed to improve their poor living conditions, were put down brutally through a cooperation of factory owners and state power, as it was the case during the Silesian Weaver's Uprising in 1844. These new rising means of production and its complicated connection between productive resources and productive relationship were analysed by *Karl Marx* (1818–1883) in his magnum opus "Capital. Critique of Political Economy" (*"Das Kapital. Kritik der politische Ökonomie"*). Marx described an antagonism of interests between the working class and the owners of the production facilities, the capitalists. While the capitalists would become rich and influential by the surplus value of the workers' labour, the workers themselves would only receive what is required for reproducing their own manpower. Thereby, this connected the misery of the workers, and this misery would continue until the workers would take power over production facilities from the capitalists and form a society of equality without classes: The communism.

Marx's theory gave the workers an own sense of consciousness for the situation they were in. Realising themselves being a unified class, they formed organisations to fight for their interests. One of these organisations was the General German Workers' Association (*Allgemeiner Deutscher Arbeitverein, ADAV*) founded in 1863 by *Ferdinand Lasalle* (1825–1864), which later became the Social Democratic Party of Germany (*Sozialdemokratische Partei Deutschlands, SPD*) in 1890. From this party the Communist Party of Germany (*Kommunistische Partei Deutschlands, KPD*) separated in 1918.

VII. Bismarck and the Founding of the German Empire in 1871

After the liberals failed in founding a German Empire, the absolutistic German states commenced a restoring policy once again in the 1850s. But soon thereafter, they faced the necessity for political reforms caused by the social changes of the industrial revolution, namely the advancement of the bourgeois class and the increasing number of working-class people living under the most impoverished conditions. *Otto von Bismarck* (1815–1898), a Prussian noblemen and politician, realised these social changes and ascertained that the dynastic monarchy would not be enough in the future to maintain the unity among the people. The state had to become a national state for keeping all classes of the people in one unified body.

However, Bismarck understood the term national state as an authoritarian state, not a parliamentarian party state. For achieving his political goals, he cooperated with almost any political party as long as it was advantageous for him. Considering national power was the key for social order and national security, both internally and externally, Bismarck was working on the national unity of Germany under the rule of Prussia.

After being appointed as Prussian minister of the interior and external in 1862, he carried out an aggressive external policy striving for Prussian dominance within Germany. After the war of 1864 against Denmark, Prussia acquired the Northern German province of Schleswig in 1865 and after the war against Austria and its German allies in 1866, Prussia also acquired Hannover, Hesse, Holstein and other German territories. Aiming to unify Germany, in 1870, Bismarck provoked the French Emperor Napoleon III to declare war against Prussia, which acquired assurance of mutual defence for the Southern German states in favour of Prussia by treaties. With great enthusiasm, huge segments of German people from all German states went to war against the French "hereditary enemy" (*"Erbfeind"*). Under the command of General *Helmuth Karl Bernhard von Moltke* (1800–1891), the German armies defeated the French armies rapidly. On the 18th of January 1871, the Prussian King *Wilhelm I.* (1797-1888) was proclaimed Emperor of the German Empire in the Hall of Mirrors at the Palace of Versailles near Paris. Bismarck's plan had worked out.

The newly founded German Empire (*Deutsches Reich*) needed a constitution, and at this point Bismarck was leading it. In the Constitution of the German Empire from 1871, the emperor of the German Empire was the executive body, while parliament had hardly any influence on government policy. Actually, the most important policy figure under this constitution was the Imperial Chancellor (*Reichskanzler*), who was Bismarck himself. All government acts of the emperor required the countersignature of the Imperial Chancellor and all ministers who were responsible to him. In national parliamentary elections, votes were equal, in contrast to the elections for the Prussian assembly, where votes were not equal but assessed by the amount of taxes the voter paid (Prussian three-calls franchise, *Dreiklassenwahlrecht*).

In domestic affairs, Bismarck started a campaign against the forces he considered as internal political enemies after the founding of the empire. In the "cultural struggle" (*"Kulturkampf"*) in the early 1870s, Bismarck turned against Catholics, especially the Centre Party (*Zentrumspartei*), for being suspicious of being "ultramontane" (*"ultramontan",* agents of the Pope in Rome). Bismarck also aimed during this campaign at reducing the influence of the Catholic Church in schools while expanding the influence of the state in these institutions. The upcoming socialist movement Bismarck tried to oppress by the Anti-Socialist Law (*Sozialistengesetz*) of 1878, which criminalised almost any kind of labour movement activity.

However, observing the misery of the working class and thereby the dangers of social disturbances and political radicalisation, Bismarck introduced a policy of social insurances as a national accident insurance and an insurance in case of sickness, invalidity and poverty among the elderly in the 1880s.[2] The costs of these insurances were distributed on the workers as well

2) *See also* the principle of the social state in Germany, Chapter 1.

as on the employers. Germany proceeded with this social legislation ahead of all the other European nations.

VIII. Wilhelminsm, World War I and German Revolution of 1918–1919

In 1888, *Wilhelm II.* (1859–1941) ascended to the throne of the German Empire. Soon, political differences appeared between the young emperor and Bismarck about external and socio-political questions, which finally led to Bismarck's dismissal in 1890.

Wilhelm II was driven for personal prestige as well as very conservative monarchic values. In opposition to Bismarck, Wilhelm II favoured, just as other European powers and the U.S., an aggressive imperialistic policy for accomplishing a "Place in the Sunshine" ("*Platz an der Sonne*") for the German Empire. The most conservative and pro-monarchic press supported these intentions as they supported him strongly for creating a positive image of himself to the public, which gave him the nickname "The Media Emperor" ("*der Medienkaiser*").

Meanwhile, technical progress advanced, too. In 1886, *Gottlieb Daimler* (1834–1900) and *Carl Benz* (1844–1929), engineered independently from each other the first automobiles, and *Otto Lilienthal* (1848–1896) designed a lighter-than-air-aircraft, which made him a pioneer of aviation before he was killed in an accident with one of his own flying machines.

In addition, social and cultural progress advanced. A new art form called Expressionism (*Expressionismus*) set colours and forms, which expresses the mental state of the individual in opposition to an emotionless mechanisation, which was taken by many as a thread. Within the working-class movement, its own working-class culture developed through choral societies, athletic and educational clubs.

Another political movement came up by the Question of Women's Rights (*Frauenfrage*). For instance, the League of German Women, founded in 1894, grew into an organization of half a million members by 1913.

This progress, however, could not stop the European elites from warmongering. The assassination of the Austrian heir apparent Ferdinand in Sarajevo in June 1914 generated the final crisis, which led after years of tensions between the European Great Powers to World War I. The Social Democratic Party of Germany, SPD, was not only unable to stop the catastrophe but instead, they supported the outbreak of the war actively by granting war loans in parliament. Great enthusiasm for the war had captivated the people of Germany, carefully prepared in the years before, and hundreds of thousands of young men who volunteered to fight on the front.

The war, which became known as World War I (*Erster Weltkrieg*) later, lasted more than four years. Around 17 Million people died by the actual battles in the war or by its side effects, among them 1.8 million German soldiers. The horrors the soldiers lived through in the German Western front (*Westfront*) were depicted clearly by *Erich Maria Remarque* (1898–1970) in his novel "All Quiet on the Western Front" ("*Im Westen nichts Neues*").

From 1917, especially the people of Europe became very war-weary. In Germany, the people were suffering from food shortages, and the workers in the ammunition factories went on strikes. On 4th October 1918, the government of the German Empire was asking for an armed truce. From this point onward, everybody in Germany knew that the war was officially lost. However, the admirals of the German Navy desired for one last great battle, in which the German Navies would sink "heroically" as they considered it. However, the German marines assessed this plan differently; at the beginning of the German Revolution (*Novemberrevolution*), on the 3rd of November 1918, a mutiny broke out in the harbours of Kiel, which quickly spread to the other German naval ports in the cities of Lübeck, Hamburg, Cuxhaven and Bremen and other German seaports. Between the 6th and the 9th November 1918, the revolutionary wave swept through Germany. At huge public meetings the speakers demanded:

> We want peace! Stop the bloodshed! Away with the emperor! Down with the monarchy! All power to the workers' and soldiers' councils!

The soldiers in the cities refused to shoot on the demonstrators and fraternised with them instead. On 9th November 1918, Reichskanzler *Prince Max von Baden* (1867–1929) declared the abdication of the emperor. Hence, the monarchy had been abolished in Germany. When these events took place, Wilhelm II had already left Germany. On the 29th October 1918, he travelled to Spa in Belgium, the seat of the German army command, and from Spa into his final exile in the Netherlands. Never returning to Germany, he died there in 1941.

But the abdication of the emperor did not put an end to the riots. Moreover, the question which political path the new German Empire was supposed to follow came up. In December 1918, reactionary monarchist militaries attempted a coup d'état in Berlin, which was put down by revolutionary soldiers and armed workers. In January 1919, an uprising for a German *Räterepublik*[3] took place in Berlin, after the interim government of social democratic leaders attempted to disarm the revolutionaries which were controlling the city as other German cities since the 9th November (January

3) The term *Räterepublik* (engl.: Soviet republic) described a system of direct democracy before Stalin where the will of the people was formed in assemblies.

Uprising (*Januaraufstand*) often deceptively called Spartacist Uprising (*Spartakusaufstand*) for the communist opposition group Spartacus League (*Spartakusbund*), which participated in the uprising but not initiating it). Other revolutionary attempts such as the Bremen Soviet Republic (*Bremer Räterepublik*) and the Bavarian Soviet Republic (*Bayerische Räterepublik*) were also overthrown in the first half of 1919, marking the end of the *Novemberrevolution*.

IX. The Weimar Republic (1919–1933)

After the elections for the National Assembly (*Nationalversammlung*, the national parliament of the German Empire) on 19th January 1919, which were the first elections in Germany where women were allowed to vote, the sitting Reichskanzler *Friedrich Ebert* (1871–1925) summoned the members of parliament to begin consultations for a new constitution. This event took place in the City of Weimar in Thuringia because of the on-going troubled political situation in Berlin. The new Weimar Constitution was comparable to the French or U.S. constitution, containing a very strong political position for the Imperial President (*Reichspräsident*) including the possibility of appointing or dismissing the government and authorising emergency decrees in cases of constitutional emergency under Section 48 of the Constitution. In the beginning of the 1930s, when no government was able to achieve a majority in the parliament and the monarchistic orientated former field marshal Hindenburg held the office of the *Reichspräsident*, this emergency decree legislation became a reason for the downfall of democracy.

The German Empire was a parliamentary democracy now, but not a beloved one. In fact, there was only a minority of people who supported the new system. This became obvious by the number of attempts to overthrow the government. In 1923 alone, there were armed communist uprisings for a German soviet republic in Hamburg, Saxony and Thuringia, attempts at separatism supported by France in Palatinate and the Rhineland, and a putsch attempt in Munich by a coalition of right-wing extremists under the leadership of the former imperial general *Erich Ludendorff* (1865-1937) and the by then hardly known politician *Adolf Hitler* (1889-1945) for abolishing democracy.

One reason for this rejection of the Weimar Republic among large parts of the population was the Treaty of Versailles (1919), the peace treaty, which brought a formal end to World War One. Enforced by the French government, the treaty stated in Article 23 that the blame for the war would be placed on the German Empire and demanded very high reparation payments from Germany. After the defeat in 1918, this was another form of indignation to many Germans, who blamed irrationally the Ebert government not only for this unfair treaty but also the social democrats in common for losing the war ("stab-in-the-back-myth", *"Dolchstoßlegende"*).

In addition, the economic situation became very grave for large parts of the population. When the German Empire was unable to pay the reparations of coal and wood dictated by the Treaty of Versailles in January 1923, the French army invaded and occupied the Ruhr, back then the main industrial heartland of Germany. Next, the German currency, the *Reichsmark*, broke down, and heavy inflation took place as a result.

However, in the years between 1924 and 1929, the economic situation could be stabilised and thereby the political situation as well. Moreover, as the policy of reconciliation between the German Empire and France was being conducted, promoted by the French foreign minister *Aristide Briand* (1862–1932) and the German foreign minister *Gustav Stresemann* (1878–1929). Germany was finally admitted to the League of Nations in 1926.

But aside all the political troubles and economic difficulties, the age of the Weimar Republic was a time of a flourishing culture, a time also known as "The Golden Twenties" (*"die goldenen zwanziger Jahre"*). After the horrible experiences of World War One, many artists drew the conclusion that the whole world and also the picture of human beings had to be reconsidered. Led by this perception, *Walter Gropius* (1883–1969) established the *Bauhaus School of Arts* in 1919. Bauhaus modernised the ideas of architecture, craftwork and interior design by orientating on clear forms and colours, all concentrating on the purpose of the object. In theatre, the playwright and poet *Bertolt Brecht* (1898–1956) developed a new form of theatre, which was not only supposed to entertain the audience but challenge them with political and social topics Epic theatre (*Episches Theater*). The graphic artist *John Heartfield* (1891–1968) joined the *Dada*-movement, which provoked intolerant coevals on purpose with senseless sentences and other apparent nonsense, and developed the collage as new form of visual art. The journalist and author *Kurt Tucholsky* (1890–1935) wrote satirical texts on socio-political topics and became one of the most important writers of the Weimar Republic. Media forms such as movies, radio, and LP, too, spread rapidly in their popularity and thereby formed mass media.

But the optimism of the years between 1924 and 1929 evaporated from the people after the stock market crash in October 1929, which meant a deep disturbance of the global economy. Thereby, banks did not grant credit to corporations anymore, resulting in a reduction of production, which was the reason for laying employees off. Mass unemployment followed as a consequence. Although the crisis was international, it affected Germany in a very unique way. Unlike other countries, it was a signal of the collapse of the political experiment called the Weimar Republic for many Germans. The masses, whose hopes for the future had been blighted by the crisis, became, after being politically centred in the years of stability, radicalised. The hope for a secure existence in this republic had finally left them.

While most of the working class people rushed to the *Kommunistische Partei Deutschlands* (KPD), led by its chairman *Ernst Thälmann* (1886–1944), aiming on establishing a German soviet republic, the petit-bourgeoisie switched from the right-winged, anti-democratic and pro-monarchistic German People's Party (*Deutsche Volkspartei, DVP*) and German National People's Party (*Deutschnationale Volkspartei, DNVP*) to the National Socialist German Workers' Party (*Nationalsozialistische Deutsche Arbeiterpartei, NSDAP,* abbr. *Nazis*) under the leadership of Adolf Hitler. The NSDAP was extremely aggressive in its opinions. Extreme nationalistic and anti-Semitic attitudes came together with a glowing anti-Marxism and the idea of the Germans as a nation without having enough "space to live" (*"Lebensraum"*). Even when being anti-monopolistic in words, their program of eliminating all kinds of left-wing activities had some attractiveness to the German upper class, especially after the beginning of the world economic crisis in 1929, when everybody was sure that the republic would pass away soon. Hence, solely in 1931, thc NSDAP received five million Reichsmarks by industrial tycoons such as *Fritz Thyssen* (1873–1951).

The political crisis became also obvious on the streets as countless street fights took place between the paramilitary organisations of different political parties, especially the Alliance of Red Front-Fighters (*Roter Frontkämpferbund, RFB*), the street-fighting organisation of the KPD, and the Storm Division (*Sturmabteilung, SA*) which were battling each other mercilessly on the streets of the cities of the German Empire.

Additionally, as a further result of this radicalisation, the parties of the political centre lost votes in the elections to the right and left. Thereby, it was not possible for the centre parties to form a majority government anymore, meaning that they could not pass laws. So, the *Reichspräsident Paul von Hindenburg* (1847–1934) appointed and dismissed governments by his own discretion, while laws were no longer put into effect as parliament laws, but as constitutional emergency decrees. On the 30th of January 1933, Hindenburg appointed Adolf Hitler to the Office of the Reichskanzler. Getting Hitler in government was supported by a coalition with the DNVP. The upper-class leaders of this party thought that the petit-bourgeois Nazis would be soon overstrained with government responsibility, which would give them the chance to govern from behind. This false calculation was a horrible mistake.

X. The National Socialist Dictatorship (1933–1945)

After the National Socialists came to power, they directly commenced to secure their position by thinning out their enemies. In the evening of the 27th February 1933, the *Reichstag*, the seat of the German Parliament in Berlin, was set ablaze. Without hesitation, Hitler blamed the act as being the result of a communist conspiracy. On the very same night, *Reichspräsident* Hindenburg signed the emergency decree "For the Protection of the People and the State" (*"Zum Schutz von Volk und Staat"*), which abrogated the most important basic rights of the Weimar constitution. From then on, it became officially legal to arrest political opponents as communists and social democrats, to ban newspapers and public meetings, to control and censor mail and phone calls and much more. Thousands were arrested in the following days, among them the chairman of the Communist Party, Ernst Thälmann. After being locked away in solitary confinement for eleven years in the concentration camp of Buchenwald, Thälmann was executed by the Nazis in 1944. In the German Democratic Republic, the socialist government made him a kind of a national saint posthumously.

After the elections on the 5th of March, 1933, the NSDAP became the strongest party remaining in parliament. Then on 23rd March, 1933, Hitler demanded the parties remaining in parliament (the KPD was already forbidden) to agree to the Enabling Pact (*Ermächtigungsgesetz*), which would place executive and legislative power in his hands. While the SPD refused to agree, the parties of the political centre catered to his demands. This was the end of the republic.

In the following months in the year of 1933, Germany became "synchronised" (*"gleichgeschaltet"*). The SPD was banned, the workers' unions smashed and their locations were confiscated. *Joseph Goebbels* (1897–1945) became Minister for Propaganda, controlling radio broadcasts, the press, arts and culture. Towards the end of June 1934, the Nazi elites continued to get rid of their political opponents by switching off their rivals on the right side, namely the leaders of the SA, who disturbed their politics with their "revolutionary" plebeian attitude, as also the conservative-monarchistic elites, which helped them to get into power by accusing them for preparing a putsch attempt (so-called *Röhm-Putsch*). In the following years, the Nazis would win over large segments of the population for supporting their policies. This was caused by many facts, but mainly by their effective strategies on how to present themselves and manipulate the masses. For example, the Nazis came to power at the moment when the economic crisis came to an end. The following economic rebound was presented as a result of their policies. Also, they took a lot of international capital and invested them not only in a huge armament campaign, but also into the economy and infrastructure projects, never sparing a thought about paying these credits back. The propaganda was done very professionally, focusing on achievements while not mentioning any bad news about themselves but only about their internal and external opponents. Anti-Semitic campaigns were especially a main spot of propaganda, as also the narrative of foreign states which would threaten the German people in order to put them down.

Those who did not believe in the Nazi propaganda apparatus, seeing that horrible things happened and even more would happen, were scared by the Nazi Terror. Particularly the Secret State Police (*Geheime Staatspolizei, Gestapo*) who spied on people and arrested anyone deemed suspicious of being an opponent for the slightest of reasons. Many of those who were deported then to a concentration camp never came back and were murdered there by the Protection Squadron (*Schutzstaffel*, *SS*), a fact that everyone knew. Nevertheless, brave people attempted to resist. To name one of many, *Georg Elser* (1903–1945) attempted to blow up the whole Nazi leadership including Hitler and Goebbels with a homemade bomb on 8th November 1939. The Nazi leaders survived by chance. Elser was caught the same day and arrested, and detained in a concentration camp, first in Buchenwald and later in Dachau. There, he was executed on 9th of April 1945, a few days before the U.S. Army liberated the concentration camp. He was 42 years old.

The Nazis were also trying to involve as many people as possible into their policies. For example, the boys should all join the Hitler Youth (*Hitlerjugend*), a paramilitary youth organisation preparing boys for the coming war. Giving people the feeling of being part of a community which would care for them, made the people follow – and thereby obtain accomplices associated with the later crimes committed by the Nazis. In fact, people did not enjoy a better quality of life as salaries decreased while the weekly working hours increased. Nevertheless, after years of instability of the Weimar Republic many Germans especailly from the petit bourgeoisie liked to believe the propaganda, which told them that it was going for the better now.

While people's approval increased, the Nazis turned to another focus of their political goals; the extermination of the Jews. Hitler and his followers thought in paranoid fashion that there was an international Jewish conspiracy causing all troubles with the goal of destroying Germany. While the terror of the Nazis against the Jews had sharply increased since 1933, it reached its preliminary peak on 9th November 1938 in a fanatic but organised pogrom against Jewish citizens and institutions, which lasted several days. In the following years, as before all kind of political opponents, people stigmatised of being Jewish were deported to concentration camps, where they were murdered, based on the aim of the complete extermination of all Jewish lives. Apart from the Jews, the Nazis murdered gypsies, Jehovah's witnesses, "anti-socials," homosexuals, disabled persons and many more in these camps. Solely the number of Jewish victims from all-over Europe killed in concentration camps in the name of Nazi ideology is estimated to be up to 6 million lives.

While having the Holocaust as one main focus, the Nazis focused on the other main goal of their policy, which was ensuing a war for the domination of Europe, beginning with invading Poland on the 1st of September 1939. In the following years, the *Wehrmacht* (name of the German army during the Nazi dictatorship) was able to conquer large swaths of Europe, including France, Belgium, the Netherlands, Denmark, Norway, Poland, Greece etc., before the Red Army of the Soviet Union could stop the advances of the Nazi army in the battle of Stalingrad in the beginning of 1943. From this point on, step-by-step, the Wehrmacht was forced to fall back. On the 6th of June 1944, the western Allies landed on the coast of Normandy (Operation Overlord), opening a two-front war against Nazi Germany, which continued from this point another eleven months. On the 29th of April 1945, surrounded by the Soviet Red army and facing defeat, the German dictator Adolf Hitler committed suicide in his bunker in Berlin. A few days later on the 8th of May 1945, the Wehrmacht completely surrendered to the Allies. The war later known as World War II (*Zweiter Weltkrieg*) was finally over along with the Nazi reign of terror. Even though the European casualties of this war started by the Nazis are hard to estimate, it is estimated up to 62 million lives.

XI. A Divided Germany

1. 1945–1949: From Four Zones to Two Zones

After the war, Germany was completely destroyed and the people were broken morally by their private sufferings and the sense of guilt for the crimes committed by a government many had supported, of which were revealed to the public at that time. Germany became occupied and divided into four occupation zones: A British zone in the north, an American zone in the south, a French zone in the west and Soviet zone in the east. The European borders were rearranged after the end of war. Germany lost its eastern territories to Russia, Poland, and Czechoslovakia. Most of the ethnic Germans inhabiting those territories were expelled. Around 10 million Germans were hit by this expulsion, being exiled to the destroyed Western Germany.

Soon thereafter, the political differences between the Soviet Union and the Western allies made any promise of cooperation difficult to achieve. Thereby, a reunification of the Soviet occupied eastern part of Germany, and the allied occupied western part was not confirmed. Moreover, the two parts of Germany were driven away from each other. At the preliminary peak of the development in the west, the Federal Republic of Germany (*Bundesrepublik Deutschland*) was founded on 23rd May 1949, while the German Democratic Republic (*Deutsche Demokratische Republik*, *DDR*) was founded in the east on 7th October 1949, eradicating hope of any quick reunification of the newly-divided Germany.

2. 1949–1989: The Development of the Two States

a. The Federal Republic of Germany

The West German economy recovered quickly from the damages of war. This was also a result of the Marshall Plan (also known as the European Recovery Program, abbr. ERP), a program initiated by the U.S. Government, with primary focus on building up the Western European economies into full recovery. This happened not only out of compassion, but also based on the reason that the USA needed a selling market for their products as well as for preventing the spread of communism in the war-ravaged nations. By the mid 1950s, the economic boom was noticeable for many West Germans, as they had a part in it through the economic policy of social market economy (*soziale Marktwirtschaft*). Cities were rebuilt, people were employed, food shortages did not occur anymore, luxury products such as cars, TV's, holidays, or even houses became affordable to many. This era of the economic boom in the 1950s was called the "Economic Miracle" (*"Wirtschaftswunder"*) in Germany. While the economic boom continued into the 1960s, a larger amount of labour forces was needed by the West German economy, which effected large scale migration, first from Italy, Spain and Yugoslavia and later also from Turkey.

The most important West German politician during those early years of the Bundesrepublik was *Konrad Adenauer* (1876–1967). Adenauer, former mayor of Cologne and member of the catholic democratic *Zentrumspartei*, joined the newly-founded Christian Democratic Union (*Christlich-Demokratische Union, CDU*) in 1946. In 1948, he became President of the Parliamentarian Council (*Parlamentarischer Rat*), which was working on drafting a new constitution for the West German state and finally adopted the Basic Law for the Federal Republic of Germany (*Grundgesetz*). After the first elections to the Federal Parliament (*Bundestag*, the Lower House of the German parliament), on 14th August 1949, members of parliament elected him as the first Federal Chancellor (*Bundeskanzler*) of the Federal Republic of Germany. He was re-elected in 1954 and 1959 and remained in office until 1963. Adenauer's foreign policy strived for west-integration of the Federal Republic towards Western Europe and the U.S., while being well-aware of the fact that this would deepen the differences with the GDR and thereby making a German reunification impossible not only in the short but also in the long-term. In this context Germany, France, Belgium, the Netherlands, Luxembourg, and Italy formed the European Coal and Steel Community, ECSC (*Europäische Gemeinschaft für Kohle und Stahl, EGKS*) in 1952. Other than for economic cooperation to the benefit of the national industries, reasons of peace-keeping by checks and balances in the field of these strategic materials were of big importance when concluding this contract. Eventually, this pact became the basis for future-oriented and closer European cooperation such as the European Atomic Energy Community (*Europäische Atomgemeinschaft*, *Euratom*) and the European Economic Community (*Europäische Wirtschaftsgemeinschaft*, *EWG*) in 1957. In the coming years, more and more European states joined this European cooperative experiment, which finally became the European Union (*Europäische Union*, *EU*) through the ratification of the Maastricht Treaty in 1993, with a total number of 28 member-states present.[4] As part of west-integration policy, Adenauer also furthered the Federal Republic by joining the western military alliance NATO (North Atlantic Treaty Organisation), in 1955. This was carried out alongside a rearmament program (*Wiederbewaffnung*) of Western Germany, which proved to be very controversial among the West German public.

In domestic politics, Adenauer leaned toward conservativism. Under his governance, the *Kommunistische Partei Deutschlands (KPD)* was banned by the Federal Constitutional Court (*Bundesverfassungsgericht*) in 1956. However, his anti-communist attitude did not prevent him from establishing diplomatic relations with the Soviet Union in 1955. In return, the Soviet Union released the last German prisoners of war. Also, diplomatic relations with Israel were established during his governance for the first time.

Important for the process of the West German nation building in matters of establishing an own identity was the triumph of the German national football team in the football World Cup tournment in 1954 in Switzerland, and it is also known as "The Miracle of Bern" ("*das Wunder von Bern*"). Starting as complete outsiders in every imaginable way into the tournament, the German team won the final against the Hungarian team, the favourite of the tournament, 3-2). In the collective memory of the German people, this event remained as an absolute highlight of a lifetime.

In the 1960s, the call among the younger generation for reform of the very conservative culture in Germany, which had its roots in the Nazi era, or even for a revolution became loud and clear. The Movement of 1968 (*68er-Bewegung*) demonstrated, in particular, on the streets of West Berlin against U.S. involvement in Vietnam and for a societal shift towards democratic socialism. The later militant Red Army Fraction (*Rote Armee Fraktion*, *RAF*) had its origins in this movement, as did the Anti-nuclear movement (*Anti-Atomkraftbewegung*), the Peace movement (*Friedensbewegung*) and indirectly the Green Party (*Bündnis 90/Die Grünen*). The wish for an immediate change in politics and culture made *Willy Brandt* (1913–1992),

4) For further information see Chapter 9.

SPD, chancellor in 1969. Among his biggest achievements was a policy of dialog and reconciliation with the Eastern European states and the Soviet Union during the Cold War.

Outstanding by its judicial importance were the Frankfurt Auschwitz Trials (1963–1965), where participants were accused for being involved in the Nazi massacre at the concentration camp of Auschwitz. After the Nuremberg Trials in 1945–1946, these trials were another attempt of judicial "overcoming the past" (*"Vergangenheitsbewältiung"*) of the times of Nazi dictatorship.

b. The German Democratic Republic (DDR)

After the end of World War II, in the East of the German territory, which was occupied by the Soviet Union, a government formed by members of the KPD (*Gruppe Ulbricht*) were placed into power by Stalin. After the *Bundesrepublik* was founded, and it was certain that there would be no quick reunification, the German Democratic Republic was founded on 7th October 1949. In the following years, the governing party within the democratic centralist one-party system, the Socialist Unity Party (*Sozialistische Einheitspartei Deutschlands, SED*), started to establish a socialist state in eastern Germany. The noble grand landowners were dispossessed, heavy industries were established, education and culture were promoted, for political-ideological reasons as well, and a free medical health care system was established. The exertions, which were demanded by the socialist government from the people for this, were not going without protests, as for example on 17th June 1953, when the Soviet Army put an end to protests, which mostly took place in East Berlin.

In the beginning of the 1960s, the government of the GDR was facing a big social problem; while many young people enjoyed the opportunity of getting professional job education in the GDR, they left the country after finishing their exams in order to take part in the economic boom occurring in West Germany. Another reason which led many to desperately depart was the narrow-minded attitude of the SED government, which took every person they considered as not being a part of their mainstream as somebody suspicious of counter activities. On 13th August 1961, the DDR government reacted to this crisis by ordering to close the borders to the *Bundesrepublik* for DDR citizens. Border facilities were built, in Berlin in the form of a wall between East and West Berlin. Anyone who tried to reach the western side was in risk of losing their life. Until the fall of the wall in 1989, approximately more than 200 people were killed at the border.

In the middle of the 1970s, the GDR had reached its summit: The material quality of life of its citizens had improved clearly, a housing program took place, whereby more than half a million new modern apartments were built, and culture and art policies were liberalised. But from the beginning of the 1980s, the economy of the GDR saw one crisis after another. The attempt of a liberal culture policy stuck in ideological dogmas, and the people of the GDR became more and more frustrated about the lack of consumer goods and civil liberties. Thereby, the GDR government was losing its legitimacy and the support of its citizens.

3. The Fall of the Wall and the German Reunification (1989–1990)

In summer of 1989, many citizens of the GDR started to leave the country, a development that came completely unexpected for everyone including the secret services in the East as in the West. Deprived of hope for change in their country, they travelled over Hungary and Czechoslovakia to the Federal Republic of Germany. The government of the GDR under *Erich Honecker* (1912–1994) was unable to react to this movement. On the evening of the 9th of November 1989, they informed the public about the opening of the borders of the GDR with West Germany. This happened rather unexpectedly than being part of a concept. Within minutes, masses of people gathered together at the border crossings at West Berlin, celebrating the event. The GDR government lost the rest of its authority, alongside its complete legitimacy among the people.

In the first multi-party elections on the 18th of March 1989, the Alliance for Germany (*Allianz für Deutschland*), the extension of the West German CDU to the east, became the strongest party in the country. By concept of the West German CDU Chancellor *Helmut Kohl* (1930–2017), a way for a fast reunification was chosen now without a consideration of any concerns and was heavily supported by a euphoric, nationalist mood among parts of the population, especially in the East. On the 3rd of October 1990, the two Germanys officially became reunited into the Federal Republic of Germany. The GDR (1949–1990) ceased to exist.

XII. Germany after 1990

The reunification was less about two nations becoming one, but more of a takeover of the East by the West. Chancellor Kohl promised the people of the former GDR literally “blooming landscapes” (*“blühende Landschaften”*), but the reality was a far cry from everything promised. The East German production facilities, which were suddenly in a single market with the West German companies, collapsed almost entirely within weeks or months. Mass unemployment increased as a result. The social structures in the East, which had been developing for a period of over 40 years at that time, were demolished together with the East German state. Job biographies simply ended and people from the West took the high positions in the East. Allover the people in the East were told that they had been living "the wrong life" until now, which felt unfair and degrading to many. As a result of the social crash, gangs of Neo-Nazis became strong and terrorised whole cities such as Dresden with violent terror. It would take until the end of the 1990s for the social situation to be settled a bit.

After 16 years of chancellorship, Helmut Kohl was voted out in the federal parliamentary elections in 1998. His successor was *Gerhard Schröder* (SPD), who was elected in parliament by a majority of social democrats and delegates from the Green Party. As the policy of the new government developed, it was disappointing to many of their voters. During the time of the "red-green coalition" (*"Rot-Grüne Koalition"*, by the colours of the two parties) from 2003–2005, the social state was reformed, which meant a policy of reducing social benefit entitlements. Also, in spring of 1999, Germany became an active waring party in the Yugoslav wars for the first time since 1945. Under this policy, more and more voters from the social democrats lost faith in their party. The SPD, which gained more than 40% of the votes in 1998, gains around 20% of the vote nowadays, and performs even less satisfactorily in the polls. However, the time of the red-green coalition was also a time of a cultural shift. The years of Helmut Kohl were marked by a conservative petit-bourgeois mood in society. After the elections of 1998, this mood changed by becoming more socially liberal. The Germany of today, which is a very cosmopolitan and tolerant country in many places, laid the foundation in this era.

In 2005, *Angela Merkel* of the CDU became Chancellor of Germany. Her government attained its majority mostly through a Big Coalition (*Große Koalition*, by the two biggest parties in parliament) of CDU and SPD, with an exception during the years between 2009–2013, when the CDU was in a coalition with the neoliberal Free Democratic Party (*Freie Demokratische Partei, FDP*). The time of Merkel's government is marked by many German, European and also worldwide crises, such as the Bank Run of 2007 ff., the Greek Government Debt Crises in 2013 ff., the Refugee Crisis in 2015 ff., and also the Brexit Crises in 2016 ff., the rise of the neoliberal right wing populist party Alternative for Germany (*Alternative für Deutschland, AfD*), the Corona Crises starting in 2020 and many others. Merkel's way of governing is debated controversially in Germany. Merkel has announced to the public that she will not seek candidacy for the office of the chancellor again.

(Note: For references and further readings see the bibliography at the end of the book.)

Chapter 3

The German Legal System

I. Introduction to the German Legal System

The legal system of the Federal Republic of Germany is based on the civil law. It is a comprehensive compendium of statute laws (*Gesetzbücher*) compared to the other law systems, especially the common law systems. In contrast, common law systems, like in the United Kingdom or the United States of America, are mainly based on the case law, which is a law made by judges.[1] Nevertheless, statute law, besides the case law, exists in the common law system as well. Although statute law is the major legal source within the German legal system, court decisions, especially by higher courts, also play an important role regarding the interpretation of the codified law. While custom (*Gewohnheitsrecht*) is also recognised within the German legal system, it has actually no relevance these days compared to federal statue law.

Historically, the German Law is influenced by its own history[2] and also by the Roman Law (*Römisches Recht*).[3] Especially, in the field of private law, (Civil Law Code) the German Law is shaped by the reception of Roman Law. Examples would be regulations on possession (*Besitz*) and property (*Eigentum*).

1) Florian Haase, "Einführung in die Methodik der Rechtsvergleichung," *JA* 2005, p. 232 (234); Susanne Augenhofer, in: Julian Krüper (Ed.), *Grundlagen des Rechts*, 2017, p. 215.

2) *See* Chapter 2.

3) *See* Dieter Blumenwitz, *Einführung in das anglo-amerikanische Recht*, 2003, p. 12.

II. Legal Sources

1. Statute Law

The codified statute law is the main legal source within a civil law system. A statute law is the basis for reliable justice whose task is to provide a secure point of reference. The legislator intends to use a wording and structure that is clear and understandable for ordinary citizens. Usually, norms are structured very clearly and consist of the *facts of case* (*Tatbestand*) and the *legal consequence* (*Rechtsfolge*). This can be explained by the example of the regulation of a theft (*Diebstahl*) under section 242 para. 1 German Criminal Code:

> Whosoever takes chattels belonging to another person away from another person with the intention of unlawfully appropriating them for himself or a third person shall be liable to imprisonment not exceeding five years or a fine.

This example illustrates that *whosoever takes chattels belonging to another person away from another person with the intention of unlawfully appropriating them for himself or a third person* are the facts of the case that are required by this regulation. If all these facts are shown in the concrete case, then the legal consequence of *imprisonment not exceeding five years or a fine* will be applied by public authorities.

Then, in the area of private law statutes, the structure of the *facts of the case* and the *legal consequence* can be illustrated by the regulation of the claims of the former possessor (*Ansprüche des früheren Besitzers*) under section 1007 para. 1 German Civil Code:

> A person who has had a movable thing in his possession may require the possessor to return the thing if the possessor was not in good faith when he acquired possession.

While the facts of the case refer to a person who has had a movable item in his possession such as to the possessor who was not in good faith when he acquired possession, the legal consequence states that the former possessor may require the possessor to return the item. Again, only if all facts of the case are proven, the claimant can demand for the legal consequence.

Besides federal statute laws in a formal sense enacted by the parliament, other legal sources are recognized as codified law like delegated legislation (*Rechtsverodnungen*) made by the executive power, the by-laws of federal organs (*Satzungen*) and moreover equivalents at the level of the states are relevant legal sources of German law.[4]

2. Court Decisions

Due to the codified law system in Germany, court decisions actually do not count as law in a narrow sense like it is in the common law system. However, court decisions are considered as a relevant legal source, especially in terms of interpretation of the statute law. In fact, a statute law, as a general abstract rule, cannot anticipate all the possible situations which might arise in practice. Therefore, court decisions are necessary in order to concretise the abstract wording of codified rules.

The legislator often even deliberately avoids overly specific regulations of specialist problems and leaves the development of the law to the courts to make a statute applicable to many cases and to make it flexible for interpretation and development in the future.[5]

The idea of binding the courts by the decision of courts above them (strict doctrine of binding precedent like in the Common Law) is unknown in German doctrine,[6] except the binding effect of the Federal Constitutional jurisprudence.[7] Court decisions only have the force of law between the parties (*inter partes*) to that particular dispute. Consequently, the courts are only bound by the law itself such as jurisprudence interpreting the law. In contrast to common law, however, a German court is not directly bound by any previously similar decision of another (higher) court. An exception to that is of course the appeal procedure. This means that if a higher court in deciding a case on review has set aside the decision of the lower court and referred the case back for a new decision, it is the decision of the higher court (in that specific case) binding.[8]

In practice the decisions of the superior courts have a decisive influence on all court decisions since in most cases the lower courts follow the decisions and argumentations of the higher courts, which is reasonable as the higher court would always have the opportunity to amend a differing judgement in an appeal procedure.[9] The superior courts often formulate a kind of headnote containing the *ratio decidendi* (*Leitsatz*) of the case which is printed at the head of the published version of the decision and has by now a quasi-normative effect.[10]

4) Nigel Foster/Satish Sule, *German Legal System and Laws*, 2010, p. 49.
5) Gerhard Robbers, *German Law*, 2017, p. 18.
6) *See also* Florian Haase, "Einführung in die Methodik der Rechtsvergleichung," *JA* 2005, p. 232.
7) *See* Nigel Foster/Satish Sule, *German Legal System and Laws*, 2010, p. 105.
8) *See* Gerhard Robbers, *German Law*, 2017, p. 19.
9) *See* Gerhard Robbers, *German Law*, 2017, p. 19.

III. Fields of Law — Substantive and Adjective Law

The German legal system is divided into three major categories. These are Private Law (*Privatrecht*), Public Law (*Öffentliches Recht*), and Criminal Law (*Strafrecht*). While Public Law such as Criminal Law always involves the state power, Private Law occurs between private persons.[11] All these fields of law are codified in various statute laws. Overall, there is a plenty of statutes provided to the public in books.

The most relevant statutes in Private Law are:

German Civil Code (*BGB, Bürgerliches Gesetzbuch*)
German Civil Law Procedure Code (*ZPO, Zivilprosessordnung*)
Courts Constitution Acts (*GVG, Gerichtsverfassungsgesetz*)
Commercial Code (*HGB, Handelsgesetzbuch*)
Limited Liability Companies Act (*GmbHG, GmbH-Gesetz*)
Act Against Unfair Competition (*UWG, Gesetz gegen den unlauteren Wettbewerb*)
Copyright Act (*Urheberrechtsgesetz*)

Labor Law (*Arbeitsrecht*) is connected to Private Law and also consists of various statute laws as follows:

Works Constitution Act (*BetrVG, Betriebsverfassungsgerichtsgesetz*)
Working Time Act (*ArbZG, Arbeitszeitgesetz*)
Minimum Wage Act (*MiLoG, Mindestlohngesetz*)
Protection Against Dismissal Act (*KSchG, Kündigungsschutzgesetz*)

Then, the most relevant statutes in Public Law are:

Code of Administrative Court Procedure (*VwGO, Verwaltungsgerichtsordnung*)
Administrative Procedure Act (*VwVfG, Verwaltungsverfahrensgesetz*)
Federal Building Code (*BGG, Baugesetzbuch*)
Federal Regional Planning Act (*ROG, Raumordnungsgesetz*)
Federal Constitutional Court Act (*BVerfGG, Bundesverfassungsgerichtsgesetz*)
Weapons Act (*WaffG, Waffengesetz*)
Nationality Act (*StAG, Staatsangehörigkeitsgesetz*)

Finally, Criminal Law consists merely of a few statutes, which are:

---

10) *See* Gerhard Robbers, *German Law*, 2017, p. 19.
11) Richard Haase/Rolf Keller, *Grundlagen und Grundformen des Rechts*, 2003, note 54.

Criminal Code (*StGB, Strafgesetzbuch*)
Criminal Procedure Code (*StPO, Strafprozessordnung*)
Youth Courts Act (*JGG, Jugendgerichtsgesetz*)
Act on Regulatory Offences (*OWiG, Ordnungswidrigkeitengesetz*)

The examples given to illustrate the various contents of the three fields of law are all related to substantive law (*materielles Recht*). Basically, substantive law has to be distinguished from adjective law (*formelles Recht*), which is actually the procedure law (*Verfahrensrecht).*[12] Substantive law refers to the law rules itself. Therefore, these kinds of regulation state rights and duties. In contrast, adjective law or procedural law can be described as the way and manner in which these rights and duties are enforced within the legal system. Adjective law for example provides several rules for the conduct of litigation. All the fields of law obtain their own procedure law which provides special regulations on legal procedure in the various fields of law. The procedure law within the German legal system will be explained in the 8th Chapter of this book.

IV. State Power with the German Legal System

1. Separation of State Power

In Germany, the principle of separation of powers (*Gewaltenteilung*) is an important element within the state structure. In Article 1 para. 3 Basic Law, the constitution refers explicitly to the three state powers which are the executive, the legislative and the judiciary, and it sets all these state powers under the area of application of the basic rights. Due to the idea of *Montesquieu* (1689-1755), the separation of powers means that the legislative makes the laws, the executive enforces and puts the law into effect, and the judiciary settles disputes and imposes sanctions for breaking the law.[13] The system of checks and balances is one of the most important elements within this concept.[14] Moreover, it should enable the jurisprudence to control the executive which is often very powerful. The separation of powers is accepted and practised in most Western democracies worldwide.

12) For more information *see* the term "Verfahrensrecht" Gerhard Köbler, *Juristisches Wörterbuch*, 2012, p. 447.
13) John Alder, *Constitutional Law and Administrative Law*, 2011, p. 137.
14) *See* Andreas Voßkuhle/Ann-Katrin Kaufhold, "Grundwissen - Öffentliches Recht: Der Grundsatz der Gewaltenteilung", *JuS* 2012, p. 314.

2. Independence of the Judiciary and Judicial Review

Legal disputes are decided exclusively by judges (*Richter*) who are subject to nothing other than the requirements of law and justice. The judges in the German legal system have received a high reputation, not just in their official role. They are also well respected in society. Article 92 Basic Law defines the judicial power in the German state [The courts]:

> The judicial power shall be vested in the judges; it shall be exercised by the Federal Constitutional Court, by the federal courts provided for in this Basic Law, and by the courts of the Länder.

The independence of the judiciary (*Unabhängigkeit der Justiz*) is characteristic to the German legal system. This principle is stated under Article 97 para. 1 Basic Law. Judicial independence is related to the idea of the separation of powers. It is actually the concept that the judiciary needs in order to be kept away from the other branches in public life. So, courts should not be subject to improper influence from other branches like the government or from private interests like economy or the media. The role of the judges is very important since they affect legal consequences to citizens and within the state. For that reason, they have to judge neutral and just refer to facts of the case.[15] Moreover, under the principle of the independence of the judiciary, no decision or other exercise of his judicial function can have personal consequences for the judge.[16] This is caused by the fact that judges are essentially appointed for life at a named court and cannot be dismissed or sent to retirement or even be transferred to a different court against their will.[17]

The jurisprudence on all levels is based on judicial review. This is generally a process under which state actions are subject to review by the judiciary, which is relevant especially if state powers exceed their authority. A court with judicial review power may invalidate laws and decisions that are incompatible with a higher authority. An executive decision may be invalidated for being unlawful. A statute may be invalidated for violating a provision of a written constitution. However, only the German Constitutional Court (*Bundesverfassungsgericht*) has the power to invalidate statute law.[18]

---

15) Richard Haase/Rolf Keller, *Grundlagen und Grundformen des Rechts*, 2003, note 109.
16) Gerhard Robbers, *German Law*, 2017, p. 24.
17) Gerhard Robbers, *German Law*, 2017, p. 24.
18) *See* Nigel Foster/Satish Sule, *German Legal System and Laws*, 2010, p. 105.

V. The German Court System

1. Hierarchy and Categories of Courts

Courts (*Gerichte*) are the major institution of the judiciary in terms of state power. The German Court System (*Gerichtssystem*) is clearly hierarchically structured. The primary legislation concerning court organization is the Courts Constitution Act (*Gerichtsverfassungsgesetz–GVG*). The courts are characterised by being specialist, regional, and hierarchically integrated at the federal level.

In fact, there are five categories of courts which are the ordinary courts (*ordentliche Gerichte*), the labour courts (*Arbeitsgerichte*), the administrative courts (*Verwaltungsgerichte*), the social courts (*Sozialgerichte*) and the fiscal courts (*Finanzgerichte*).[19] All these courts are respectively established on a local, state and federal level, except for the latter which is only installed on a state and federal level. Within these categories, there is a hierarchical division into various instances since the courts are organised regionally and by the single states up to the second highest instance which is always the highest instance in a certain state (*Bundesland*). Above these highest courts in the single states, there is a federal court in each of the five or categories.

Ordinary courts are the most numerous by far. Therefore, it is the main category of courts that is responsible for criminal matters, civil cases, and voluntary jurisdiction (*Freiwillige Gerichtsbarkeit*). The name of the ordinary courts is historical and comes from the beginning of 19th century when the jurisdiction of these courts was the only field that had been entrusted to independent and regular courts, while other courts have not been really independent at that time.[20]

The category of ordinary courts consists of four levels: the local court (*Amtsgericht*), the regional court (*Landgericht*), the higher regional court (*Oberlandesgericht*) and the Federal Court of Justice (*Bundesgerichtshof*). As already mentioned, jurisdiction of the regular courts includes the civil and the criminal jurisdiction. In criminal cases, depending on their nature, each of the first three courts can have jurisdiction, whereas in civil proceedings it will be either the local court or the regional court. One or two other courts may be appealed to on points of fact or law.

Within the hierarchy of ordinary courts, local courts which hear cases involving minor criminal offences or small civil suits are at the lowest level. Most cases in the local courts are decided by a single judge. In criminal cases in which the sentence is expected to exceed two years but no more than

---

19) *See* Nigel Foster/Satish Sule, *German Legal System and Laws*, 2010, p. 82.
20) Gerhard Robbers, *German Law*, 2017, p. 26.

4 years, the professional judge is assisted by two lay judges (*Schöffen*) with equal rights as the professional judge.[21]

Above the local courts are the regional courts which are divided into two sections, one for major civil cases and the other for criminal cases. Regional courts are organized in chambers of three judges but for reasons of efficiency, most cases are heard by single judges. Regional courts function as courts of appeals for decisions from the local courts and hold original jurisdiction in most major civil and criminal matters.

At the next level, higher regional courts primarily review points of law raised in appeals from the lower courts. These courts also hold original jurisdiction in cases of treason and anti-constitutional activity. They are divided into panels of judges who are arranged according to legal specialization.

On the highest level within the system of the ordinary courts is the Federal Court of Justice (*Bundesgerichtshof*) located in Karlsruhe, which represents the final court of appeals for all cases originating in the regional and appellate courts and holds no original jurisdiction. But actually, the German Federal Constitutional Court (*Bundesverfassungsgericht*), which is also located in Karlsruhe, is the court of the highest rank within the whole German legal system. The main difference between the Federal Constitutional Court and the Federal Court of Justice is that the Federal Constitutional Court may only be called if a constitutional matter within a case is in question like if a possible violation of human rights in a criminal trial is in question. The Constitutional Court exclusively concentrates on specific violations of the German Constitution by not taking breaches of ordinary law into account. In contrast to that, the Federal Court of Justice is the highest instance of the regular court structure and can be called as an appeal court in every case regarding this branch. Compared to other countries like the United Kingdom this structure is quite special. The British Supreme Court combines the jurisprudence of both types of superior courts, while the German Federal Constitutional Court (*Bundesverfassungsgericht*) is completely separate from all the other branches of jurisdictions.

Outside German court structure and the domestic court hierarchy in Germany, there are the European Court of Justice (ECJ) and the Court of First Instance. These institutions deal only with questions regarding the EU or the interpretation of EU Law by national courts in a special procedure when national courts in a conflict situation have to question the European Court to interpret the EU law to guarantee a unified interpretation of the EU law all over the member states.[22] However, the European Court is neither a highest court of appeal nor is it for bringing up cases such as after failing on national level.

---

21) Nigel Foster/Satish Sule, *German Legal System and Laws*, 2010, pp. 83–84.

22) *See also* Chapter 9.

2. Trials

Basically, the German legal system provides three types of remedies when bringing a case to court. Usually, it starts with the appeal on questions of the facts (*Berufung*) when one of the party requests for a formal change of the outcome of the decision. This remedy is followed by proceedings that prove exclusively the legal aspects of the case (*Revision*). Moreover, a request for relief from a court order is possible (*Beschwerde*).

Court cases are generally oral and public to guarantee the public control (*Grundsatz der Öffentlichkeit*). This principle also incorporates the provision for public access to the courts and requires judgements to be read out in open courts.[23] Only in special circumstances can the public be excluded from the proceedings, for reasons of the protection of the parties, but only after a decision of a court regarding this question.

Then, a ban is imposed on radio and live television transmission from the court. Therefore, no kind of "Court TV" like in the US is allowed in Germany. The reason is, firstly, to avoid any influence or pressure on the judges by media or public meaning.[24] Secondly, it is for protecting the parties, the witnesses and especially the accused in criminal court from publicity and possible severe consequences which can occur from this publicity.[25] But, of course, the media, as a part of society, is allowed to observe the proceeding when the trail is public. Under the constitutional guarantee of the freedom of press, journalists can make notes and report afterwards about the hearing at court.

3. Legal Aid

Proceeding before the court (usually civil courts) charges the claimant for court fees (*Gerichtskosten*). The amount of payment is determined with reference to the Court Fees Act (*GVG; Gerichtskostengesetz*) and its progress, depending on the value of dispute, which is determined by the court.[20] Even in the courts where self-representation is possible, the complexity of both the material and procedural law makes representation virtually a necessity.[27] Since costs arising by court actions can be very high, the German legal system provides legal aid (*Prozesskostenhilfe*) if a person is economically unable to afford a trail before German courts. In fact, legal aid is paid by the

23) Nigel Foster/Satish Sule, *German Legal System and Laws*, 2010, p. 139.
24) Gerhard Robbers, *German Law*, 2017, pp. 24–25
25) Gerhard Robbers, *German Law*, 2017, pp. 24–25.
26) Gerhard Robbers, *German Law*, 2017, p. 246.
27) Nigel Foster/Satish Sule, *German Legal System and Laws*, 2010, p. 128.

state and covers all the costs that arise by bringing a case to court including the costs for an attorney. Section 114 Civil Law Procedure Code (*ZPO; Zivilprozessordnung*) provides the basic regulation on the principle of legal aid:

> (1) Any parties who, due to their personal and economic circumstances, are unable to pay the costs of litigation, or are able to pay them only in part or only as instalments, will be granted assistance with the court costs upon filing a corresponding application, provided that the action they intend to bring or their defence against an action that has been brought against them has sufficient prospects of success and does not seem frivolous. (...)
>
> (2) The action being brought or the defence against an action is maliciaus where a party that has not taken recourse to assistance with the court costs would desist, upon having judiciously assessed all circumstances, from bringing an action or defending against an action in spite of sufficient perspectives of succeeding.

VI. Hierarchy of Norms

1. Supranational Law

Within the German legal system there is a special order of hierarchy and priority between legal rules, which results in various types of legal rules standing below the other in a strict hierarchical relationship. This order of hierarchy appears within a multi-level legal system since the German legal system is interwoven with the legal system of the European Union and the system of the European Convention of Human Rights.

On the top of the ladder structure of the German legal system is the level of supranational law which is the European Union Law. The European Union Law consists of primary legislation which are treaties and of secondary legislation which are regulations, directives and others.[28] In fact, the European Union Law has a direct effect which means that it is directly applicable in the German legal system.[29]

28) *See* Chapter 9.

29) For more information *see* Chapter 9.

2. National Law

Federal law (*Bundesrecht*) in Germany consists of several laws with the following hierarchy:

- federal constitution which is the Basic Law (*Grundgesetz*)
- federal statute laws which are Acts by the Federal Parliament (*Bundesgesetze*)
- federal delegated legislation (*Rechtsverordnungen*)

The Law of the states is ranked under the federal level with the following hierarchy:

- all Laws of the Federal States (*Landesrecht*)
- acts passed by the parliaments of the federal states (*Landesgesetze*)
- delegated legislation of the federal states (*Landesrechtsverordnungen*)[30]

Each regulation must be compatible with the law on the higher level within the hierarchy. If not, the lower rule is null and void (*nichtig*), from the moment the rules are in collision (*ex tunc*).[31] The hierarchy of norms generally roots in the regulations of the Basic Law. Article 1 para. 3 Basic Law states that the Basic Law with its provisions on Basic Rights binds legislation, executive and judicial decisions as law with immediate effect. Consequently, the Basic Law is necessarily on the highest level within the national legal system. Moreover, in terms of Article 20 para. 3 Basic Law, the legislature is bound by the constitutional order, executive authority, and the courts are bound by law and justice.[32]

Then, Article 20 para. 1 Basic Law states that the Federal Republic of Germany is a federal state. In fact, the federal structure is one of the most relevant principles. It means that the fulfilment of the functions of the German state are a matter of the various states of the federation, as long as there is not an exception in the constitution, which arises in areas of competences which are explicitly listed in the constitution itself.[33] In 2006, by a reform (*Föderalismusreform*), several competences were transferred to the state level.[34] While the states shall have the right to legislate under Article 70 para. 1 Basic Law insofar as this Basic Law does not confer legislative power on the Fed-

30) *See also* Richard Haase/Rolf Keller, *Grundlagen und Grundformen des Rechts*, 2003, note 74.

31) Gerhard Robbers, *German Law*, 2017, p. 20; for the term "ex tunc" *refer to* Gerhard Köbler, *Juristisches Wörterbuch*, 2012, p. 137.

32) Gerhard Robbers, *German Law*, 2017, p. 20.

33) Gerhard Robbers, *German Law*, 2017, p. 20.

34) Walter Schön/Rainer, Holtschneider, *Die Reform des Bundesstaates*, 2007, p. 9.

eration, the practical experience shows that most of the legislation is made on a federal level. Actually, there are only a few matters on public administration law like building law (*Baurecht*), police law (*Polizei- und Ordnungsrecht*) and assembly law (*Versammlungsrecht*) left to the states.

Due to the fact that there are laws both on the federal level and on the level of the states, collisions of rules can occur. In order to prevent any conflict between the levels, the German constitution states the rule of the supremacy of the federal law under Article 31 Basic Law explaining that federal law shall take precedence over land law (*Bundesrecht bricht Landesrecht*).[35]

VII. Governance and Public Administration

In Germany, the political governance is on the federal level. While the federal chancellor (*Bundeskanzler*) makes the main political decisions, the federal president (*Bundespräsident*) is actually the head of the state. More information on this structure of political governance and especially the federal government (*Bundesregierung*) will be provided in Chapter 4 as it is a relevant part of German public law.

The public administration in Germany is mainly determined by the principle of federalism as explained above. Good governance is a very important issue in German public policies. The law of public administration is also a comprehensive framework of regulation in order to provide the best rules for the public life in Germany.[36]

1. The Basic Structure of Public Administration

The organisation of the public administration is characterized by the federal structure of Germany as explained above. The organisation of the public administration in Germany is primarily characterized by this federal structure consisting of two levels of federation (*Bund*) and states (*Länder*). Both federation and states have their own administration (*Landesverwaltung and Bundesverwaltung*).

The federation of the different states in Germany is divided, which means that almost each state is divided into districts (*Kreise*) and communes (*Gemeinden*). Each of these legal bodies is an administrative authority in its own rights. Each institutional unit in these different levels is described as a public authority (*Behörde*). This includes every structure which performs tasks of

35) Richard Haase/Rolf Keller, *Grundlagen und Grundformen des Rechts*, 2003, note 75.

36) For the latest developments *see* Carsten Tegethoff, "Die Entwicklung des Verwaltungsverfahrensrechts in der Rechtsprechung," *NVwZ* 2018, p. 1081.

public administration, for example, the Public Order Office (*Ordnungsbehörde*), the State Bureau for the Preservation of public documents (*Denkmalschutzbehörde*), the Federal Ministry for Labour and Social Affairs (*Bundesministerium für Arbeit und Soziales*).

Some of these public authorities are established on the level of the different states such as on the level of the federation, like Federal Commissioner for Data Protection and Freedom of Information (*Bundesbeauftragter für den Datenschutz*) and Chief Privacy Office (*Landesbeauftragter für den Datenschutz*).

2. Duties and Organisation of the Public Administration

In earlier times, the public administration had the role as a mere guarantor of the citizen's safety. Insofar, in former days people feared that it could operate as an instrument of oppression but this fear is groundless today.[37] Now, the image of the administration is determined by its comprehensive welfare activities on behalf of the population. In this respect, one important point of the public administration is that the state provides the basic necessities of life (*Daseinsvorsorge*[38]).[39] However, this idea is not very dominant in the citizen's real life.

Due to the increasing privatisation of the State's activities, the structure of administrative law is also changing and the concepts and categories of the administrative law are only gradually adapting to its reality.[40] There is a strong tendency, to transfer more and more administrative services from the sovereign, the German state, to the private sector.

3. Principles of Administrative Law

In administrative law, the German citizen is not merely an object but rather an individual with subjective rights. Subsequently, if the authorities act by an administrative act (*Verwaltungsakt*) which is the most common form of legal administrative action, then the affected individual must be given a hearing to let him or her argue for the own position and interests.

Then, for all the actions of the public administration there is the principle

37) Gerhard Robbers, *German Law*, 2017, p. 67.

38) For further explaination of the states' duty to care for the citizens social needs *see* Robert Keller/Mara Hellstern, "Das öffentliche Interesse und Wettbewerb in der Daseinsvorsorge," *NZBau* 2018, p. 323 (324).

39) Gerhard Robbers, *German Law*, 2017, p. 67.

40) *See* Gerhard Robbers, *German Law*, 2017, p. 67.

that legitimate expectations to be protected (*Vertrauensschutz*).[41] This generally means that individuals can relay on certain procedures if they are always the same or if certain behaviour has been tolerated over years, the state has to give more justification for its action.

In fact, the decision-making process in public administration is also specially regulated.[42] In most of the decisions, the public administration has a discretion (*Ermessen*[43]). If this is the case and certain prerequisites are met, the authority may make whichever decision seems appropriate to it.[44] Within the decision process, the public authorities have to take all circumstances into account and draw a conclusion resulting in effects that are proportional, especially referring to the citizens' individual rights.

Moreover, there are some more principles in German administrative law. On the one hand, the public administration is bound by the principles of effectiveness in its action (*Effektivitätsgrundsatz*) and its limits of budgetary (*Sparsamkeit der Verwaltung*).[45] On the other hand, in all decisions the public administration is bound. That also means that the administration power is limited in this respect. It is always a challenge of the public administration to make decisions by balancing these two sides. Wrongdoings in administrative action can be claimed before the administrative courts.

41) *See* Sylvia Calmes-Brunet, "Rechtssicherheit und Vertrauensschutz im Verwaltungsrecht," *JuS* 2014, p. 1077.

42) Gerhard Robbers, *German Law*, 2017, p. 72.

43) Richard Haase/Rolf Keller, *Grundlagen und Grundformen des Rechts*, 2003, p. 358.

44) Gerhard Robbers, *German Law*, 2017, p. 72.

45) *See* Federal Administrative Court (Bundesverwaltungsgericht), Decision from 13.02.2013, *NVwZ* 2013, p. 1082.

Chapter 4

Public Law

I. Introduction to German Public Law

Public law (*öffentliches Recht*) is one of the three main fields in German law, besides criminal law and private law. While private law is defined as to be relevant between private persons, public law always involves actions of the state. This also means that the German state is limited in its action by the German constitution (*Grundgesetz*) and other laws. If the state violates certain rights guaranteed in the constitution, the state power must present a specific justification for this concrete action. This is usually a matter of constitutional law (*Verfassungsrecht*). In fact, constitutional law is one of the major parts of public law. The law of the organization of the state (*Staatsorganisationsrecht*) is closely linked to constitutional law. Both fields are concentrated under the legal term state law (*Staatsrecht*). Due to the broad understanding of the term state law in education and academia, the terms of the categories constitutional law and law of the organization of the state are used more frequently. Beside state law, German public law consists of administrative law (*Verwaltungsrecht*) of which the practical relevance lies in public life within society. However, this chapter will focus on constitutional law because of the fact that the German constitutional law and constitutional jurisprudence had a strong impact on other legal systems worldwide, especially in East-Asia. The Korean constitutional law and jurisprudence is shaped by its consistent orientation on the German constitutional law.

II. The Law of the Organization of the State

1. The Legal Framework

The law of the organization of the State (*Staatsorganisationsrecht*) can be seen as linked to the constitutional law since it also refers to constitutional matters such as rights and duties of the organs of the German State and regulations on elections. This part of public law is actually a framework of various legal sources. Most important is the German Constitution, the Basic Law (*Grundgesetz*), which regulates the existence and legitimation of the various state organs and constitutional organs. The functioning of the organs is usually subject to statute laws on a federal basis such as standing orders (*Geschäftsordnungen*) as internal regulations made by these organs themselves.

2. State Organs and Constitutional Organs

The President of the Federal Republic of Germany (*Bundespräsident*) is the formal head of the state (*Staatsoberhaupt*). However, in contrast to the Chancellor (*Bundeskanzler*) who acts with strong political power, the President holds rather representative functions. This is the result of the historical experience in Germany during the *Weimarer Republic* when the President obtained so much power that it allowed the NSDAP (National Socialist German Worker's Party) and Adolf Hitler to gain political power. Today, the weak political power of the President is rather the opposite from the time of the *Weimarer Republic*.[1] In order to avoid any abuse of political power within the German state, various institutions are integrated in a transparent process of decision making and legislation. The term of office for the President is five years while he can only be re-elected once.[2] Moreover, unlike the *Weimarer Constitution*, the Basic Law does not entitle the parliament to dissolve itself.[3]

Under Article 60 para. 2 Basic Law, the President appoints and dismisses the Chancellor after he or she has been elected or deposed by the Bundesrat and also appoints the federal ministers proposed by the Chancellor.[4] Furthermore, the President appoints and dismisses the federal judges, federal civil servants and the officers and non-commissioned officers of the armed forces. Moreover, under Article 59 para. 1 Basic Law, the President represents Germany in international affairs. This means that he signs treaties with foreign countries in the name of the Federal Republic of Germany and accredits

1) *See* Josef Isensee, "Brauch die Republik einen Präsidenten?" *NJW* 1994, p. 1329.
2) Peter Badura, *Staatsrecht*, 2018, p. 676.
3) Nigel Foster/Satish Sule, *German Legal System and Laws*, 2010, p. 196.
4) Helge Sodan/Jan Ziekow, *Grundkurs Öffentliches Recht*, 2016, p. 124.

and receives their diplomatic representatives.[5] Then, the President plays a relevant role within the formal process of legislation. Under Article 82 para. 1, sentence 1 Basic Law, the President signs into law statutes that have been passed by the Bundestag and the Bundesrat, which are the legislator. This right within the process of legislation can be compared to the Royal Assent by the Queen of England in the United Kingdom.[6]

The German Federal Government consists of the Chancellor and the Federal Ministers. Each minister directs his department independently and is responsible for its action. This is the principle of ministerial responsibility (*Ressortprinzip*).[7] However, under Article 65 Basic Law the chancellor has the legal power to set government policy (*Richtlinienkompetenz*). All ministers are bound by the decisions of the Chancellor on board, fundamental issues of policy and the Chancellor can also decide specific questions of particular importance.[8] The role of the German Chancellor these days can be compared with the role of a Prime Minister in other Western democracies. According to the *Kollegialprinzip,* the federal government has to decide collectively, namely cabinet (*Bundeskabinett*).[9] In the case of contradicting opinions between ministers on points that do not fall within the Chancellor's general policy-setting powers, a decision on the matter is made by the government as a whole.[10]

The *Bundestag* is the German parliament on a federal level. It is located in Berlin, the capital city. As the federal parliament, the delegates of the Bundestag also elect the chancellor. Together with the *Bundesrat,* it constitutes the legislative body. The *Bundesrat* provides an opportunity for the states to participate in legislation and administration at the federal level and consists of the members of the states' governments.[11] Therefore, all German states are represented in the *Bundesrat*. Depending on the size of the population, each state is allocated with a minimum of three and a maximum of six votes.[12] The main purpose of the *Bundesrat* is to play a role in the passing of statute law on a federal level. Compared to other political systems worldwide, this structure of two legislative bodies is quite unique. The procedure of legislation is regulated in the Basic Law such as in the standing orders of Bundestag and Bundesrat (*Geschäftsordnungen des Bundestages und des Bundesrates*).

5) Gerhard Robbers, *German Law*, 2017, p. 55.
6) *See* John Alder, *Constitutional Law and Administrative Law*, 2011, p. 307.
7) Herzog, in: Maunz/Düring (Editor), *Grundgesetzkommentar*, 2018, Art. 65 No. 53.
8) Gerhard Robbers, *German Law*, 2017, p. 60.
9) Nigel Foster/Satish Sule, *German Legal System and Laws*, 2010, p. 204.
10) Gerhard Robbers, *German Law*, 2017, p. 60.
11) *See* Helge Sodan/Jan Ziekow, *Grundkurs Öffentliches Recht*, 2016, p. 116.
12) Martin Morlock/Lothar Michael, *Staatsorganisationsrecht*, 2019, p. 340ff.

3. Elections and the Right to Vote

The German parliament consists of delegates (*Bundestagsabgeordnete*) who are elected in democratic elections. The term for these elections is four years.[13] In fact, the complete procedure of this election is determined in the federal statute law by the Federal Elections Act (*Bundeswahlgesetz*) and by the Federal Elections Ordinance (*Bundeswahlordnung*). Half of the number of delegates prescribed by this legislation are elected according to a majority vote (*Mehrheitswahl*) while the remaining delegates are elected on the basis of representation (*Verhältniswahl*) and therefore every voter has two votes.[14] This combination of giving two votes is the basic structure determining the German parliamentarianism[15], which is completely different from those of other European countries, the one in the United Kingdom for example.[16] In fact, the whole of Germany is divided into constituencies (*Wahlkreise*), each of which includes approximately the same numbers of voters. In each constituency, candidates stand for election usually as a member of a political party. The candidate winning this election by achieving the most votes obtains the direct mandate which is decided on the winner-takes-all basis by counting each voter's first vote (*Erststimme*).[17] However, the first vote is not terminating the result of the election as a whole. This is due to the fact that the other delegates of the Bundestag are elected according to the system of proportional representation by voting for lists of candidates in each state. In this respect, the second vote (*Zweitstimme*) of each voter is counted towards one of the state lists. The proportion of the total vote won by each list determines how many of the candidates on a particular list are finally elected for the federal parliament.[18]

The state lists are under a regulation that states that a party's lists have to receive at least 5% of the total number of second votes in respect to all votes in Germany in order to enter the German Bundestag (*Fünfprozentklausel/ Sperrklausel*).[19] This rule aims to prevent splinter groups from obstructing the work of the Bundestag and gaining disproportionate influence in the event that a coalition government must be formed due to a circumstance in which no party has a majority.[20]

13) Helge Sodan/Jan Ziekow, *Grundkurs Öffentliches Recht*, 2016, p. 106.

14) Gerhard Robbers, *German Law*, 2017, p. 57.

15) *See also* Stefan Marschall, *Parlamentarismus*, 2016, p. 51.

16) *See* John Alder, *Constitutional Law and Administrative Law*, 2011, p. 296.

17) Gerhard Robbers, *German Law*, 2017, p. 57 para. 185.

18) Gerhard Robbers, *German Law*, 2017, p. 57 para. 186.

19) Bundesverfassungsgericht, Decision from 23.1.1957–2 BvE 2/56, *NJW* 1957, p. 377; *see also* Ann Kathrin Kaufhold, "Grundwissen — Öffentliches Recht: Die Wahlgrundsätze," *JuS* 2013, p. 1078.

20) Alexander Thiele, "Neugestaltung des Wahlrechts zur Wiederbelebung der Demokratie," *ZRP*

Delegates are elected in a general, direct, free, equal and secret balloting process as it is regulated in Article 38 Basic Law. The right to vote (*Wahlrecht*) applies to all Germans over the age of 18.[21] This right comprises both the right to vote in an election (*aktives Wahlrecht*) such as the right to candidate in an election (*passives Wahlrecht*). The right to vote maintains that nobody is legally forced nor is it a duty to vote. However, some people see voting in elections as a so-called unofficial duty of citizens. Compared to other states, there is high voter participation. The fight for citizens voting rights has a long tradition in Germany.[22] Regarding the election principles under Article 38 Basic Law, a *general* (*allgemein*) election requires that voting rights apply to *all* German citizens nationwide.[23] *Direct* (*unmittelbar*) means that the imposition of any sort of electoral college in other intermediary, which in turn decides on the composition of the parliament, is not permissible.[24] The right of a *free* (*frei*) election demands that no pressure or force may be exerted to make the electorate vote in a certain way.[25] *Equal* (*gleich*) means that each vote must have the same value and the same chance of success.[26] Each voter must have the same number of votes and each vote must be of equal weight to the vote of any other voters in determination of the result. Finally, the act of voting itself must be *secret* (*geheim*). In this respect, an open ballot is never permissible.[27]

4. The Rights of Political Parties

Political parties are a fundamental element of public life in the Federal Republic of Germany. They play a significant role in forming the political will of the people. The role of political parties is regulated in Article 21 Basic Law [Political Parties]:

> (1) Political parties shall participate in the formation of the political will of the people. They may be freely founded. Their internal organization must conform to democratic principles. They must publicly account for their assets and for the sources and use of their funds.
>
> (2) Political parties that, by reason of their aims or the behavior of their

2017, p. 105; Gerhard Robbers, *German Law*, 2017, p. 57.

21) Helge Sodan/Jan Ziekow, *Grundkurs Öffentliches Recht*, 2016, p. 50.

22) *See* Martin Kriele, *Einführung in die Staatslehre – Die geschichtlichen Legitimitätsgrundlagen des demokratischen Verfassungsstaates*, 2003, pp. 200–203.

23) Stefan Marschall, *Parlamentarismus*, 2016, p. 36.

24) Gerhard Robbers, *German Law*, 2017, p. 57; Stefan Marschall, *Parlamentarismus*, 2016, p. 37.

25) Peter Badura, *Staatsrecht*, 2018, p. 601; Stefan Marschall, *Parlamentarismus*, 2016, p. 37.

26) *See also* Nigel Foster/Satish Sule, *German Legal System and Laws*, 2010, pp. 172–173.

27) Gerhard Robbers, *German Law*, 2017, p. 57.

adherents, seek to undermine or abolish the free democratic basic order or to endanger the existence of the Federal Republic of Germany shall be unconstitutional. The Federal Constitutional Court shall rule on the question of unconstitutionality.

(3) Details shall be regulated by federal state laws.

Article 21 Basic Law does not only describe the role of political parties, but also prescribes certain organizational requirements to which they must conform. The internal structure of a political party has to be in accordance with democratic principles. However, within this legal frame of regulations citizens are free to bring up their own political party. This concept is called party privilege (*Parteienprivileg*).[28]

Parties that, in terms of their goals or behavior of their supporters are directed towards the impairment or destruction of the basic system of freedom and democracy or that endanger the existence of the Federal Republic of Germany are unconstitutional (*verfassungswidrig*) and may be banned (*Parteienverbot*).[29] However, the ban can only be made by the Federal Constitutional Court. The aim of this regulation is to prevent the government from banning the opposition parties for opportunistic reasons. In former times two political parties were banned. These were the Socialist Reichs Party, a National Socialist Party, in 1952[30] and the German Communist Party (*Kommunistische Partei Deutschlands*) in 1956.[31] Moreover, there were a few attempts to ban the National Democratic Party of Germany (NPD), which is a far-right party. For several times, the NPD was accused of neo-Nazi links but the German Constitutional Court found that there was a lack of evidence to prove that the accused party is violating the German Constitution. The members of this political party were deemed too ineffective to pose a real threat to democracy. Although the party AfD is also right-winged, a ban of this party has not been attempted yet. Members of this party are supporters of movements like the anti-Islam *Pegida* and other protests against the liberal asylum politics of the German state during the refugee crises in Europe.

The financing of political parties (*Parteienfinanzierung*) in Germany is also a controversial discussion issue. As social groups, they must be primarily self-financing, relying in membership fees and donations. Additional financing from public funds is possible to a limited extent. It is discussed whether it is possible to suspend anti-democratic political parties from public funds which could also be a way to fight against these parties if a ban is not possible for formal reasons.[32]

28) Michael Klöpfer, "Über erlaubte, unerwünschte und verbotene Parteien," *NJW* 2016, p. 3003.
29) Friderike Stiehr, "Das Parteiverbotsverfahren," *JuS* 2015, p. 994.
30) *BVerfGE* 2, p. 1.
31) *BVerfGE* 5, p. 85 – *KPD-Verbot*.

III. The Concept of German Constitutional Law

1. History and Concept of the German Constitution

As already mentioned in chapter two, Germany was divided into four occupational zones after its defeat in World War II. On 23rd May 1949, the Federal Republic of Germany was founded on the territory of the three western occupational zones. On the day of the formation of this West German State, the constitution of this state was also adopted, which was named the Basic Law. This name was used instead of constitution to emphasize the provisional character of the Western German State, which, as the preamble of the Basic law stated, should exist until the German people would achieve the unity and freedom of Germany in free determination.[33]

A few months later, on 7th October 1949, on the territory of the Soviet occupational zone the German Democratic Republic, the GDR (*Deutsche Demokratische Republik,* DDR) was founded. The GDR had an own constitution, too, which also immediately stated the reunification of the two German states as a national objective. However, in later years this goal was erased from the constitution.

After the reunification on 3rd October 1990, the GDR accessed the territory of the Federal Republic of Germany. Thereby, since 1990, the Basic Law is the one and only German constitution, which covers now the whole of Germany.

As regards content, this German constitution is shaped very much by the historical experiences Germany went through. In fact, the fate of the democratic Weimar Constitution and the time of the National Socialist dictatorship (*Nationalsozialismus*) and the determination for preventing similar events from occuring again are strong influences in German law that last even today. The Basic Law is thoroughly pervaded by this desire, and these experiences are also fundamental for the internal self-understanding of Germany as a country and its modern liberal society. The political debates in Germany – even today –, the law making and all merits and weaknesses of it cannot be understood without bearing this background in mind.

Otherwise, by its conception, the Basic Law is a very modern constitution that includes a broad and liberal catalogue of freedoms, rights, guarantees and national objectives (*Staatsziele*). Beginning with the Guarantee of

32) Michael Klöpfer, "Parteienfinanzierung und NPD-Urteil — Zum Ausschluss der staatlichen Teilfinanzierung für verfassungsfeindliche Parteien," *NVwZ* 2017, p. 913; Kyrill-A. Schwarz, "Der Ausschluss verfassungsfeindlicher Parteien von der staatlichen Parteienfinanzierung," *NVwZ-Beilage* 2017, p. 39.

33) Gerhard Robbers, *German Law*, 2017, p. 35.

Human Dignity under Article 1 Basic Law,[34] the constitution offers a wide range of freedom rights and equality rights. Moreover, it is open to new developments and challenges of a modern society. One example for the modern standard of the German constitution is the clause which reads "Protection of natural foundations of life and animals" under Article 20a Basic Law.

2. Interpretation of the Basic Law as a Living Constitution

Historically, the scholar *Rudolph Smend* (1882–1975) saw the constitution as a legal medium for integration and even today, the Basic Rights are particularly seen as an expression of a community of culture and values.[35] Such integration in principle takes in all people living within the area in which the constitution is in force, that is the whole of Germany.[36] Consequently, nobody is excluded by the application of constitutional rights within this area. The Basic Law gains the highest rank within the German law system and limits the state power by guaranteeing Basic Rights[37] which is very significant in respect to the historical experiences under the Nazi-Regime.

The constitution is a basis for unity and must itself be understood and interpreted as a unified whole.[38] Therefore, it must also be understood as imposing an obligation to realize its postulates. Here, the tendency is rather towards the preservation of general principles of law that precede the constitution and take the form of constitutional government under the rule of law. In this respect, the constitution also tends to bind the constitution-making power of the people to cultural values which have developed over the time.[39] Finally, all courts in Germany tend to interpret statute law provisions which are questionable in the light of the constitution in favour for the values of the Basic Law (*verfassungskonforme Auslegung*).[40]

Today, the nature of the German constitution is basically defined by the Federal Constitutional Court in Karlsruhe. Since the beginning, this court has been deemed the constitution in general and the Basic Rights in particular as a complete value system. In fact, the constitution itself provides the basis for

34) *See also* Martin Kriele, *Einführung in die Staatslehre – Die geschichtlichen Legitimitätsgrundlagen des demokratischen Verfassungsstaates*, 2003, pp. 181–186.

35) Gerhard Robbers, *German Law*, 2017, p. 37; for *Rudolph Smend*, *see also* Ino Augsburg/Sebastian Unger (Editors), *Basistexte: Grundrechtstheorie*, 2012, pp. 160–170.

36) Gerhard Robbers, *German Law*, 2017, p. 37; Peter Badura, *Staatsrecht*, 2018, pp. 21ff.

37) Reinhold Zippelius/Thomas Würtenberger, *Deutsches Staatsrecht*, 2008, p. 41.

38) Gerhard Robbers, *German Law*, 2017, p. 37.

39) Gerhard Robbers, *German Law*, 2017, p. 38.

40) Christoph Möllers, "Scope and Legitimacy of Judicial Reviwe in German Constitutional Law – the Court versus the Political Process," in: Hermann Pünder/Christian Waldhoff (Editors), *Debates in German Public Law*, 2014, p. 9.

arguments in favour of a comprehensive protection of individual freedoms. By the time, the development of the constitutional jurisdiction received more and more importance. Without abandoning its emphasis on the protection of individual freedom, the idea of a closed system was broken open and the Federal Constitutional Court spoke of Basic Rights merely as fundamental principles determining the values of the whole legal system (*wertentscheidende Grundsatznormen*).[41] Subsequently, the Basic Rights of the German Constitution also play an important role when it comes to the interpretation of the ordinary law, such as private law or criminal law.[42]

As a very modern constitution, the document of the Basic Law is interpreted openly[43] as a "living constitution." The text of the German constitution is mostly written in broad and flexible terms to create a dynamic and "living document." Such a document requires a flexible understanding of the rights and guarantees that are codified in the text of the constitution. The idea behind that interpretation refers to the views that contemporary society should be taken into account when interpreting constitutional phrases and values.

IV. Major Principles of the German Constitution

1. The Nature of Basic Rights

The Basic Law guarantees a variety of specific rights. This concept refers to the European and US-tradition of human rights discourse and the meaning of freedoms. The rights codified in the Basic Law are Fundamental Rights which are called Basic Rights (*Grundrechte*) within the German legal system. Other rights that are scattered throughout the constitution are called Quasi-Basic Rights (*grundrechtsgleiche Rechte*). These rights can also offer individual positions and guarantees like the right that states that "no one may be removed from the jurisdiction of his lawful judge" (*Recht auf den gesetzlichen Richter*) under Article 101 para. 1 Basic Law. Another example would be the right that states that "in the courts every person shall be entitled to a hearing in accordance with law" (*Recht auf rechtliches Gehör*) under Article 103 para. 1 Basic Law. The value and meaning of these Quasi-Basic Rights within the concept of the constitution is similar to the Basic Rights. Both Basic Rights and Quasi-Basic Rights can be subject to a constitutional complaint before the Federal Constitutional Court in Karlsruhe.[44]

---

41) Gerhard Robbers, *German Law*, 2017, p. 38.

42) *See also* Herdegen, in: Maunz/Düring (Editors), *Grundgesetzkommentar*, 2018, Art. 1 No. 16–18.

43) *See* offene Verfassung Reinhold Zippelius/Thomas Würtenberger, *Deutsches Staatsrecht*, 2008, p. 65.

44) *See* above.

First of all, Basic Rights are understood as the so-called defensive rights (*Abwehrreche gegen den Staat*).[45] This means that the state authorities may not interfere with the subjective legal position of a person unless there is a specific reason to do so. Then, a significant element of Basic Rights is that they are designed to function as individual and subject rights. Thus, basically, every person can complain an inference of the rights before the Federal Constitutional Court. In some cases, however, besides individual persons, legal artificial persons (*juristische Personen*) can also refer to the protection of Basic Rights. Legal artificial persons like companies that are constituted as bearers of legal rights (*Rechtsinhaber*) by the legal system are also bearers of basic rights, insofar as the particular basic right in question is of such a nature that it can be applicable to them. This is said in Article 19 para. 3 Basic Law: "*The basic rights shall also apply to domestic artificial persons to the extent that the nature of such rights permits*." For example, a legal person can have property and is therefore entitled to the protection under Article 14 Basic Law (*Eigentumsgarantie*). However, it cannot have a conscience and therefore basically cannot make any claim based on the freedom of conscience under Article 4 Basic Law (*Glaubensfreiheit*).

German Basic Rights can be classified in two different categories; either as freedom rights (*Freiheitsrechte*) or as equality rights (*Gleichheitsrechte*). Freedom rights are, for example, the personal freedoms (*Freiheit der Person; allgemeine Handlungsfreiheit*) under Article 2 Basic Law, Freedom of Faith and Conscience (*Glaubens- und Gewissensfreiheit)* under Article 4 Basic Law, Freedom of Expression, Arts and Sciences under Article 5 Basic Law (*Meinungsfreiheit, Pressefreiheit, Rundfunkfreiheit, Filmfreiheit, Kunst und Wissenschaftsfreiheit*), the Protection of Marriage – Family – Children under Article 6 Basic Law (*Schutz von Ehe von Familie*), Freedom of Assembly under Article 8 Basic Law (*Versammlungsfreiheit*) and Occupational freedom under Article 12 Basic Law (*Berufsfreiheit*). Equality rights are especially the Equality Guarantee (*allgemeiner Gleichheitsgrundsatz*) which is codified in Article 3 para. 1 Basic Law.

2. Constitutional Principles and the Rule of Law

As mentioned above, most of the constitutional principles in German Constitutional Law find their basis for legitimation in Article 20 Basic Law [Constitutional principles – Right of resistance]:

(1) The Federal Republic of Germany is a democratic and social federal

45) Helge Sodan/Jan Ziekow, *Grundkurs Öffentliches Recht*, 2016, p. 180.

state.

(2) All state authority is derived from the people. It shall be exercised by the people through elections and other votes and through specific legislative, executive and judicial bodies.

(3) The legislature is bound by the constitutional order, the executive and the judiciary by law and justice.

(4) All Germans attempting have the right to resist any person seeking to abolish this constitutional order, if no other remedy is available.

In fact, Article 20 of the Basic Law contains several different aspects. Para. 1 explains the structure of the German state clearly by using just a few words. Referring to that, Germany is a democratic and social federal state. In terms, these are the principle of democracy (*Demokratieprinzip*), the principle of the social state (*Sozialstaatsprinzip*) and the structure of federalism (*Föderalismus*).[46] The political system of federalism means that there are different levels of legal and political powers within the federal state of Germany. In fact, the major political power is concentrated on the federal level. However, every state in Germany has its own state constitution (*Landesverfassung*) which is in part modelled on the basic law and in part establishes an identity of its own. The principle of homogeneity, which is laid in Article 28 para. 1 Basic Law, obliges the state constitutions to comply with the fundamental principles of the Basic Law.

Article 20 para. 3 Basic Law provides perhaps the most significant principle in German Constitutional Law because it states that all the state power is bound by these principles which are mentioned above such as by the rule of law (*Rechtsstaatsprinzip*).[47] This principle stands in complete contrast to the law in National Socialism. Together with the comprehensive protection of Basic Rights, this principle expresses the ideal self-image of the Federal Republic of Germany to an even greater extent than the principle of democracy.[48] In a legal state under the rule of law, violations of law are identified and punished, while unjustness (*Unrecht*) only occurs if the law is generally ignored.[49] Consequently, legal decisions are binding and have to be followed, even if the final result is not accepted by the moral standards of the majority in society. The basic idea of this principle is to guarantee justice and legal certainty (*Rechtssicherheit*). The guarantee of human rights is the content of the principle itself. The supremacy of the law (*Vorrang des Gesetzes*) demands that all possibility of executive authority should be bound by statute

46) Bernd Grzeszick, in: Maunz/Düring (Editors), *Grundgesetzkommentar*, 2017, Art. 20 No. 1.

47) Andreas Voßkuhle/Katrin Kaufhold, "Öffentliches Recht: Das Rechtstaatsgebiet," *JuS* 2010, p. 116.

48) Gerhard Robbers, *German Law*, 2017, p. 50.

49) Andreas Voßkuhle, "Rechtsstaat unter Druck," *DIE ZEIT*, no. 40, 2018, p. 6.

law.[50] This excludes the possibility of executive prerogative or innate powers of the courts. The necessity of law (*Vorbehalt des Gesetzes*) means that any intrusion into the sphere of the individual's rights and all the important administrative decisions are only permissible if they have a statutory basis.[51] Both principles are of the same importance.

3. Changes of the Basic Law

The Basic Law has been deliberately designed to be particularly difficult to change. The aim is to ensure that there is a broad consensus supporting any change and to remove the constitution as far as possible from the influence of short-term political tendencies. Article 79 para. 1 Basic Law contains this regulation:

> (1) This Basic Law may be amended only by a law expressly amending or supplementing its text. An international treaty concerning a peace settlement, the preparation of a peace settlement, or the phasing out of an occupation regime, or designed to promote the defence of the Federal Republic, it shall be sufficient, for the purpose of clarification that the provisions of this Basic Law do not preclude the conclusion and entry into force of the treaty, to add language to the Basic Law that merely makes this clarification.

This means that the Basic Law can be amended only by a law which expressly alters or adds to the text of the basic law. In fact, the only way to change the constitution is when two thirds (*Zwei-Drittel-Mehrheit*) of the members of the *Bundestag* and two thirds of the members of the *Bundesrat,* which together built up the legislative body in the state, vote in favor.

4. Guarantee of Eternity

As explained above, changes of the German constitution are possible. However, certain fundamental positions cannot not be subject to a change at all. Such immutability is the guarantee of eternity (*Ewigkeitsgarantie*)[52] under Article 79 para. 3 Basic Law:

50) Martin Morlock/Lothar Michael, *Staatsorganisationsrecht*, 2019, p. 164.

51) Gerhard Robbers, *German Law*, 2017, p. 50.

52) *See* Matthias Herdegen, in: Maunz/Düring (Editor), *Grundgesetzkommentar*, 2017, Art. 79 No. 74–76.

> An amendment to this Basic Law by which the organization of the Federation into states, the basic cooperation of the states in legislation or the basic principles laid down in Articles 1 and 20 are affected, shall be not permissible.

To sum up, the principle of eternity applies to the following aspects:

the federal structure of Germany (*Bundesstaat*);
the respect of human dignity (*Menschenwürde*);
the protection of basic rights and human rights (*Schutz der Grundrechte*);
the principle of the constitutional government under the rule of law (*Rechtsstaatsprinzip*);
democracy and sovereignty of the people (*Demokratieprinzip*);
the principle of the social state (*Sozialstaatsprinzip*)
and the principle that the state of Germany must take a republican form.

In addition, this provision itself cannot be abolished because of the internal log of Article 79 para. 3 basic law.

V. The Protection of Basic Rights

1. Basic Rights in Constitutional Jurisprudence

As explained above, the Basic Rights are notably interpreted by constitutional jurisprudence. From the beginning on, the Federal Constitutional Court determined the scope and interpretation of each Basic Right codified in the Articles of the Basic Law. Leading decisions (*Leitentscheidungen*) of the German Federal Constitutional Court are available in the official collection of decisions under the acronym BVerfGE (*Bundesverfassungsgerichtsentscheidung*) combined with the successive numbers of the volumes such as the first page of a certain decision. Usually, names are given to leading decisions. To give an example, this can be found and cited like BVerfGE 34, 269 – Soraya.

2. Human Dignity

The Guarantee of Human Dignity (*Menschenwürdegarantie*) is codified in Article 1 para. 1 Basic Law:

> Human dignity is inviolable. To respect and to protect it is the duty of all state authority.

The provision for the protection of Human Dignity is the basic requirement for all people to have fundamental rights under the German Constitution. Due to the terrible historical experiences under the Nazi-Regime and during the World War II, there has always been a strong emphasis on this guarantee ever since.[53] The importance of this guarantee is obvious due to the order of the Articles in the Basic Law beginning with the Guarantee of Human Dignity.[54] Moreover, it is argued that all fundamental rights are rooted in this principle.[55] One major value protected by the Guarantee of Human Dignity is human life. However, the state's capability of human life protection is rather relative and it is possible only under certain circumstances, that the state can even take a person's life away legally. This might be the case for security reasons, and especially to save someone else's life. Still, the question of the limits of an admissible action by the state is hard to ans-wer. Consider, for example, an airplane hijacked by terrorists is shot down together with crew and passengers to avert danger from community. In this situation, it is not only a decision on the right to live of the persons responsible for the attack, who would have had to face the defensive measures anyway, but also on the rights of all uninvolved and innocent persons on board of the plane. When the German Federal Constitutional Court had to deal with this dilemma in 2006, it held that the authority to shoot down a hijacked plane is the violation of Article 1 Basic Law and therefore unconstitutional.[56]

3. The General Freedom Right

The German Constitution comprises several freedom rights. In fact, they are all designed as specific freedom rights. But there is just one exception. However, this exception is very relevant within the concept of Human Rights Protection in the German legal system. Article 2 para. 1 Basic Law protects the free development of personality. In fact, Article 2 Basic Law is the core provision for personal freedoms:

> (1) Every person has the right to free development of his personality insofar as he does not violate the rights of others or offend against the constitutional order or the moral law.
> (2) Every person has the right to life and physical integrity. Freedom of the person is inviolable. These rights may be interfered with only pur-

53) *See* Reinhold Zippelius/Thomas Würtenberger, *Deutsches Staatsrecht*, 2008, p. 228.

54) *See also* Friedhelm Hufen, "Die Menschenwürde," Art. 1 I GG, *JuS* 2010, p. 1.

55) Dieter Grimm, "Proportionality in Canadian and German Constitutional Jurisprudence," *57 University of Toronto Law Journal*, 2007, p. 383, (387).

56) *BVerfGE* 115, p. 118 – *Luftsicherheitsgesetz*.

suant to a law.

To some extent Article 2 para. 1 Basic Law (*allgemeine Handlungsfreiheit*) is a catch-all right which operates whenever the numerous freedom rights are not applicable (*sogenanntes Auffanggrundrecht*).[57] This right is used as a general freedom right. This also means that whenever a lawyer has to examine the applicability of a certain basic right in a concrete case, he has to consider these extra special freedom rights first.

4. Equality Rights

As explained above, there are two categories of Basic Rights, which are Freedom Rights and Equality Rights. The most relevant Equality Right is Article 3 para. 1 Basic Law due to its broad scope of protection. Due to its wording, this right guarantees that all people are equal before the law. The issues raised by the requirement of equal treatment are particularly visible as far as the obligations of legislators are concerned. In fact, this Equality Right is also a catch-all right behind a number of specific equality provisions[58] such as the guarantee of equality of men and woman under Article 3 para. 2 Basic Law, the Protection against discrimination under Article 3 para. 2 Basic Law or equal voting rights under article 38 para. 1 Basic Law (*gleiches Wahlrecht*). Insofar, Article 2 para. 1 Basic Law and Article 3 para. 1 Basic Law together provide the legal basis for the comprehensive protection of the values for freedom and equality.

The wording of Article 3 [Equality before the law] Basic Law is quite comprehensive:

(1) All persons are equal before the law.
(2) Men and women have equal rights. The state shall promote the actual implementation of equal rights for women and men and take steps to eliminate disadvantages that now exist.
(3) No person shall be favoured or disfavoured because of sex, parentage, race, language, homeland and origin, faith, or religious or political opinions. No person shall be disfavoured because of disability.

Article 38 Basic Law provides the relevant regulation regarding elections. In para. 1, it contains a specific equality right regarding voting rights.

57) *BVerfGE* 80, p. 137 – *Reiten im Walde.*
58) Hans D. Jarass/Bodo Pieroth (Editors), *GG Kommentar*, 2018, Article 3 note 4.

(1) Members of the German Bundestag shall be elected in general, direct, free, equal and secret elections. They shall be representatives of the altogether people, not bound by orders or instructions, and responsible only to their conscience.

5. Specific Freedom Rights

Each of these Freedom Rights comprises a specific field of law. Freedom of Expression, Arts and Sciences under Article 5 Basic Law (*Meinungsfreiheit, Pressefreiheit, Rundfunkfreiheit, Filmfreiheit, Kunst und Wissenschaftsfreiheit*) is one of the core freedoms securing the democracy within the state. While simply the term Freedom of Speech is used in other democratic legal systems, the German legislator choose a comprehensive and precise wording:

(1) Every person has the right freely to express and disseminate his opinions in speech, writing and pictures, and to inform himself without hindrance from generally accessible sources. Freedom of the press and freedom of reporting by means of broadcasts and films shall be guaranteed. There shall be no censorship.
(2) These rights shall find their limits in the provisions of the general laws, in provisions for the protection of young persons, and in the right to personal honour.
(3) Arts and sciences, research and teaching are free. The freedom of teaching shall not release any person from allegiance to the constitution.

Under this provision, every person has the right to express freely his or her opinion in own words, writings or images. The scope of protection comprises not only opinions (*Meinungen*) but also statements of facts (*Tatsachenbehauptungen*), as the two are often not clearly separable.[59] Of course, this includes expressions on the internet. Especially in the political context, the right to express the most severe criticism has thus continuously been protected. In a leading decision of *Lüth* from 1958, the Federal Constitutional Court declared that a call to boycott the screening of a film by a director who had previously worked for the National Socialists was legitimate under a broad interpretation of freedom of speech under Article 5 para. 1 Basic Law.[60] This broad interpretation also applies to all the other forms of expressions as well.

---

59) Nigel Foster/Satish Sule, *German Legal System and Laws*, 2010, p. 253; Hans D. Jarass/Bodo Pieroth (Editors), *GG Kommentar*, 2018, Article 5 note 5–8.
60) *BVerfGE* 7, p. 198 – *Lüth*.

The limitation provision of Article 5 para. 2 Basic Law has also proved to be important on numerous occasions, not only for the practical definition of legal rules, but also for the pervasive influence of the Fundamental Rights.[61] However, the article regulates that freedom of expression can be limited by law (*Einschränkungsmöglichkeiten*). Due to the wording, the rights can be limited under Article 5 para. 2 Basic Law by "general laws" (*allgemeine Gesetze*). The phrase "general laws" in this context means that those provisions are not directed against the expression of a specific opinion, but are rather for the protection of a legal good which is worthy to be protected. Laws limiting the freedom rights regarding expression have to be interpreted narrowly in order to give regard to the importance of free speech within a free and democratic state.[62]

Another core freedom securing the democracy within the state is the Freedom of Assembly under Article 8 Basic Law (*Versammlungsfreiheit*):

> (1) All Germans have the right to assemble peacefully and unarmed without prior notification or permission.
> (2) In the case of outdoor assemblies, this right may be restricted by or pursuant to a law.

The Freedom of Assembly is guaranteed in Article 8 Basic Law and regulated in detail in the Federal Assembly Act or Assembly Acts of states (*Gesetz über Versammlungen und Aufzüge)* (*Versammlungsgesetz*) as ordinary statute laws. Freedom of assembly is the individual right or ability of persons to come together and collectively express, promote, pursue, and defend their ideas.[63] Referring to the jurisprudence, a public music event, like the techno parade called Love Parade, is not qualified to be protected under this law.[64] The typical type of an assembly is the public protest in form of a demonstration. In fact, the freedom is recognized as a civil liberty, a political right and a civil liberty. Although no permission for an assembly is required under the basic law, assemblies outside in the public must be annouced to the authorities 48 hours beforehand; otherwise they might be dispersed by the police. Details of limitations are regulated in the Assembly Acts. In the case of a spontaneous demonstration in which the participants take part without preparation, it is not necessary to report the assembly to the police. In some

61) Gerhard Robbers, *German Law*, 2017, p. 47.

62) *BVerfGE* 7, p. 198 (208) – *Lüth*.

63) *See* Wilfried Peters/Norbert Janz, "Aktuelle Fragen des Versammlungsrechts — Rechtsprechungsübersicht," *LKV*, 2016, p. 193 (194).

64) Bundesverfassungsgericht, Decision from 12.07.2001–1 BvQ 28/01 and 1 BvQ 30/01 – *Love Parade*.

respect, the provisions of the Assembly Acts become quite explicit and provide several forms of limitations on the Freedom of Assembly for the sake of the public order and security. Accordingly, it is legally possible to prohibit an assembly if this is necessary for security reasons. However, due to its impact for a democratic society, limitations of this freedom like a ban in general have to be in proportion to the legal purpose and therefore "ultima ratio.[65]

6. Justification of Rights Violation — the Balancing Test

Basic Rights are not absolute. Their task is to guarantee freedom and equality. However, there might be some cases in which the Basic Rights can be limited, especially when they violate other interests or for security reasons.

There are four steps to examine this (*verfassungsrechtliche Prüfung*); firstly, there must be a violation of a certain Basic Right or several Basic Rights in question. The so-called sphere of protection (*grundrechtlicher Schutzbereich*) of each of the various Basic Rights determines the scope of the protection of the specific right or freedom. For example, under Article 8 Basic Law the sphere of protection compraises every peaceful and unarmed assembly without prior registration or permission.[66] Armed or non-peaceful assemblies are not protected and therefor do not fall in the sphere of protection. Secondly, there must be an infringement of the sphere of protection referring to the relevant Basic Right. The violation must be done by the state power. This could be any act of the executive, legislative or judicative within the Federal Republic of Germany (*Eingriff*). Thirdly, the legislator designed Basic Rights with several limitations. The reason behind such a construction is that for a satisfactory life it is necessary to limit certain freedoms and reconcile them with one another. Insofar, there are several limitations (*Schranken*) codified in some Articles themselves to legitimate the limitation of Basic Rights. However, and as a last step, the limitation has to be justified for special reason. Otherwise, the infringement of the particular Basic Right would be unconstitutional and therefore also unlawful. One of the most relevant rulings in the constitutional jurisprudence is that any infringements on the sphere of protection of any Basic Right always needs a special justification (*verfassungsrechtliche Rechtfertigung*). The principle of justification is a result of the rule of law. Within this justification, the infringement of the basic law done by the state power needs necessarily a good reason (*legitimer Zweck*) first. In the next step, the court asks whether the law is suitable to reach it (*Geeignetheit*). Then, in the following step, the court asks whether the law is necessary to reach this aim or whether a less intrusive means exists

65) *See BVerfGE* 69, p. 315 – *Brokdorf.*
66) *See* the wording of the Article above.

that will likewise reach to the aim (*Erforderlichkeit*) while the last step is actually a cost-benefit analyses (*Kosten-Nutzen-Erwägung*) that requires a balancing between the fundamental rights interests and the good reason in which interest the basic right is limited.[67] Accordingly, the conflicting interests – the Basic Right on the one side and the reason for limiting this right on the other side – have to be pointed out, evaluated and finally balanced. All aspects of the concrete case must be taken into account (*Einzelfallbetrachtung*). In the end, any violation of Basic Rights can only be justified if it is proportional (*verhältnismäßig*) to its reason of limitation (*Angemessenheitsprüfung*) in the concrete case. In fact, the proportionality test aims to give full effect on the Basic Rights.[68] For this reason, the rights and interests of both sides have to be balanced that carefully. In order to achieve a result corresponding to the idea of the constitution, a comprehensive argumentation focusing on various factors is necessary. In the end, this balancing process including all arguments and positions is an important part of interpretation of Basic Rights.[69]

VI. Administrative Law

As mentioned above, administrative law (*Verwaltungsrecht*) in Germany is of substantial practical relevance. In fact, this part of law consists of the general administrative law providing all basic regulations for the administrative procedure and the part of special administrative law which deals with different sections of administrative law, like public construction law (*öffentliches Baurecht*), police and security law (*Polizei- und Ordnungsrecht*) or environmental law (*Umweltrecht*). The main principles and regulations of general administrative law also apply to the various specified sections of administrative law. However, to avoid collisions of norms, if there is such a specific provision, it will take precedence over the general provisions of administrative law.

1. The Administrative Procedure Act as the Major Legal Source

To begin with, the federal Administrative Procedure Act (*Verwaltungsverfahrensgesetz – VwVfG*) from 1977 contains all relevant provisions regulat-

67) Dieter Grimm, "Proportionality in Canadian and German Constitutional Jurisprudence," 57 *University of Toronto Law Journal*, 2007, p. 383 (387).

68) Dieter Grimm, "Proportionality in Canadian and German Constitutional Jurisprudence," 57 *University of Toronto Law Journal*, 2007, p. 383 (396).

69) Axel Tschentscher, "Interpreting Fundamental Rights – Freedom versus Optimization," in: Hermann Pünder/Christian Waldhoff (Editors), *Debates in German Public Law*, 2014, p. 43.

ing the procedure regarding the federal bureaucracy in administrative matters. Besides this law, the states provide similar laws or simply declare the federal Administrative Procedure Act to be governing the activities of their respective bureaucracies. Furthermore, referring to the different sections of administrative law which are mentioned above, there are other statues which regulate specialised administrative procedures.

2. Legal Forms of Administrative Action

Public administrative recognizes different legal forms of administrative action (*Verwaltungshandeln*) while most of them are regulated in the federal Administrative Procedure Act. Administrative activities range from making a formal decision determining the amount to be paid to a person in need by way of social security payments to publishing guidelines of general application dealing with specific details of the procedures followed in deciding whether to approve building plans.[70]

Actually, there is a wide range of possibilities of administrative actions. The three main possibilities are the administrative act (*Verwaltungsakt*), public contract (*öffentlich-rechtlicher Vertrag*) and forms of delegated legislation like laws made by the executive (*Rechtsverodnung*).

The classical form of administration is the administrative act (*Verwaltungsakt*) which is explicitly defined in section 35 sentence 1 of the federal Administrative Procedure Act. In terms of this provision an administrative act is any direction (*Verfügung*), decision (*Entscheidung*) or other sovereign act (*hoheitliche Maßnahme*) on the part of an administrative body that is directed at dealing with a specific factual situation in the field of public law.[71] The administrative act applies mostly to private persons, so to citizens of the German state. However, it is important to highlight that not only private persons may be addressed by this legal instrument but also public bodies, even if the exercise of public authority is concerned. A typical administrative act could be, for example, an instruction by a policeman or some order from the authorities such as an approval of plans in public construction law or other sovereign acts in the fields of public law.

Another form of administrative action is the public agreement or public contract (*öffentlich-rechtlicher Vertrag*) with the affected person regulated in section 54 federal Administrative Procedure Act.[72] This legal form can be

---

70) Gerhard Robbers, *German Law*, 2017, p. 70.

71) Gerhard Robbers, *German Law*, 2017, p. 70; for further information *see* Stelkens, in: Stelkens/Bonk/Sachs (Editors) *VwVfG* 2018, section 35 no. 2–10.

72) Bonk/Neumann/Siegel, in: Stelkens/Bonk/Sachs (Editors) *VwVfG* 2018, section 54 no. 1; Richard Haase/Rolf Keller, *Grundlagen und Grundformen des Rechts*, 2003, p. 367.

used instead of a proceeding by an administrative act. In several situations, the authorities have the choice to do so. Section 54 federal Administrative Procedure Act states:

> A legal relationship under public law may be constituted, amended or annulled by agreement (agreement under public law) in so far as this is not contrary to legal provision. Especially, the authority may, instead of issuing an administrative act, conclude an agreement under public law with the person to whom it would otherwise direct the administrative act.

Under section 56 federal Administrative Procedure Act, the exchange agreement is described with all its details:

> (1) An agreement under public law within the meaning of section 54, second sentence and under which the party to the agreement binds himself to give the authority a consideration may be concluded when the consideration is agreed in the contract as being for a particular purpose and serves the authority in the fulfilment of its public tasks. The consideration must be in proportion to the overall circumstances and be materially connected with the contractual performance of the authority.
>
> (2) If a claim to the performance of the authority exists, only such considerations may be agreed which might form the subject of an additional stipulation under section 36, were an administrative act to be issued.

Finally, due to section 57 federal Administrative Procedure Act, the public contract has to be concluded in a written form, except where another form is described by law.

Moreover, as in other law systems, the executive is able to make own laws as so-called delegated legislation. The executive has to be empowered by the legislator to do so. These types of rule (*Rechtsverodnung*) is even regulated in the German constitution under Article 80 Basic Law.

Apart from situations in which public bodies act to affect the legal position, there are also situations in which they simply perform some act, for example when the security guard patrols with his or her dog such as other simple activities (*schliches Verwaltungshandeln*) or merely factual activities (*Realakte*).

Chapter 5

Private Law

I. Introduction to German Private Law

1. The History of Private Law

From the second half of the 18th century on, the European bourgeoisie won on social and political influence by the development of trade and industry.[1] One of the political goals of this class, which was not at least consisting by merchants, was a legal system which would serve their interest of making business. The feudalistic law with its privileges for the nobility and their restrictions for non-aristocratic people, which also affected business, were constricting this interest in many ways, hence a new form of law had to set into practice. For that purpose, the *Ancient Régime* of the nobility had to be overthrown, which commenced in Europe by the French Revolution in the years from 1789 on. Already in 1793 during the years of the revolution, a *code civil* was created in France which was set into practice by Napoleon Bonaparte after usurping power in 1799. With the wars of Napoleon and his conquests, the *code civil*, also known as *code Napoleon*, was spread all over Europe, which was setting a fundament to the bourgeois class for increasing business and profits and thus for their social and political advancement. In 1900, in Germany the *code civil* was replaced by the advanced German Civil Code (*BGB, Bürgerliches Gesetzbuch*), which is still valid today as the major source of German private law.

---

1) *See* Chapter 2.

2. Legal Sources of German Private Law Germany

Beside the German Civil Code as the major source of German private law, there are many other statutes belonging to Private Law, concretizing specific fields of private law as the Commercial Code (*HGB, Handelsgesetzbuch*), the Limited Liability Companies Act (*GmbHG, GmbH-Gesetz*), the Act Against Unfair Competition (*UWG, Gesetz gegen den unlauteren Wettbewerb*), the Product Safety Act (*Produkthaftungsgesetz*), the Copyright Act (*Urheberrechtsgesetz*) and also the Labor Law (*Arbeitsrecht*), as Private Law is understood broadly. Therefore, like the other main fields of law, German Private Law consists of a framework of different statutes.

3. The Principle of Private Autonomy (Privatautonomie)

Private autonomy (*Privatautonomie*) is one of the major principles of the German Civil Code. Basically, the term of private autonomy means that the contract partners can design their contractual relationship as they want to. This contains, for example, the freedom of contract, which means that every person can conclude a contract with any content, and with whomever. Furthermore, the term of private autonomy includes the freedom of property, the right of disposing and also the right of marriage. But granting these rights and freedoms limitlessly, as it was done in the beginning of the civil law, would mean to promote the right of the strong because the contract partners are not always in equal positions when bargaining about the terms of contract. Moreover, as e.g. in employment law between employer and employee, there will be often one party in a strong position, and another party in a weak position. Therefore, the principle of private autonomy is limited at many spots of the law for avoiding a right of the strong and hence avoiding circumstances that would violate the peoples feeling for justice and thereby endangering the whole legal system by losing moral authority. Today, aside employment law especially commercial law and consumer law provide several regulations in order to protect the structural weaker part of the contract in specific constellations.

II. The Structure of the German Civil Code

As already mentioned, the German Civil Code is the major legal source of German private law. The German Civil Code is one of the most comprehensive statutes within the German legal system, consisting of five books. The code itself starts with several rather abstract and general provisions in the first book and then continues with specific regulations on fields of Private Law in the other four law books.

The first book (*Allgemeiner Teil*), from section 1 to section 240, contains general provisions, which are applicable to all the following books of the German Civil Code. These are, for example, definitions and regulations on legal persons, things and animals. It further contains regulations on legal transactions, agency and limitations.

The second book (*Schuldrecht*), from section 241 to section 853, concerning the Law of Obligations comprises firstly a general part, applicable to all obligations and secondly a special part with rules for various particularly important types of obligations, as e.g. sales contracts, service contracts or lease contracts. The second book also contains unjustified enrichment law (*Bereicherungsrecht*) and tort law (*Haftungs- und Schadensrecht*).

The third book (*Sachenrecht*), from section 854 to section 1296, is about the Law of Things. This applies to regulations on possession, right of property and real estate property rights, as different matters on ownership.

Then, the fourth book (*Familienrecht*), from section 1297 to section 1921, provides regulations on engagement, civil marriage, divorce, parental custody and other family matters.

Finally, the fifth book (*Erbrecht*), from section 1922 to section 2385, provides detailed regulations on succession law. This concerns universal succession, the capacity to inherit, legal positions of the heir, the claim to inheritance and it also clarifies the relationship of the heirs between themselves.

III. General Provisions of the Civil Code

The book of general provision consists of fundamental provisions relating to persons and things as the subjects and objects of the law. These are followed by rules concerning legally relevant declarations of will (*Willenserklärung*) and legal transactions (*Rechtsgeschäft*) as the basic elements of legal activity. In addition, the book of general provisions contains provisions relating to limitation of actions.

The legal capacity to perform juristic acts (*Geschäftsfähigkeit*) is one of the major legal instruments in private law since it enables a person to enter valid legal transactions and therefore, it comprises the ability to conclude a contract. This must be distinguished from the capacity to have rights and duties (*Rechtsfähigkeit*) and also the capacity to be liable in tort (*Deliktsfähigkeit*).

1. Legal Capacity to Perform Juristic Acts

Under section 104 German Civil Code, the legal capacity to perform juristic acts depends necessarily on the age and mental capacity of the acting person. Subsequently, anyone who has attained the age of majority (in Germany on the 18th birthday) has a legal capacity to perform juristic acts by law. However, the legal situation unfolds differently if a person is under that age. Generally, a minor who has not yet turned the age 7 years, has no capacity to perform juristic acts at all under section 104 no. 1 German Civil Code. The voidness of declaration of intent (*Nichtigkeit der Willenserkärung*) is stated under section 105 German Civil Code:

> (1) The declaration of intent of a person incapable of contracting is void.
> (2) Void is also a declaration of intent that is made in a state of unconsciousness or temporary mental disturbance.

Under this regulation, a declaration of will, which purports on having legal consequences, is void in case it is made by a person concerned by section 104 German Civil Code. This leads to the legal consequence that the declaration of this person has no legal effect.

In contrast, under section 106 German Civil Code, a minor has a limited capacity (*beschränkte Geschäftsfähigkeit*) to perform juristic acts, starting at his or her 7th birthday. This means that this declaration is not void but requires the prior consent (*Zustimmung*) of the legal guardians, usually the parents, for being legally binding. If such a prior consent is missing, section 108 German Civil Code (*Vertragsschluss ohne Einwilligung*) gives detailed regulations on an entry into a contract without consent as an exemption to the general rule that a prior consent is required:

> (1) If the minor enters into a contract without the necessary consent of his legal representative, the effectiveness of the contract is subject to the ratification of the legal representative.
> (2) If the other party requests the representative to declare that ratification, the declaration can only be made to the other party; a declaration or refusal of ratification made to the minor before the request of the other party is ineffective. The ratification can only be declared before the expiry of two weeks after receipt of the demand; if ratification is not declared, it is considered to have been refused.
> (3) If the minor has become fully capable of contracting, the ratification of the minor replaces the ratification of the representative.

This regulation states that without a legal guardian's consent before the transaction is concluded, it is suspensively invalid (*"schwebend unwirksam*) and can be ratified subsequently only by the guardian to achieve a legal binding. Yet, if the guardian denies the content, it becomes (finally) invalid. An exception to this rule is for the case that the transaction is exclusively of legal benefits for the minor and without legal obligations.[2]

Moreover, section 110 German Civil Code provides some exception in cases of payment by minor with inherent means (*Bewirken der Leistung mit eigenen Mitteln*) by stating:

> A contract entered into by the minor without the approval of the legal representative is deemed effective from the beginning if the minor effects performance under the contract with means that were given to him for this purpose or for free disposal by the legal representative or by a third party with the ratification of the representative.

This regulation is the so-called "pocket money provision" (*Taschengeldparagraph*) since it allows certain legally binding contracts of minors in cases in which they are able to perform the obligation of the contract as payments with resources that the guardian has made available for him to dispose of freely as e.g. buying candies or going to the cinema.[3]

2. Declaration of Will

One of the essential structural characteristics of German private law is the declaration of will (*Willenserklärung*). Actually, the system of the German Civil Code is based on this legal instrument. The idea of private autonomy finds its expression in the declaration of will since the individual has the right to enter a legal transaction by expressing one's own will.

Although both legal instruments, the declaration of will as also the legal transaction, are closely connected with each other, they also have to be distinguished from each other. Actually, private autonomy consists of at least one declaration of will and often of several other additional elements. Therefore, a contract is a legal transaction, which comes into existence by several valid declarations of will. Moreover, the declaration of will is an expression, which aims at the achievement of some legal consequence (*Rechtsbindungswille*). This requires firstly an outer act of expression, which could have any kind of form, also implicitly, and secondly at an internal state regarding the intention achieving a concrete legal consequence.[4] The internal state of a

2) For further inforation *see* Dieter Medicus/Jens Petersen, *Bürgerliches Recht*, 2017, p. 75.

3) Ansgar Staudinger/Björn Steinrötter, "Minderjährige im Zivilrecht," *JuS*, 2012, p. 97 (99).

4) *See* Jörg Neuner, "Was ist eine Willenserklärung?" *JuS*, 2007, p. 881.

declaration of will is further distinguished in two aspects; first of all, there is the desire to act (*Handlungswille*), which is a conscious and deliberate act, however, is e.g. absent when speaking while sleeping. Secondly, there is the consciousness of declaration (*Erklärungsbewusstsein*). The consciousness of declaration is the awareness that acting in a certain way affects a concrete legal consequence such as the desire to enter a specific legal transaction. Basically, silence will not constitute a declaration of will.[5]

Then, there is an important distinction between declarations of will requiring a receipt by another party before taking effect (*empfangsbedürftige Willenserklärung*) and those that do not need to be received (*einseitige Willenserklärungen*). Declarations of will requiring a receipt become effective only when they have been delivered to the addressee. If the declaration of will is for a person who is not present, this means that it has to be placed in the sphere of control of the addressee in such a way that under normal circumstances he would be in a position to receive it.[6] This can be for a letter containing a declaration of will if it is placed in the addressee's letterbox or e-mail inbox. Section 130 German Civil Code (*Wirksamwerden der Willenserklärung gegenüber Abwesenden*) provides comprehensive regulations on the effectiveness of a declaration of intent to absent parties:

> (1) A declaration of intent that is to be made to another becomes effective, if made in his absence, at the moment when this declaration arrives at him. It does not become effective if a revocation reaches the other previously or at the same time.
> (2) The effectiveness of a declaration of intent is not affected if the person declaring dies or loses capacity to contract after making a declaration.
> (3) These provisions apply even if the declaration of intent is to be made to a public authority.

3. Legal Transactions

One of the key concepts in German Civil Law is the legal transaction (*Rechtsgeschäft*). The most relevant example of a legal transaction is the contract. A legal transaction is an expression of the idea of private autonomy and individual freedom. This means that it is the most important tool that the legal system defines for the individual to structure his private affairs on his own initiative. A declaration of will forms the core of a legal transaction to which the further elements are added, like requirements of form or special compensation. A legal transaction usually involves two or more parties. In

5) Nigel Foster/Satish Sule, *German Legal System and Laws*, 2010, p. 431.
6) Frank Weller, "Der Zugang von Willenserklärungen," *JuS*, 2005, p. 788 (791).

the case of a contract, there are mostly two parties and, therefore, a contract consists of two corresponding declarations of will. This will usually be an offer (*Angebot*) and an acceptance of this offer (*Annahme*) that can be a 'yes' or by obvious behaviour, by nodding one's head for example.

The abstraction principle (*Abstraktionsprinzip*) and the principle of separation mean that there is a strict distinction between obligation transaction (creates rights in personam) and disposition transaction (creates rights in rem).[7] This principle is very characteristic to the German Civil Law. It means that the validity of the disposition transaction is, in principle, independent of the validity of the obligation transaction to unwind through law of unjustified enrichment (restitution).

The validity of a disposition presupposes a particular power on the part of the person claiming to make the disposition of, for example, the owner's ability to transfer ownership. Alongside, the validity of the obligation transaction does not depend on a power of disposition. Insofar, it is possible for a seller to sell one thing several times and thus enter several valid obligation transactions. However, the owner can only fulfil one selling contract with one buyer and will be liable in damages to the other buyers.

4. Form Requirements

Generally, legal transactions and declarations of will are legally binding without fulfilling any requirements of a special form. This is also an outcome of the principle of private autonomy. Therefore, the German Civil Code states certain form requirements (*Formerfordernisse*) only as exemptions from the general rule that contracts and all the other legal transactions are not under the obligation of certain form requirements. An oral agreement or even mere obvious behaviour may be sufficient in most cases. However, in some special constellations certain forms must be complied with. One of the major reasons for that is warning of factors such as security reasons for both parties of the contract. A written and signed contract can always prove the agreement of the contract before court. From a practical point of view, this is also the reason why it is often recommended to have a written contract, moreover signed by the parties, to provide evidence for any kind of possible dispute in the future.

If a contract or any other legal transaction requires a certain form, this is explicitly codified in the German Civil Code. Form requirements are stated under section 126 German Civil Code for the written form (*Schriftformerfordernis*), section 126a German Civil Code for the electronic form and

7) *See* Dieter Medicus/Jens Petersen, *Bürgerliches Recht*, 2017, 18, p. 259.

section 127 German Civil Code for the text form. The most relevant form is a written contract that requires the personal signature of each party due to section 126 para. 1 German Civil Code.[8] Moreover, there is the requirement that the parties have to conclude the contract in front of a public notary (*Notar*) for special kind of contracts. This official documentation by a notary (*notarielle Beurkundung*) is the strictest form requirement by law, mostly involving contracts on real estate. The notary as an official person gives further information and warning regarding the legal consequences to the parties.

Finally, section 125 German Civil Code states the voidness resulting from a defect of form:

> A legal transaction that lacks the form prescribed by statute is void. In case of doubt, lack of the form specified by legal transaction also results in voidness.

IV. Law of Obligations

The law of obligations (*Schuldrecht*) in the 2nd book of the German Civil Code is of high importance since it provides a comprehensive collection of general regulations which refer to a broad scope of legal scenarios. The contract (*Vertrag*) with all its regulations is actually the core aspect of this field of law. Basically, parties can develop atypical and hybrid contracts as well as completely new types of agreements under the principle of private autonomy.[9] Typical types of contracts are codified in separate regulations providing particular regulations for specific scenarios. These are sales contract (*Kaufvertrag*), leasing contract (*Mietvertrag*), contract of personal service or contract of employment (*Dienstvertrag*). Most relevant is the sales contract. Accordingly, the chapter will put a focus on this.

1. Contracts and Obligations

Since parties can develop atypical and mixed contracts, even contracts without any specification are foreseen in the German Civil Code. Section 311 German Civil Code refers to contracts in general terms and provides regulations on obligations created by legal transaction and obligations similar to legal transactions:

8) *See also* Mansel, in: Stürner, Rolf (Editor) Jauernig, *Bürgerliches Gesetzbuch*, 2018, p. 126 no. 4.
9) Richard Haase/Rolf Keller, *Grundlagen und Grundformen des Rechts*, 2003, note 190.

(1) In order to create an obligation by legal transaction and to alter the contents of an obligation, a contract between the parties is necessary, unless otherwise provided by statute law.
(2) An obligation with duties under section 241 (2) also comes into existence by
1. the commencement of contract negotiations
2. the initiation of a contract where one party, with regard to a potential contractual relationship, gives the other party the chance of affecting his rights, legal interests and other interests, or entrusts these to him, or
3. similar business contacts.
(3) An obligation with duties under section 241 (2) may also come into existence in relation to persons who are not themselves intended to be parties to the contract. Such an obligation comes into existence in particular if the third party, by laying claim to being given a particularly high degree of trust, substantially influences the pre-contract negotiations or the entering into of the contract.

Section 311 German Civil Code refers to section 241 para. 2 German Civil Code several times. As shown later, section 241 para. 2 German Civil Code refers to several constellations of contractual and pre-contractual situations in which the personal interests of both parties are protected besides the actual contractual obligation (*nichtleistungsbezogene Nebenpflichten*).[10] Insofar, section 241 para. 2 German Civil Code also refers to duties arising from an obligation, therefore, by any kind of contract:

(1) By virtue of an obligation an obligee is entitled to claim performance from the obligor. The performance may also consist in forbearance.
(2) An obligation may also, depending on its contents, oblige each party to take account of the rights, legal interests and other interests of the other party.

Due to this regulation, the contract law is quite flexible. However, this does not mean that these types of contracts are not under the same protection of law. All contracts are generally binding under the principle "pacta sunt servanda" which means that agreements must be kept.

Referring to the general principles of the law of contract, firstly, obligations come into existence by legal transaction. These legal transactions are usually contracts, or they arise by law, like tort law (*Haftungs- und Schadensrecht*) and unjustified enrichment law (*Bereicherungsrecht*). Secondly, there are several regulations limiting the private autonomy. The freedom of

10) Dieter Medicus/Jens Petersen, *Bürgerliches Recht*, 2017, p. 96.

contract, and especially the misuse of any superior position, is limited by the general clauses of section 242 German Civil Code (*"Treu und Glauben"*) which regulates that everyone has to act with regard to normal business practice. Section 242 German Civil Code – *Performance in good faith* – says:

> An obligor has a duty to perform according to the requirements of good faith, taking customary practice into consideration.

Another important regulation in this context is section 138 German Civil Code. This regulation provides that transactions which are contrary to public policy are void due to their unconscionability (*Sittenwidrigkeit*). This section aims to protect in situations of obvious disparity. Section 138 German Civil Code (Legal transaction contrary to public policy; usury) states that:

> (1) A legal transaction that is contrary to public policy is void.
> (2) Especially, a legal transaction is void by which a person, by exploiting the predicament, inexperience, lack of sound judgement or considerable weakness of will of another, causes himself or a third party, in exchange for an act of performance, to be promised or granted pecuniary advantages that are obviously disproportionate to the performance.

Usually, section 138 para. 1 German Civil Code refers to spousal guarantees for high amounts of money (*Ehegattenbürschaft*),[11] which is viewed as violating moral standards since it could be a burden for the whole family.

These provisions are important not only for the German Civil Code but the whole private law since these regulations open the private law to the influence of Fundamental Rights as fundamental value judgements as already explained above. The ideas of "good faith changed and still change the social development, which makes the law flexible for changes of new interpretation.

2. Sale Contract

For daily life, the sale contract (*Kaufvertrag*) is the most relevant. The sale contract under section 433 German Civil Code is also the core regulation for typical contractual duties in a purchase agreement:

> (1) By a sale contract, the seller of a thing is obliged to deliver the thing to the buyer and to supply ownership of the thing for the buyer. The

11) *See BGHZ* 151, p. 34.

seller must supply the thing for the buyer free from material and legal defects.

(2) The buyer is obliged to pay the seller the agreed purchase price and to accept delivery of the thing purchased.

This provision states clearly both obligations and rights of the parties regarding the object of purchase. In the following provision section 434 German Civil Code, the law gives definitions of material defects (*Sachmangel*), and section 435 German Civil Code explains legal defects (*Rechtsmangel*).[12]

Material defects under section 434 German Civil Code are defined as follows:

(1) The thing is free from material defects if, upon the passing of the risk, the thing has the quality agreed in the contract. To the extent that the quality has not been agreed, the thing is free of material defects

1. if it is suitable for the use intended under the contract,
2. if it is suitable for the customary use and its quality is usual in things of the same kind and the buyer may expect this quality in view of the type of the thing.

Quality under sentence 2 no. 2 above includes features that the buyer can expect from the public statements on specific characteristics of the thing that are made by the seller, the producer (section 4 (1) and (2) of the Product Liability Act [Produkthaftungsgesetz]) or his assistant, including without limitation in advertising or in identification, unless the seller was aware of the statement and also had no duty to be aware of it, or at the time when the contract was entered into it, had been corrected in a manner of equal value, or it did not influence the decision to purchase the thing.

(2) It is also a material defect if the agreed installation by the seller or persons whom he used to perform his obligation has been carried out improperly. However, there is a material defect in a thing intended for installation if the installation instructions are defective, unless the thing has been assembled without any error.

(3) Supply by the seller of a different thing or of a lesser amount of the thing is equivalent to a material defect.

In fact, the most relevant scenario would be a damage of the object of purchase under section 434 para. 1 German Civil Code. However, due to the jurisprudence of the German Supreme Court, a material defect could also be

12) Richard Haase/Rolf Keller, *Grundlagen und Grundformen des Rechts*, 2003, pp. 118–119.

the wrong colour of a car[13], the poor state of health of a dressage horse[14] such as other various cases. Then, legal defects under section 435 German Civil Code are defined as follows:

> The thing is free of legal defects if third parties, in relation to the thing, can assert either no rights, or only the rights taken over in the purchase agreement, against the buyer. It is equivalent to a legal defect if a right that does not exist is registered in the Land Register.

The seller is under the obligation to transfer the object of the sale to the buyer free of any claims of third parties.[15] Otherwise this could be classified as a legal defect of the object of purchase. Actually, material effects and legal effects can be claimed at the same time. These categories are not mutually exclusive. For judicial argumentation in legal dispute, it has to be preciously described what concrete type of defect is in question.

If the seller does not fulfil these obligations, the buyer has the right to resort to the general remedies applicable to bilateral transactions set out in sections 320-326 German Civil Code.[16] Basically, the seller is liable for the fact that the goods are defective (not of merchantable quality) while the buyer has a number of possible remedies.[17] These possible remedies like rescinding the contract (*Rücktritt*) or reducing the price of purchase (*Minderung*) such as compensation for damages (*Schadensersatz*) are regulated in section 437 German Civil Code. However, if the seller does not fulfil the obligations under a valid sale contract by selling a defective good, the buyer has to continue to demand for the fulfilment of the contract, first by asking to repair the object of purchase or to repair it. This cure (*Nacherfüllung*) as supplementary performance is an important legal construction within the law of obligations as on the one hand it provides a right for the seller still to fulfil his contractual obligations while it gives the buyer the right to insist on the fulfilment of the contract on the other hand.[18] Only if the seller also fails with this, can the buyer refer to several other remedies. As cure the buyer may, at his choice, demand that the defect is remedied or a new item free of defects is supplied, due to section 439 para. 1 German Civil Code.

In case where the supplementary performance has failed, the buyer can rescind the contract due to sections 437 no. 2, 440, 323, 326 German Civil

13) Bundesgerichtshof, Decision from 17.02.2010 – *VIII ZR* 70/07, *NJW-RR* 2017, p. 1289.
14) Bundesgerichtshof, Decision from 18.10.2017 – *VIII ZR* 32/16, *NJW* 2018, p. 150.
15) Gerhard Robbers, *German Law*, 2017, p. 177; Hans Brox/Wolf-Dietrich Walker, *Besonderes Schuldrecht*, 2015, pp. 9–10.
16) Gerhard Robbers, *German Law*, 2017, p. 177.
17) Gerhard Robbers, *German Law*, 2017, p. 177; *see also* Palandt, *Bürgerliches Gesetzbuch*, 2018, Section 437, note 2.
18) *See also* Palandt, *Bürgerliches Gesetzbuch*, 2018, Section 437, note 2.

Code. Alternatively, the buyer can also demand that the price for which the goods were sold be reduced to the extent that the defects in the goods diminish the value.[19]

Besides this, a claim for compensation is also possible due to section 325 German Civil Code. Claims for damages can be made under section 437 no. 3, 280, 281, 283, 284, 311a German Civil Code. The main principle is that the defect or lack of performance is due the fault of the seller. Within the concept of the law of obligations, all damages for the breach of duty find their legal basis in section 280 para. 1 German Civil Code requiring the responsibility (*Vertretenmüssen*) of the party:

> If the obligor breaches a duty arising from the obligation, the obligee may demand damages for the damage caused thereby. This does not apply if the obligor is not responsible for the breach of duty.

This regulation on the compensation is one of the core regulations in the law of obligations since it refers to all irregularities in the performance of a contract. This could also occur in any other kinds of contract like leasing contract, contract of personal service or contract of employment. Basically, the most relevant examples for compensation are impossibility of performance (*Unmöglichkeit der Leistung*), the failure to perform within the prescribed time (*Verzögerung* and *Verzug*), and positive malperformance (*positive Vertragsverletzung*).[20] The latter example of *positive malperformance* is special in the respect that the contract is fulfilled but damages occur besides the actual obligations of the contract. This is basically the case if one party violates the rights, legal interests and other interests of the other party as protected under section 241 para. 2 German Civil Code. This could be, for example, if a delivered good is in perfect condition but several other interiors gets destroyed or damaged by installing it in the customers home.

A violation of section 241 para. 2 German Civil Code is also relevant for the last example of compensation, which is the pre-contractual liability (*culpa in comprahendo*). Even before a contract is concluded, the parties have these obligations and a violation of these can lead damages on the ground of sections 311 para. 2, 241 para. 2 German Civil Code.[21] To give an example, interior in the customers home this could be damaged or destroyed by the first inspection visit of the company's workers who prepare the delivering of the purchased good, such as furniture for example. In this case, the buyer can claim for compensation, although there is no defect on the object of purchase itself.

---

19) Gerhard Robbers, *German Law*, 2017, p. 177.

20) *See also* Bundesgerichtshof, Decision from 27.03.2009–V ZR 30/08, *NJW* 2009, p. 2120.

21) Gerhard Robbers, *German Law*, 2017, p. 174.

3. Law of Torts

Besides the law of contracts, the law of torts (*Deliktsrecht*) is also a relevant aspect of German private law, especially when it comes to compensation. In fact, the law of obligations regarding contracts is more special but it can be applied besides tort law as well. While in the law of contract the anchor is the contractual relationship itself, tort law refers to the wrongful act.

a. The Basic Principles of Tort Law

Someone who commits a legally wrongful act, in other words, an act contrary to the law, and thereby causes damages to the protected legal interests of another person, will generally be liable to compensate the injured party for the resulting harm.[22] Even limited use of a protected good would be concerned to be compensated.[23] However, the obligation arising by this is not penal in nature.[24] Punitive damages (*Strafschaden*) in private law like in the US-American law[25] are basically not acknowledged in German private law. The German law of torts focuses rather on compensation for different scenarios of wrongful acts.

b. Tortious Liability of Minors

The tortious liability of minors is one of the most relevant aspects in German tort law. First of all, children under the age of seven lack tortious liability. Consequently, they are not liable for any wrongful act due to section 828 para. 1 German Civil Code. Then, under section 828 para. 2 German Civil Code, children between seven and eighteen are fully liable for the damage they have caused,[26] at least negligent (*fahrlässig*), if they had sufficient insight to discern their responsibility.[27] Section 828 German Civil Code provides the regulation on tortious liability of minors in German law:

> (1) A person who has not reached the age of seven is not responsible for any damage caused to another person.
>
> (2) A person who has reached the age of seven but not the age of ten is not responsible for any damage that he inflicts on another party in an accident involving a motor vehicle, a railway or a suspension railway. This

22) Gerhard Robbers, *German Law*, 2017, p. 188.

23) Eduard Picker, "Das Deliktsrecht im Zivilrechtssystem," *ZfPW*, 2015, p. 385 (409); *see also* *BGHZ* 55, p. 153 – *Fleet Fall.*

24) Gerhard Robbers, *German Law*, 2017, p. 188.

25) *See also* Michael Klode, "Punitive Damages - Ein aktueller Beitrag zum US-amerikanischen Strafschadensersatz", *NJOZ*, 2009, p. 1762.

26) *See* *BGHZ* 161, p. 180.

27) *See* Ansgar Staudinger/Björn Steinrötter, "Minderjährige im Zivilrecht," *JuS*, 2012, p. 97 (103).

does not apply if he intentionally caused the injury.

(3) A person who has not yet reached the age of eighteen is, to the extent that his responsibility is not excluded under subsection (1) or (2), not responsible for any damage he inflicts on another person if, when committing the damaging act, he does not have the insight required to recognise his responsibility.

c. Liability for Damages under Section 823 Para. 1 German Civil Code

A person who, intentionally or negligently, unlawfully injures the life, body, health, freedom, property or another right of another person is liable to make compensation to the other party for the damage arising from this.

Section 823 para. 1 German Civil Code states clearly that anyone who, contrary to law, deliberately causes a harm to the life, person, health, liberty, property or other rights of another person has an obligation to compensate that person for the resulting damage.[28] Duc to the wording of the law, some rights (*Schutzgüter*) are expressively mentioned to be protected and further the so-called other rights which can be possession (*Besitz*) or the general right of personality (*allgemeines Persönlichkeitsrecht*) for example.[29]

The general right of personality arises from Article 1 para. 1 and Article 2 para. 1 basic law is recognized as one of the most relevant "other rights" within the scope of section 823 para. 1 German Civil Code. Besides different aspects such as the right to one's image (*Recht am eigenen Bild*) or personal honour (*Ehrschutz*), the general right of personality contains the protection of privacy (*Schutz der Privatsphäre*).[30] This is mostly relevant in cases of mass media reporting on famous people.[31] In addition, these rights become also more relevant between ordinary private persons when they communicate in the internet and infrige other persons' personality rights.

A claim for damages thus depends on the proof of damage to one of various specific rights of another person for which the infringement of rights and the resulting damage must be attributable (*kausal*) to some culpable act on the part of the defendant.[32] Regarding the infringement of expressively mentioned rights under section 823 para. 1 German Civil Code, there is a presumption (*Vermutung*) that the act causing the harm was wrongful. For

---

28) Gerhard Robbers, *German Law*, 2017, p. 188.

29) Hans Brox/Wolf-Dietrich Walker, *Besonderes Schuldrecht*, 2015, pp. 527–535.

30) *See* BGHZ 131, p. 332 – *Caroline von Hannover*.

31) *See* Judith Janna Märten, "Personality Rights and Freedom of Expression – A Journey through the Development of German Jurispridence under the Influence of the European Court of Human Rights," *Journal of Media Law* (2) 2012, p. 333.

32) Gerhard Robbers, *German Law*, 2017, pp. 188–189.

example, it is rebuttably presumed that the defendant owed the claimant a duty of care.[33] However, it is possible to justify the wrongful act due to several reasons provided by the law such as self-defence, defence of property or basic rights. Referring to the example of the violation of famous persons' privacy in the media, justification is always grounded on freedom of speech under Article 5 para. 1 basic law.[34]

d. Liability for Damages under Section 823 Para. 2 German Civil Code

Section 823 para. 2 German Civil Code provides the second legal ground for tortious liability:

> The same duty is held by a person who commits a breach of a statute that is intended to protect another person. If, according to the contents of the statute, it may also be breached without fault, then liability to compensation merely exists in the case of fault.

Section 823 para. 2 German Civil Code imposes an obligation to pay damages on anyone who wrongfully infringes against any law which its purpose is the protection of other persons and by this, it refers to specific protective statutes (*Schutzgesetze*).[35] These specific protective statutes can be any statute law in this respect, for example fraud (*Betrug*) under section 263 Criminal Code.

V. The Law of Property

The law of Property (*Sachenrecht*) is also one of the major fields in private law. While the law of obligations (*Schuldrecht*) regulates the legal relationship between persons, the law of property (also called law of things) deals with real rights (*dingliche Rechte*).[36] From this distinction the principle of abstraction (*Abstraktionsprinzip*) arises by keeping these two parts completely separated from each other in German civil law.[37]

The next important distinction made in German property law is the one between possession (*Besitz*) and ownership (*Eigentum*). Receiving property

33) Gerhard Robbers, *German Law*, 2017, p. 188.

34) *See* Judith Janna Märten, "Personality Rights and Freedom of Expression – A Journey through the Development of German Jurispridence under the Influence of the European Court of Human Rights," *Journal of Media Law* (2) 2012, p. 333.

35) Hans Brox/Wolf-Dietrich Walker, *Besonderes Schuldrecht*, 2015, p. 558; Gerhard Robbers, *German Law*, 2017, p. 190.

36) Gerhard Robbers, *German Law*, 2017, p. 196.

37) *See* Dieter Medicus/Jens Petersen, *Bürgerliches Recht*, 2017, pp. 18, 259.

does not necessarily mean receiving possession and vice versa.

> To give an example: The tenant of a house will be in possession of the house but actually it is the landlord who (usually) is the proprietor owner.

Another example would be:

> If A lends his bike to B for a couple of days, he does not cease to be owner. B is merely possessor of the bike. However, if C steals the bike from B, he now becomes the possessor, as he has the factual control over the bike. This still does not affect A's ownership.[38]

All these real rights are enforceable against the whole world, so against everybody, and not against another party of a particular legal transaction. That also means that these rights are absolute in their nature. The transfer of ownership is the most relevant. It is possible by law or legal transaction.

The transfer of ownership is regulated in section 929 German Civil Code:

> For the transfer of the ownership of a movable thing, it is necessary that the owner delivers the thing to the acquirer and both agree that ownership is going to be passed. If the acquirer is in possession of the thing, agreement on the transfer of the ownership suffices.

Due to this regulation, the transfer of ownership has basically two requirements. Firstly, an agreement on the passing of ownership is required. This consists of two corresponding declarations of will. Then, the thing in question must be handed over.

Regarding real estate and land, for example, there are different and stricter requirements for a valid transfer of ownership. However, the first requirement of an agreement on the passing of ownership is the same. Moreover, however, the agreement must be declared formally before an authorised official in presence of both parties, regularly before a public notary (*Notar*).[39] Then, the thing in question also must be handed over which means for real estate that the alteration of the legal position (*Rechtsänderung*) must be registered in the land register (*Grundbuch*) on which the public is entitled to rely on.[40] This is because a transfer of ownership of real estate is much more momentous than other items of daily life's transactions.

---

38) Nigel Foster/Satish Sule, *German Legal System and Laws*, 2010, p. 415.

39) Palandt, *Bürgerliches Gesetzbuch*, 2018, Section 925, note 2.

40) Richard Haase/Rolf Keller, "Richtigkeitsvermutung," *Grundlagen und Grundformen des Rechts*, 2003, note 546.

VI. Other Fields of Private Law

Other fields of private law concern family law (*Familienrecht*) such as law of succession (*Erbrecht*). Both parts are regulated in the German Civil Code. From a real live perspective, these parts are closely connected. However, from a dogmatic point of view, these parts need to be separated. While succession basically concerns transfer of property, family law is quite unique by taking the special needs of family members and the family as whole into account.

In addition, there are more fields of private law that concern the economic world. These are intellectual property law (*Urheberrecht*), company law (*Gesellschaftsrecht*), trade and commercial law (*Handelsrecht*), bank law (*Bankenrecht*) and insolvency law (*Insolvenzrecht*). Closely related to these fields are labour and employment law which also play a great role in Germany. However, this field of law has to be considered separately.[41]

41) *See* Chapter 7.

Chapter 6

Criminal Law

I. Criminology and Criminal Law

Criminology (*Kriminologie*) is related to criminal law in terms of subject matter but is to be distinguished from the criminal law (*Strafrecht*) as the study of the rules governing the treatment of crime.

In contrast to criminal law, criminology firstly concerns the reasons for criminal behaviour by focusing on several aspects of crime in society as also on the individual criminal person.[1] The theories about the reasons for criminal behaviour can be differed into two big branches, the biological theories and the social theories:

Biological theories assume that the reasons for criminal behaviour are determined in the physical constitution of the criminal. Thereby, these theories suppose that some human type like a "born criminal" or an "offender by nature" exists. For naming an example, in the 1960s in the USA, a theory became popular that asserted by the example of the eightfold ripper Richard Speck that a redundant Y-chromosome in the genetic code of a person (XYY-syndrome) would lead to criminal behaviour.[2] Later, studies disproved this theory by ascertaining that the number of XYY-men among convicts has not been significantly higher than the number among non-criminal male individuals.[3] Biological theories have been favoured by fascists regimes in particular, e.g. by the National-Socialists in Germany in the 1930s. The Nazis thought that the Jewish population was dangerous to the German people not by their will but by their genetic, which would determine the Jews to a destructive behaviour. Therefore, the Nazis came to the assumption that the

1) Karl-Ludwig Kunz/Tobias Singelnstein, *Kriminologie*, 2016, p. 14.

2) Armand Mergen, *Der geborene Verbrecher*, 1968, p. 43

3) Saleeem Shah/Loren H. Roth, "Biological and psychophysiological factors in criminality," p. 137, in: Daniel Glaser (Editor), *Handbook of Criminology*, 1974, pp. 101–173.

Jewish population had to be wiped out as the only possible solution to get rid of the danger. Hence, this example demonstrates how dangerous biological theories can become when set into practice. Other studies, known as bio-chemical assumptions, attempt to ascertain if a lack of substances, which are naturally produced by the human body, stimulating the brain functions. It is supposed as well that a lack of vitamins and minerals could result in abnormal and thereby possibly criminal behaviour.[4]

On the other side, social theories concentrate on the social environment of the offender for evaluating the reasons of criminal behaviour. One of the social theories is the subculture theory, which was developed in the 1950s in the USA. Scholars asserted that in particular, young men joined criminal gangs as a reaction to failing to achieve material success as also acceptance. Inside those gangs, another system of values was appreciated, which in case of following the rules of the gang, led to the acceptance and material success the young men were seeking. But interacting within these group values would also mean violating the laws of the state, hence a criminal behaviour of the individuals.[5]

A similar theory is the social-learning theory. The individual learns by his social environment that criminal behaviour leads to success.[6] For example, a child who has been beaten by the father learns that violence turns the other individual into a favoured direction.

More into a psychological perspective, a theory exists based on the studies of *Sigmund Freud*. Freud drew the conclusion that the child is a "universal-criminal creature" because it had not learnt to control his drives by developing an Ego and also a Superego, which functions as the moral authority of the personality. But in case of e.g. a disturbed relationship to the father, the Superego cannot be developed properly by the child, which can lead to a criminal behaviour in the future. Hence, criminality appears as a result of an infant development disturbance.[7]

Another theory, which is strongly accepted in the present German criminal law relating to young offenders, is the *Labelling Approach* theory. By this theory, criminality does not appear as an objective matter of fact, but is the result of the subjective view of the society on a certain kind of behaviour. Hence, the individual, who shows a non-conform behaviour, is labelled as a criminal by his social environment for this and adopts this role. Thereby, the individual considers criminal behaviour as his personal way in life, which

---

4) Karl-Ludwig Kunz, *Kriminologie*, 2nd edition, 1998, p. 115

5) In summary: Albert K. Cohen, *Delinquent Boys. The culture of the gang*, 1951.

6) In summary: Albert Bandura, *Lernen am Modell. Ansätze zu einer sozial-kognitiven Lerntheorie*, 1976.

7) In summary: Rüdiger Herren, *Freud und die Kriminologie. Einführung in die psychoanalytische Kriminologie*, 1973.

gets him in conflict with the criminal law in the future again.[8] By acknowledging this theory, the German criminal procedures in relation to young offenders attempts to appear not too much as a criminal procedure. For example, the judge does not wear a robe of office but a suit, and instead of a criminal punishment the young offender will receive educational corrective methods by law in most of the cases. In conclusion, these theories of criminology are helpful to understand the reasons of criminal behaviour. However, none of these theories is able to explain the origins of criminal behaviour in general since the human nature is too individual for a general explanation.

In addition, criminology deals with the several reasons of punishment. Important aspects are usually crime prevention (*Prävention*), deterrence (*Abschreckung*), retribution (*Vergeltung*) and rehabilitation (*Resozialisation*).[9] The latter is the relevant goal of punishment in Germany and aims to reform the perpetrator as a preparation for re-integration into society by living without committing crimes. Rehabilitation aims to protect both the perpetrator and the society in the future. Imprisonment offers social training in special centres in which prisoners generally undergo vocational training and, moreover, they do paid work to get prepared for their future life after their imprisonment. Although rehabilitation has sometimes been criticized in society by arguing on a lack of effectiveness in real life, it still counts as the only legitimate purpose of punishment today.[10] Moreover, criminology is also relevant for the question why young offenders are punished by a different system of legal consequences under the Juvenile Courts Act (*Jugendstrafgesetzbuch; JGG*). This is going to be discussed later in this chapter.

Finally, criminology is rather an empirical discipline concerned with the causes and varieties of crime and the effects of the sanctions imposed on people who break the rules. Criminal law exclusively operates with codified statute laws that describe the requirements of a crime and state the legal consequence. Both are described in an abstract manner and have to be applied concretely for every single case.

II. The German Criminal Code and Its Structure

The major legal source of German criminal law is the German Criminal Code (*Strafgesetzbuch; StGB*). Like other statutes, and also explained related to the German Civil Code, the German Criminal Code consists of two main parts which are firstly the General Part ("*Allgemeiner Teil*") and secondly

---

8) In summary: Karl-Ludwig Kunz, *Kriminologie*, 2nd edition, 1998, 20, pp, 176–191.

9) *See also* Markus Dirk Dubber, "Theories of Crimes and Punishment in German Criminal Law," *The American Journal of Comparative Law*, Vol. 53, No. 3, 2005, pp. 679–707.

10) Michael Köhne, "Resozialisierungsunfähige Strafgefangene," *ZRP*, 2003, p. 207.

the Special Part (*"Besonderer Teil"*). In the general part, overall issues are arranged while in the special part different criminal offences and their definitions and punishments are listed.

The book of general provisions sets out structural principles applicable to all aspects of criminal law such as the area of application, general forms of punishable behaviour, such as attempts and completed crimes, and the requirements of intent or negligence. Examples are regulations on the area of the law's validity, law-related definitions, the capacity to be adjudged guilty (*Schuld*), perpetration and incitement or accessoryship (*Täterschaft*), necessary defence (*Notwehr*), general provisions for punishments such as fines and imprisonment and also the attempt (*Versuch*). All these rather abstract and general regulations can be applied to any kinds of criminal act that is set out in the special part of the German Criminal Code such as other criminal laws.

The section on specific offences determines the specific requirements of individual crimes, like murder, manslaughter, fraud, theft, bribery and many more. Offences are structured in different categories which all provide separate chapters containing regulations on specific types of criminal actions. These are the examples of crimes against the democratic rule of law, crimes against public order, crimes against the person of a sexual nature, crimes against life and crimes against another person's wealth.

III. Criminal Offences

1. Types of Offences

First of all, there are different types of criminal offence, which have to be distinguished from each other. These are lesser offences (*Ordnungswidrigkeiten*), misdemeanour (*Vergehen*) and felonies (*Verbrechen*). Secondly, the first category of lesser offences has to be distinguished from the other following categories, which are exclusively related to criminal law. In fact, the criminal law is something different in context of lesser offences since the law of lesser offences finds its roots in the punitive administrative law of the 19th century and is imposed by administrative authorities.[11] Actually, the original idea behind the concept was to decriminalize the ethically neutral disregard for administrative rule. To give an example, most traffic offences or disorderly conduct are accordingly classified as lesser offences. The various types of lesser offences are regulated in the Lesser Offences Act (*OWiG Gesetz für Ordnungswidrigkeiten*), which is a statue law on the federal level.[12] On many

11) Gerhard Robbers, *German Law*, 2017, p. 114.

respects, its structure can be compared to that of the German Criminal Code. However, as a legal consequence, it only states monetary fines (*Geldstafen*) and can apply to juristic persons, which is not possible under the German Criminal Code.

Then, section 12 German Criminal Code[13] provides a clear distinction between felonies and misdemeanour as it states:

> (1) Felonies are unlawful acts that are punishable by a minimum sentence of one year's imprisonment.
> (2) Misdemeanours are unlawful acts that are punishable by a lesser minimum term of imprisonment or by fine.
> (3) Aggravations or mitigations provided for under the provisions of the General Part, or under especially serious or less serious cases in the Special Part, shall be irrelevant to this classification.

This provision defines that felonies are offences punishable by imprisonment for at least one year. Severe criminal offences like a murder under section 211 German Criminal Code are usually felonies. Different from that, misdemeanours are unlawful acts that are punishable for under one year imprisonment, which are crimes like theft under section 242 German Criminal Code.

2. The Structure of the Criminal Offence and Crimes by Omission

The structure of the criminal offence (*Aufbau einer Straftat*)[14] is one of the most elementary aspects in criminal law. First of all, there must be a person who committed a criminal act. Secondly, however, the concrete act of the accused person has to be unlawful and thirdly, the accused person has to have acted in a culpable state of mind. Therefore, three essential elements must be present before an offence is committed. To sum up, these are the physical and mental elements of an offence (*Tatbestand*), unlawfulness (*Rechtswidrigkeit*), and guilt (*Schuld*).[15] Only when all three elements are given, would punishment of the accused person be the legal result.

To complete the structure of a criminal offence and refer to the first step, it is important to have a criminal act. This could be if the accused person shoots the victim or takes a thing of his or her possession.[16] However, the accused

12) Richard Haase/Rolf Keller, *Grundlagen und Grundformen des Rechts*, 2003, pp. 425–427.
13) *See also* Volker Krey/Robert Esser, Deutsches Strafrecht – Allgemeiner Teil, 2012, p. 82.
14) *See also* Volker Krey/Robert Esser, *Deutsches Strafrecht – Allgemeiner Teil*, 2012, pp. 255–278.
15) Nigel Foster/Satish Sule, *German Legal System and Laws*, 2010, p. 341.
16) Gerhard Robbers, *German Law*, 2017, p. 116.

person may also become guilty of a crime by omission (*Unterlassungsdelikt*[17]) if he or she fails to act in a situation in which the law imp- oses a duty to do so.[18] The so-called "genuine crimes by omission" impose penalties on the failure to fulfil a duty to act that is expressively imposed by law.[19] The most relevant example would be the regulation section 323c German Criminal Code (*Unterlassene Hilfeleistung*) as a *real* crime by omission (*echtes Unterlassungsdelikt*) under which certain duties to help another person in emergency cases is stated.[20] There is a second group of crimes within this category which are kind of imitated crimes (*unechte Unterlassungsdelikte*).[21] They are present if by an omission an act that generally requires positive action is committed but section 13 German Criminal Code provides that not taking steps to prevent an act or situation that fulfils the factual requirements of a crime is in itself a crime, if the accused has a legal duty to prevent the act or situation occurring.[22] This could be the case if the accused person is under a special obligation due to a close relationship to the victim, for example family-members, or a special responsibility arising from a certain profession, like a teacher has in respect to the pupils (*Garantenpflicht*).[23]

3. Intent and Negligence

Most crimes require that the perpetrator (*Täter*) should have acted intentionally to be liable.[24] This is due to the regulation on intent (*Vorstatz*) and negligence (*Fahrlässigkeit*) of section 15 German Criminal Code: "*Unless the law expressly provides for criminal liability based on negligence, only intentional conduct shall attract criminal liability.*"

To act intentionally, the perpetrator must know that his or her actions fulfil the objective elements of the crime and he or she must have desired this.[25] In contrast to that, some offences are fulfilled with mere negligence. In those cases, the legislator intended to punish a lack of care. The liability for negligence has to be explicitly stated in the regulation due to legal security. A prominent example would be section 229 German Criminal Code – Causing

17) Kristian Kühl, "Das Unterlassungsdelikt," *JA*, 2014, p. 507.
18) Gerhard Robbers, *German Law*, 2017, p. 117.
19) Gerhard Robbers, *German Law*, 2017, p. 117.
20) Kristian Kühl, "Das Unterlassungsdelikt," *JA*, 2014, p. 507.
21) Kristian Kühl, "Das Unterlassungsdelikt," *JA*, 2014, p. 507 (508–511).
22) Gerhard Robbers, *German Law*, 2017, p. 117; *see also* Andreas Ransiek, "Das unechte Unterlassungsdelikt," *JuS*, 2010, p. 490 (491).
23) Richard Haase/Rolf Keller, *Grundlagen und Grundformen des Rechts*, 2003, pp. 382–383.
24) Gerhard Robbers, *German Law*, 2017, p. 118.
25) Gerhard Robbers, *German Law*, 2017, p. 118; Richard Haase/Rolf Keller, *Grundlagen und Grundformen des Rechts*, 2003, p. 384.

bodily harm by negligence (*Fahrlässige Körperverletzung*) – by stating: *Whosoever by negligence causes bodily harm to another shall be liable to imprisonment not exceeding three years or a fine.*

IV. Attempt and Withdrawal

Crimes could be completed or just attempted. The attempt (*Versuch*) could also be punishable if either the concrete law says so or if a felony is attempted. Section 23 para. 1 German Criminal Code states the liability for attempts by saying: *"Any attempt to commit a felony entails criminal liability; this applies to attempted misdemeanours only if expressly provided by law.* Insofar, the question on whether an attempt is punishable is quite easy to answer and has to be concerned as a first step. Then, section 22 German Criminal Code preciously defines the liable attempt by law in the following words: *"A person attempts to commit an offence if he takes steps which will immediately lead to the completion of the offence as envisaged by him."*

1. Attempt

The requirements for an attempt are satisfied once the perpetrator subjectively sees himself or herself as having begun to carry out his or her plan to do an act which satisfies the elements of a crime (*Tatentschluss*).[26] This aims to complete the crime.[27] An outside observer must be able to perceive that the intentions of the perpetrator are serious and that, at least in the mind of the perpetrator, the elements of a crime are about to be satisfied (*unmittelbares Ansetzen zur Tat*).[28] This element is given once the perpetrator thinks "I start now" ("*Jetzt geht es los*").[29]

2. Withdrawal

However, in order to protect the victim by motivating the perpetrator to stop his or her action,[30] a withdrawal (*Rücktritt*) from the liable attempt of a crime is possible under section 24 German Criminal Code:

26) Gerhard Robbers, *German Law*, 2017, p. 120.
27) Klaus Hoffmann-Holland, in: *MüKoStGB*, 2017, StGB Section 22, notes 34–3.
28) Gerhard Robbers, *German Law*, 2017, p. 120.
29) Holm Putzke, "Der strafbare Versuch," *JuS*, 2009, p. 985 (986); *see also* Bundesgerichtshof, Decision from 25.10.2012 – 4 StR 346/12, *NStZ*, 2013, p. 156.
30) *See also* Bundesgerichtshof, Decision from 29.6.2016 – 2 StR 588/15, *NStZ*, 2016, p. 664.

(1) A person, who of his own volition gives up the further execution of the offence or prevents its completion, is not liable for this attempt. If the offence is not completed regardless of his actions, that person is not liable if he has made a voluntary and serious effort to prevent the completion of the offence.
(2) If more than one person participate in the offence, the person who voluntarily prevents its completion is not liable for the attempt. His voluntary and earnest effort to prevent the completion of the offence shall suffice for exemption from liability, if the offence is not completed regardless of his actions or is committed independently of his earlier contribution to the offence.

V. Grounds of Justification — Self-defence and Necessity

As a general rule, if a person does an act fulfilling the factual elements of the definition of a crime, the perpetrator is acting illegally which means that the illegality (*Rechtswidrigkeit*) of an act or omission is suggested by the fact that it fits the definition of a particular crime.[31] This refers to the idea that the criminal law merely intents to punish illegal acts or behaviour. In some exceptional cases, such an act may nevertheless be lawful due to some ground of justification (*Rechtfertigungsgrund*),[32] which could be self-defence (*Notwehr*) and necessity (*Notstand*) as codified in the German Criminal Code such as the scope of certain basic rights of the German constitution.

1. Self-defence

Section 32 German Criminal Code is one of the most relevant legal grounds for justification of the offence.[33] The wording of this regulation states:

(1) A person, who commits an act in self-defence, does not act unlawfully.
(2) Self-defence means any defensive action that is necessary to avert an imminent unlawful attack on oneself or another.

According to this regulation, the attack must be present and unlawful. Therefore, there must be an attack, first of all. Then, the attack has to be present, which is the case if it is about to be commenced when it has been

31) Gerhard Robbers, *German Law*, 2017, p. 121.
32) Gerhard Robbers, *German Law*, 2017, p. 121; Richard Haase/Rolf Keller, *Grundlagen und Grundformen des Rechts*, 2003, pp. 386–387.
33) *See* Thomas Fischer (Editor), *Strafgesetzgesetzbuch*, 2018, Section 32, note 2.

already started or continues.[34] In addition, the defender must be aware of the attack at the time that his action is in self-defence. His action of defence has to be proportional in the sense that it should not be more harmful than what is necessary.[35] This regulation illustrates that the legal order essentially does not require any person to tolerate an attack on his or her legal interests if the attack itself is one of which the legal order itself disapproves.[36]

2. Necessity

Section 34 German Criminal Code regulates another ground of justification which is necessity (*rechtfertigender Notstand*):

> A person who, faced with an imminent danger to life, limb, freedom, honour, property or another legal interest which cannot otherwise be prevented, commits an act to avert the danger from himself or another, does not act unlawfully, if, upon weighing the conflicting interests, in particular the affected legal interests and the degree of the danger facing them, the protected interest substantially outweighs the one interfered with. This shall apply only if and to the extent that the act committed is an adequate means to prevent the danger.

In this defence, the criminal law takes account to situations in which the infringement of a legal interest is permissible even although the person whose interest is to be infringed is not attacking the person acting out of necessity, which is in contrast to self-defence, which only applies in the case of an illegal attack.[37] An example could be if a person's dog attacks the defender; in this case, he or she is allowed to defend himself or herself which, in a severe case, would also justify to kill the dog.

VI. Guilt and Legal Culpability

As mentioned above, the accused person is only able to be punished if his or her acts fulfil the elements of a crime as an unlawful act which has necessarily be done in a culpable state of mind with the effect that the accused

34) Nigel Foster/Satish Sule, *German Legal System and Laws*, 2010, p. 348; *see also* Bundesgerichtshof, *NJW*, 1973, p. 255 – *Brusttaschenfall.*
35) Nigel Foster/Satish Sule, *German Legal System and Laws*, 2010, p. 348.
36) Gerhard Robbers, *German Law*, 2017, p. 121.
37) Gerhard Robbers, *German Law*, 2017, p. 122.

can be held personally responsible for the relevant act.[38] The concept of guilt (*Schuld*) incorporates social responsibility.[39] Basically, guilt is the core element in criminal law when justifying punishment for a criminal offence.[40] Guilt in context of law is recognized as legal culpability that depends on the individual's criminal capacity (*Schuldfähigkeit*). Due to section 19 German Criminal Code, children under the age of fourteen do not have criminal capacity and generally the criminal capacity of minors must be examined also by referring to the Juvenile Courts Act (*Jugendgerichtsgesetz*).

However, the most relevant is concerning the aspect of the individual's criminal capacity, is insanity (*Schuldunfähigkeit wegen seelischer Störungen*), which is regulated in section 20 German Criminal Code:

> Any person, who at the time of the commission of the offence is incapable of appreciating the unlawfulness of their actions or of acting in accordance with any such appreciation due to a pathological mental disorder, a profound consciousness disorder, debility or any other serious mental abnormality, is considered to act without guilt.

Section 20 German Criminal Code provides a presumption of incapacity for persons with mental disorders.[41] However, there are also other aspects like mental disturbances, and judges always have to consider all circumstances of the concrete case. In fact, drunkenness presents the greatest problems because there is no objective test as to what blood alcohol levels will result in incapacity section 20 German Criminal Code.[42] The German criminal law also recognizes the possibility of diminished responsibility arising from any of these causes with the consequence that the sentence may then be reduced appropriately due to section 21 German Criminal Code (*verminderte Schuldfähigkeit*).[43]

VII. Mistakes in the Context of Criminal Law

There are several possible mistakes in the context of criminal Law that are basically considered by the German Criminal Code. Because of the principle of culpability, it is of crucial importance in determining the legal consequences of a mistake to determine whether it affects the reprehensibility of

38) Gerhard Robbers, *German Law*, 2017, p. 123.
39) Nigel Foster/Satish Sule, *German Legal System and Laws*, 2010, p. 355.
40) For more information *see* Uwe Murmann, *Grundkurs Strafrecht*, 2017, pp. 79–83.
41) Thomas Fischer (Editor), *Strafgesetzgesetzbuch*, 2018, Section 20, note 2.
42) Nigel Foster/Satish Sule, *German Legal System and Laws*, 2010, p. 355.
43) Gerhard Robbers, *German Law*, 2017, p. 123.

the crime.[44] Most relevant are the mistakes of fact under section 16 German Criminal Code (*Tatbestandsirrtum*) and the mistakes of law under section 17 German Criminal Code (*Verbotsirrtum*).[45] For mistakes of facts, section 16 German Criminal Code states:

> (1) Whosoever at the time of commiting of the offence is unaware of a fact which is a statutory element of the offence shall be deemed to lack intention. Any liability for negligence remains unaffected.
> (2) Whosoever at the time of commission of the offence mistakenly assumes the existence of facts that would satisfy the elements of a more lenient provision, may only be punished for the intentional commission of the offence under the more lenient provision.

For mistakes of law, section 17 German Criminal Code states:

> If at the time of committing of the offence the offender lacks the awareness that he is acting unlawfully, he shall be deemed to have acted without guilt if the mistake was unavoidable. If the mistake was avoidable, the sentence may be mitigated pursuant to section 49(1).

The major difference between these two types of mistakes is dogmatic in the sense that regarding the mistakes of facts the person is not aware of a circumstance, which is one of the elements of the crime in question, while the mistake of law describes the situation in which the perpetrator sees his or her behaviour as being legal because the perpetrator is not aware of the rule prohibiting the act, or believes that it is invalid.[46]

VIII. System of Penalties

Several reasons for punishment were mentioned in the introduction of this chapter since they are closely related to criminology. In fact, the individual culpability of the perpetrator in the concrete case is both the basis and the limit of all kinds of punishment in German criminal law.

These days, the system of penalties consists basically of imprisonment and imposition of fines.[47] Due to section 46 German Criminal Code, the

44) Gerhard Robbers, *German Law*, 2017, p. 125.

45) *See also* Patrick A. Hinderer, "Tatbestandsirrtum oder Verbotsirrtum?" *JuS*, 2009, p. 864.

46) Gerhard Robbers, *German Law*, 2017, pp. 125–126; Wolfgang Joecks, in: *MüKoStGB*, 2017, StGB, Section 16, notes 115–118.

47) For historical aspects of punishment in Germany *see* Werner Gentz, "The Problem of Punishment in Germany," 22 Am.Inst. Crim. L. & Criminology, 1931/1932, pp. 873–894.

concrete sentencing is determined by the judges concerning various circumstances and traits of character of the accused person.[48] As stated in the law, there could be, for example, the motives and aims of the offender, the attitude reflected in the offence and the degree of force of will, the degree of the violation of the offender's duties, the modus operandi and the consequences caused by the offence to the extent that the offender is to be blamed for them, the offender's prior history, his or her personal and financial circumstances such as his or her conduct after the offence, particularly his efforts to make restitution and finally for the harm caused as well as the offender's efforts at reconciliation with the victim.

Because the maximum penalty is life imprisonment (*lebenslänglich*), which is fifteen years, regulated in section 38 para. 2 German Criminal Code, in other cases the term of imprisonment shall be for a fixed term depending on the concrete case as regulated in section 38 para. 1 German Criminal Code. The death penalty is abolished as codified in the German Constitution under article 102 Basic Law. Torture and corporal punishments are also not allowed due to human rights standards under the European Convention of Human Rights.

The imposition of fines obliges to pay a monetary fine. In order to regard different social and economic situations, this is not in absolute terms but rather in daily earning rates as detailly explained in section 40 German Criminal Code – Day fine units (*Tagessätze*) – and is quite relevant in practise:

> (1) A fine is imposed in daily units. The minimum fine consists of five and, unless the law provides otherwise, the maximum consists of three hundred and sixty full daily units.
> (2) The court determines the amount of the daily unit taking into consideration the personal and financial circumstances of the offender. In doing so, it shall typically base its calculation on the current average one-day net income of the offender or the average income he could achieve in one day. A daily unit shall not be set at less than one and not at more than thirty thousand euros.
> (3) The income of the offender, his assets and other relevant assessment factors may be estimated when setting the amount of a daily unit.
> (4) The number and amount of the daily units shall be indicated in the decision.

Due to this regulation, the amount must be fixed individually.[49] Therefore, firstly, the number of daily rates according to the culpability has to be determined and secondly, the amount of the single rate will be determined accord-

48) Richard Haase/Rolf Keller, *Grundlagen und Grundformen des Rechts*, 2003, p. 401.
49) *See* Bundegerichtshof, Decision from 8.12.2016 – I ZB 118/15, *GRUR*, 2017, p. 318 – *Dügida*.

ing to the economic situation.[50]

However, besides these two introduced major types of punishments, there are some other orders possible which are illustrated by the following examples. Section 63 German Criminal Code codifies the mental hospital order (*Unterbringung in einem psychatrischen Krankenhaus*). This regulation states that if a person has committed an unlawful act in a state of insanity (section 20) or diminished responsibility (section 21), the court shall make a mental hospital order if a comprehensive evaluation of the offender and the act leads to the conclusion that as a result of his condition, future serious unlawful acts can be expected of him and that he therefore presents a danger to the general public. Similar to that, section 64 German Criminal Code states the custodial addiction treatment order (*Unterbringung in Erziehungsanstalt*).[51]

IX. Examples of Criminal Offences

The special part of the German Criminal Code consists of different sections, all referring to special categories of crimes. Since the wording is generally clear, the citizen would understand the regulations. In this chapter, there is a focus on the general part of the German Criminal Code but to obtain a first understanding of special part, some selected examples of criminal acts and their wording are given in the following.

1. Murder and Manslaughter

In section 211 German Criminal Code the law punishes murder (*Mord*) as the most severe crime. It actually refers to murder under specific aggravating circumstances:

> (1) Whosoever commits a murder under the conditions of this provision shall be liable to imprisonment for life.
> (2) A murderer under this provision is any person who kills another person for pleasure, for sexual gratification, out of greed or otherwise motives, by stealth or cruelly or by means that pose a danger to the public or in order to facilitate or to cover up another offence.

Murder is thus characterised either by a set of circumstances that are par-

50) *See also* Albert Mösl, "Zum Strafzumessungsrecht," *NStZ*, 1981, p. 425.
51) *See also* Richard Haase/Rolf Keller, *Grundlagen und Grundformen des Rechts*, 2003, p. 403.

ticularly reprehensible or by reprehensible motives[52] while any killing of a human being that does not amount to murder is punishable as manslaughter (*Totschlag*) under section 12 German Criminal Code.[53] Due to the nature of both regulations, murder is special to manslaughter.[54] Manslaughter is only applicable if the killing was intentional while negligent manslaughter under section 222 German Criminal Code (*Fahrlässige Tötung*) comprises cases where the killing of the victim was not intentional. Then, section 227 German Criminal Code regulates the infliction of bodily harm causing death (*Körperverletzung mit Todesfolge*) for cases in which the offender causes the death of the victim *through* the infliction of bodily harm. This is the case when the death of the victim was not intended but happed as a result of the offender's act.

2. Theft

Theft (*Diebstahl*) under section 242 German Criminal Code is probably the misdemeanour that is committed most frequently. The legal interests protected by this provision are ownership (*Eigentum*) and custody of a thing (*Gewahrsam*) while custody describes the factual relationship of control over a thing accompanied by the will to control it.[55] Custody of a thing in criminal law does not have precisely the same meaning as possession (*Besitz*) in private law but generally speaking, the two concepts will correspond.[56] By law, the theft under section 242 para. 1 German Criminal Code is defined as:

> Whosoever takes chattels belonging to another person away from another person with the intention of unlawfully appropriating them for himself or a third person shall be liable to imprisonment not exceeding five years or a fine.

Like most of the other crimes, theft is based on the intention to take a thing away from another person, including shop-lifting. The victim's consent (*Einverständnis*) suspends the perpetrators act from being crime.[57]

Then, theft in a more severe case is possible. The first is aggravated theft under section 243 German Criminal Code (*Besonders schwerer Fall des*

52) For a more precious analasys of this *see* Thomas Fischer (Editor), *Strafgesetzgesetzbuch*, 2018, Section 211, note 6a.
53) Gerhard Robbers, *German Law*, 2017, p. 133.
54) For more information *see* Albin Eser/Detlev, Sternberg-Lieben, in: Schönke/Schröder (Editors) *Strafgesetzbuch*, 29th edition, 2014, Preface to sections 211 and further, note 5.
55) Gerhard Robbers, *German Law*, 2017, p. 135.
56) Gerhard Robbers, *German Law*, 2017, p. 135.
57) Thomas Fischer (Editor), *Strafgesetzgesetzbuch*, 2018, Section 242, note 22.

Diebstahls), and the second is theft including carrying weapons, acting as a member of a gang and burglary of private homes under section 244 German Criminal Code (*Diebstahl mit Waffen; Bandendiebstahl; Wohnungseinbruchsdiebstahl*). Section 243 para. 1 German Criminal Code states:[58]

> In especially serious cases of theft, the penalty shall be imprisonment between three months and ten years. An especially serious case typically occurs if the offender
> 1. for the purpose of the execution of the offence breaks into or enters a building, official or business premises or another enclosed space or intrudes by using a fake key or other tool not typically used for gaining access or hides in the room;
> 2. steals a property that is especially protected by a sealed container or other protective equipment;
> 3. steals for commercial purposes;
> 4. steals property for religious worship or used for religious veneration from a church or other building or space used for the practice of religion;
> 5. steals a property of importance to science, art or history or to technical development, and which is located in a generally accessible collection or is publicly exhibited;
> 6. steals by exploiting the shiftlessness of another person, an accident or a common danger; or
> 7. steals a firearm for the acquisition of which a licence is required under the Weapons Act, a machine gun, a submachine gun, a fully or semi-automatic rifle or a military weapon containing an explosive within the meaning of the Weapons of War Control Act or an explosive.

Then, section 244 German Criminal Code regulates:

(1) Whosoever

1. commits a theft during which he or another accomplice
   (a) carries a weapon or another dangerous instrument;
   (b) otherwise carries an instrument or means in order to prevent or overcome the resistance of another person by force or threat of force;
2. steals as a member of a gang whose function is the continued commission of robbery or theft under participation of another member of the gang; or
3. commits a theft for the commission of which he breaks into or enters a home or intrudes by using a fake key or other tool not typically used

58) *See also* Richard Haase/Rolf Keller, *Grundlagen und Grundformen des Rechts*, 2003, pp. 408–409.

for gaining access or hides in the dwelling

shall be liable to imprisonment between six months and ten years.

(2) The attempt shall be punishable.

(3) In less serious cases the penalty shall be imprisonment from three months and five years.

(4) In cases under subsection (1) No 2 above, section 73d shall apply.

3. Fraud

Fraud (*Betrug*) und der section 263 German Criminal Code is also one of the most relevant criminal acts. Section 263 para. 1 German Criminal Code states that:

> Whosoever with the intent of gaining for himself or a third person an unlawful material benefit damages the property of another by causing or maintaining an error by pretending false facts or by distorting or suppressing true facts is liable to imprisonment not exceeding five years or a fine.

Although fraud is considered as a misdemeanour, the attempt shall be punishable under section 263 para. 2 German Criminal Code. Then, the law states specifically qualified cases in para. 3, in which case the penalty shall be imprisonment from six months to ten years.[59] An especially serious case typically occurs if the offender

1. acts on a commercial basis or as a member of a gang whose function is the continued commission of forgery or fraud
2. causes a major financial loss or acts with the intent of placing a large number of persons in danger of financial loss by the continued committing of offences of fraud
3. brings another person in financial misery
4. abuses his powers or his position as a public official
5. pretends that an insured event has occured after he or another have for this purpose set fire to an object of significant value or destroyed it, in whole or in part, through setting fire to it or caused the sinking or beaching of a ship.

59) Richard Haase/Rolf Keller, *Grundlagen und Grundformen des Rechts*, 2003, p. 412, note 1249.

X. Criminal Law and Basic Rights

1. Limitations by the Constitution

Basically, the German Criminal Law is limited by several regulations and values of the German constitution which could be simply basic principles or the citizens' basic rights. Under the rule of law (*Rechtsstaatsprinzip*) an act can only be punished if the provision containing punishment in question was enacted before the act was committed which is actually also regulated in article 103 para. 2 Basic Law and section 1 German Criminal Code limiting the scope of criminal law.[60] Corresponding to that, any kind of retrospective effect is strictly prohibited (*Rückwirkungsverbot im Strafrecht*) under German law. Closely connected to this aspect is the prohibition on the ad hoc creation of new offences by analogy with existing crimes (*Analogieverbot*). Moreover, the various regulations of the criminal law use a clear wording in order to guarantee sufficient certainty.

2. The Conflict Between Criminal Law and Individual Basic Rights

Since criminal law always comprises limitations of personal freedom and therefore German Basic Rights, it is interesting to see examples when Criminal Law regulations conflict with constitutional right and even take precedence over Basic Rights if this can be justified under constitutional law. So, in several cases, regulations of the German Criminal Code give legitimation to limit personal freedoms. However, the German Constitutional Court emphasized the importance of freedom of speech in its early jurisprudence.[61] Under this jurisprudence it is always about the proportion within the balancing of the two sides of interests. The following examples of collisions involving freedom of speech illustrate values in German law and therefore in German legal culture in which limitations of freedom of speech are basically accepted by the jurisprudence.

The most important and sometimes controversial regulation limiting the freedom of speech is provided by section 185 German Criminal Code for an insult (*Beleidigung*):

> An insult is punished with imprisonment not exceeding one year or a fine and, if the insult is committed by means of an assault, with imprisonment

60) *See also* Gerhard Robbers, *German Law*, 2017, p. 115.
61) *BVerfGE* 7, p. 198 – *Lüth*.

not exceeding two years or a fine.

In some cases, any punishable insult could also occur if it refers to a group of people like for the term "ACAB" ("All cops are bastards") as referring to German police officers.[62] Malicious gossip (*Üble Nachrede*) under section 186 German Criminal Code and intentional defamation (*Verleumdung*) under section 187 German Criminal Code provide limitations of free speech as well.[63]

Defamation under section 186 German Criminal Code:

> Whosoever asserts or disseminates a fact related to another person which may defame him or affect public opinion about him in a negative manner, shall, unless this fact can be proven to be true, be liable to imprisonment not exceeding one year or a fine and, if the offence was committed publicly or through the dissemination of written materials, to imprisonment not exceeding two years or a fine.

Intentional defamation under section 187 German Criminal Code:

> Whosoever intentionally and knowingly asserts or disseminates an untrue fact related to another person, which may defame him or affect public opinion in a negative manner about him or endanger his creditworthiness shall be liable to imprisonment not exceeding two years or a fine, and, if the act was committed publicly, in a meeting or through dissemination of written materials to imprisonment not exceeding five years or a fine.

Utterances about facts (opposed to personal judgement) are allowed if they are true and can be proven. Yet, journalists are free to investigate without evidence because they are justified by *Safeguarding Legitimate Interests* under section 193 German Criminal Code [Fair comment; defence]:

> Critical opinions about scientific, artistic or commercial achievements, utterances made in order to exercise or protect rights or to safeguard legitimate interests, as well as remonstrations and reprimands by superiors to their subordinates, official reports or judgments by a civil servant, and similar cases only entail liability to the extent that the existence of an insult results from the profile of the utterance of the circumstances under which it was made.

---

62) Bundesverfassungsgericht, Decision from 17.5.2016 – 1 BvR 257/14 – "ACAB," *JuS*, 2016, p. 751.

63) *See also* Dirk Eppner/Antje Hahn, "Die Tatbestände der Beleidigungsdelikte," *JuS*, 2006, p. 860.

Satire and other similar forms of art, as also protected under Article 5 Basic Law, enjoy more freedom but have to respect human dignity (*Menschenwürde*) under Article 1 of the Basic Law.[64] Hate Speech may be punishable if against *segments of the population* and *in a manner that is capable of disturbing the public peace* including racist agitation and antisemitism. This refers to the comprehensive regulations under section 130 German Criminal Code [Agitation of the People]:

> (1) Whosoever, in a way capable of disturbing the public peace
> 1. incites hatred against a national, racial, religious group or a group defined by their ethnic origins, against segments of the population or individuals because of their belonging to one of these groups or segments of the population or calls for violent or arbitrary measures against them; or
> 2. offends the human dignity of others by insulting, maliciously maligning an aforementioined group, parts of the population or individuals because of their belonging to one of the aforementioned groups or segments of the population, or defaming segments of the population,
>
> shall be liable to imprisonment from three months to five years.
>
> (2) (...)
>
> (3) Whosoever publicly or in a meeting approves of, denies or downplays an act committed under the rule of National Socialism of the kind indicated in section 6 (1) of the Code of International Criminal Law, in a manner capable of disturbing the public peace shall be liable to imprisonment not exceeding five years or a fine.
>
> (4) Whosoever publicly or in a meeting disturbs the public peace in a manner that violates the dignity of the victims by approving of, glorifying, or justifying National Socialist rule of arbitrary force shall be liable to imprisonment not exceeding three years or a fine.
>
> (5) ...(7)

In fact, in German hate speech, law is mainly understood in terms of expressions regarding the historical German National Socialism under the regime of Adolf Hitler. Especially, Section 130 para. 3 German Criminal Code refers explicitly to this. Under this regulation, Holocaust denial (*Leugnung des Holocaust*) such as other forms of agitation of people in this respect (*Volksverhetzung*) are punishable.[65]

---

64) Bundesverfassungsgericht, Decision from 17.07.1984 – 1 BvR 816/82 – "Anachronistischer Zug," *NStZ,* 2016, p. 313.

65) Bundesverfassungsgericht, Decision from 4.2.2010 – 1 BvR 369/04, *NJW* 2010, 2193 – "Ausländerrückführung"; *see also* Winfried Brugger, "Hassrede, Beleidigung, Volksverhetzung," *JA,* 2006, p. 687.

XI. Law on Juvenile Offenders

The law on juvenile offenders (*Jugendstrafrecht*) is a part of the criminal law that contains different rules concerning criminal responsibility to minors. Children under 14 years of age are in lack of criminal capacity and therefore cannot be punished. However, punishment is possible for young minors from the age of 14 years and older. In fact, this on juvenile offenders aims to concern the young age of these criminal offenders. Therefore, special and separate rules apply to the criminal responsibility of minors and young adults, the latter in the age of 18 to 21 years. This part of German criminal law is regulated in the Juvenile Courts Act (*Jugendstrafgesetzbuch*). These rules of Juvenile Courts Act are supposed to take account of the special circumstances and challenges that exist while someone is growing up and to provide an appropriate reaction to the dangers and opportunities presented by this period of life.[66]

Due to section 3 Juvenile Courts Act (*Verantwortlichkeit*), a minor of 14 years or older will only be held responsible if, at the time of doing the act, his moral and intellectual development is sufficiently advanced to allow him to comprehend the wrongness of the deed and to act accordingly.[67] Regarding section 3 Juvenile Courts Act the main difference between this law and the German Criminal Code is that the former law refers exclusively to the capacity in guilt regarding the age.[68] Moreover, this law differs from the German Criminal Code in terms of the applicable penalties. The dominant value of punishment in this law refers to correctional education. Basically, three types of sanction exist which are educational measures, disciplinary measures and juvenile detention with imprisonment of minimum six month and a maximum of 10 years for severe crimes like murder for example. The concrete punishment is determined on the basis of section 17 Juvenile Courts Act.[69]

66) Gerhard Robbers, *German Law*, 2017, p. 138.
67) Gerhard Robbers, *German Law*, 2017, p. 138.
68) Friedrich Schaffenstein/Werner Beulke/Sabine Swoboda, *Jugendstrafrecht*, 2014, p. 73.
69) Albert Mösl, "Zum Strafzumessungsrecht," *NStZ*, 1981, p. 425 (428).

Chapter 7

Employment Law

I. Introduction — the Features of German Employment Law

1. The Character of German Employment

For understanding the character of the German Employment Law (*Arbeitsrecht*) it is necessary to focus on the ideas behind it. In a material method of approach, the German Employment Law acts on the assumption that there is an existing conflict of interests between employees and employers. Thus, the employees have an interest on most advantageous working conditions as high wages, a plenty of holidays, protection on dismissal, high security standards on workplaces and health protection in common. On the other hand, the employers have an interest on an economic activity in maximum efficiency and maximum flexibility for meeting the requirements of a globalised market with globalised competition.

By facts, in an employment contract situation the employer is economically seen in a stronger position than the employee because as long as the employee is not highly trained, he can be replaced easily. But in the real world the employees outnumber the employers by heads, which gives them the opportunity for fighting back by organising in trade unions and going on strike. This situation can turn socially explosive by coming to riots and political extremes as it can be seen in particular in German history.

The German Employment Law has realised this situation and hence developed a position, which can be seen as a buffer between the interests of the employers and the employees for establishing balance. This kind of solution is mostly an achievement of the activities of the German labour movement dating back to the beginning of the era of the industrial revolution, which has shaped the country's political and legal constitution. The balance of interest can also be observed as a lesson learnt from German history since situations of conflicts of interests between employers and employees has turned to political extremes in the past. Therefore, the German employment law appears actually as a protection regulation in advantage of the employees by intervening into the principle of private autonomy of the civil law.

However, the German Employment Law does not appear as something static but rather as a dynamic field of law since it is open to upcoming economic, political and social developments.

2. The Dogmatics of German Employment Law

Basically, the field of German Employment Law consists of two parts. A distinction is made between employment law in narrow sense, which refers to the contract relation between the single employee and the employer (*Individualarbeitsrecht*), and the law of collective labour law, with a collective association on employees as trade unions (*Gewerkschaften*) or works councils (*Betriebsräte*) on the one side and the employer or an employer's association of the other side (*Kollektivarbeitsrecht*).[1] Although there is such a distinction, both fields are closely connected with each other as equal parts of German Employment Law.

Dogmatically the German Employment Law is not codified in one single statute law. It is rather a patchwork of various legal acts for different matters of employment law. Some relevant examples are:

- the Maternity Protection Act (*Mutterschutzgesetz*), which regulates the employment of mothers during pregnancy and lactation time,
- the Minimum Wage Act (*Mindestlohngesetz*), which regulates the matters of minimum wage,
- the Protection against Unlawful Dismissal Act (*Küdigungsschutzgesetz*), which deals with the regulations for terminating an employment contract by the employer,
- the Employment Protection Act (*Arbeitsschutzgesetz*), which sets the frame for further working safety regulations.

Aside those many special laws, an important source of German Employment Law is the case law. Many important regulations have been developed by the jurisdiction of the German courts for employment law, in particular by the Federal Labour Court (*Bundesarbeitsgericht*) and the Federal Constitutional Court. The importance of case law for the German Employment Law

1) Gerhard Robbers, *German Law*, 2017, p. 238.

is caused by the fact that the law often works with abstract legal concepts, which have to be concretized by the jurisdiction. Around 600,000 employment law cases per year are the basis for this legal practice.

The prevailing opinion of jurisprudence (law science) is used as a source as long as prevailing view has not been formed to a legal problem by the higher labour law courts.

Furthermore, collective agreements between associations of employees, namely trade unions or works councils on the one side and single employers or employer associations on the other side are a source of employment law in Germany. This is because these agreements occur between the agreement parties as contract regulations, which employers and employees have to pay legal attention to.[2]

II. Examples of Specified German Employment Law Regulations

1. Protection against Unlawful Dismissal

Very specific about German Employment Law is the protection of the employee against (unlawful) dismissal (*Kündigungsschutz*). In times of globalisation of the markets and restructuring of companies, dismissals appear as a mass phenomenon, also in Germany.[3] While no decision of the employer hits the employee harder than his dismissal in general, it hits German people in a unique way. This is caused by the very strong relation German people have to their professional occupation. Taking their occupation very seriously, it gives them not only sense in life but also plays a big part in defining their personal identity, hence giving them a feeling of self-confidence. So, being dismissed from work means much more to German people than "only" the economical difficulties, which usually appear after the dismissal of an employment contract. While in many countries of the world, the employer can dismiss employees simply by his interest, this cannot be done so easily in Germany. Moreover, the German employment law includes regulations of protection against unlawful dismissal, which differ in a special protection regulations and in a general protection regulation.

a. Special Protections against Unlawful Dismissal by German Employment Law

The German Employment Law guarantees a special protection for certain groups of employees, when reasons exist in the person of the employee, which demand a special protection against dismissals by the employer. This

2) Wolfgang Däubler, *Arbeitsrecht: Ratgeber für Beruf-Praxis-Studium*, 2017, para. 11 ff.

3) Wolfgang Däubler, *Arbeitsrecht: Ratgeber für Beruf-Praxis-Studium*, 2017, para 789.

is the case when the person belongs to a group of employees, which could be disruptive to the interest of the employer of acting economically in the most efficient way by their physical constitution or to his interest of determining his business only by his will.

To the first named group expecting mothers belong, for instance. They are protected by the Maternity Protection Act (*Mutterschutzgesetz, abbr. MuSchG*).

Section 17 para. 1 Maternity Protection Act states for cases of dismissals:

> The dismissal of a woman is prohibited
> 1. during pregnancy,
> 2. until the expiration of 4 months after a miscarriage after the twelfth week of pregnancy,
> 3. until the end of her protection period after confinement, though four months after confinement at least,
>
> if the Employer has known about the pregnancy, the miscarriage after the twelfth week of pregnancy or the confinement or if he was informed about it two weeks after arrival of the notice of the dismissal. (...)

Even after this two-weeks period under certain circumstances, the woman can still inform her employer for getting under the protection of the Maternity Protection Act.

Section 17 Paragraph 2 Maternity Protection Act states that the appropriate highest authority of the particular federal German state can permit the dismissal “in special cases”, if those reasons forming a special case are not in relation to the condition of the woman. Actually, there are examples of employers who accuse the pregnant women of theft or offences which could be a special use in the meaning of the law. However, in the absolute majority of these cases, the authority will refuse the request, arguing that the health of the mother and the unborn child is more valuable than the interest of the employer of terminating the employment contract, which also could be executed after the protection period for mother and child.

Employees with a disability are also under a special protection against dismissal by the 9th Code of Social Law (*Sozialgesetzbuch IX*, abbr. *SGB IX*). For the dismissal of an employee with disability, the approval of the Bureau for Integration (of employees with disabilities on the employment market; *Integrationsamt*) is essential by section 168 SGB IX. As long as the Bureau for Integration has not agreed on the dismissal, it is legally ineffective and the employee can demand continued employment.

Another group, which is under special protection against dismissals are working rights activists inside a company as, for example, members of works councils (*Betriebsratsmitglieder*) or legal representatives for young employees or apprentices (*Jugend- und Auszubildendenvertreter*), thereby persons, who are representing the interests of the employees by German Employment Law. Section 15 para. 1 of the Protection Against Unlawful Dismissal Act (*Kündigungsschutzgesetz, KSchG*) states:

> The dismissal of a member of a works council, (or) a young employees and apprentices council (...) is unlawful unless circumstances exist, which entitle the employer for dismissing the employee for special causes without notice, and the required consent pursuant to section 103 Employees Representation Law has been obtained or a court decree has been obtained in lieu of such consent.

Dismissing for "a (special) cause" without notice describes a case of serious violation of the employment contract duties by the employee as e.g. theft or an insult towards the employer. These dismissals for special causes are called extraordinary dismissals (*außerordentliche Kündigung*) and are conducted without any notice period. Hence, an ordinary dismissal (see below) to a member of a works council or a representative for young employees or apprentices is basically unlawful.

b. The General Protection against Unlawful Dismissals

Owing to circumstances, employees cannot be dismissed with notice (*ordentliche Kündigung*, ordinary dismissal) only by the will of the employer by the Protection Against Unlawful Dismissal Act (*KSchG*). By section 1 para. 1 Protection Against Unlawful Dismissal Act the dismissal of an employee is legally ineffective, if the dismissal is unfair by social reasons.

However, for this kind of protection there are the requirements by section 1, according to which the employee is occupied for an uninterrupted period of at least six months in the same company, as also that the company got more than five employees in common, section 23 para. 1 Protection Against Unlawful Dismissal Act.

Section 1 para. 2 states then that a dismissal is unfair by social reasons if the dismissal is not caused

- by reasons due to the person of the employee (e.g. a long-lasting sickness of the employee without a chance of recovery), or
- by the behaviour of the employee (e.g. steadily coming to late to work or even continued staying away from work), or
- by urgent management requirements, which are opposed to a continued employment (e.g. the employer decides to go on working with less employees).

The answer to the question if these causes are present in a single case or not has been answered by the jurisdiction in a broad field of case law decisions. Especially, the element of an urgent management requirement appears as being complicated, as the employer has to conduct a social selection of who to dismiss in case he wants to reduce his staff of employees by section 1 para. 3 Protection Against Unlawful Dismissal Act. For this social selection the employer has to consider facts as e.g. the period the employer has been working for his company, the age of the employee and thereby his chances to get a new job, if the employee got children or not and many more.[4]

2. The Right of the Employee for Paid Leave

By German Employment Law, the basic regulation for a statutory leave is the Federal Paid Leave Act (*Bundesurlaubsgesetz, BUrlG*). By section 1 Federal Paid Leave Act every employee has the right for paid leave during a calendar year. In section 3 para. 1 Federal Paid Leave Act the regulations state the minimum duration of a paid leave, which is 24 working days per year, which does not include sun- or bank holidays by section 3 para. 2 Federal Paid Leave Act. However, the act assumes a weekly working time of six days per week. While it is most common in Germany that employment contracts determine a weekly working time of five days per week, the minimum paid leave duration is 20 days per week though.[5]

During the leave, the employer is not allowed to contact the employee for job reasons in any way. If he does so, the holiday is legally interrupted and the day of contact has to be repeated as a holiday. Section 13 para. 1 Federal Paid Leave Act states these regulations as compulsory law, so the parties of the employment contract are not allowed to deviate from these.

However, the regulations of the Federal Paid Leave Act are only meant to be the fundament of the right for paid leave of the employee. In practice many employment relationships in Germany provide higher leave entitlements by individual contract or by labour agreement, which then replace the statutory holiday of the Federal Paid Leave Act. For example, most collective wage agreements of the *Industriegewerkschaft Metall* (Industrial Union of Metalworkers) and of the *Industriegewerkschaft Bergbau, Chemie, Energie* (Industrial Union of mining, chemical and energy workers) contain a leave entitlement of 30 days per year during a working week of five working days.

---

4) For further information about the topic of dismissals for urgent management requirements and its legal difficulties *see* Hartmut Oetker, "Kündigungsschutzgesetz (KSchG)," Section 1, para. 211–298, in: Rudi Müller-Glöge, Ulrich Preis, Ingrid Schmidt, *Erfurter Kommentar*, 2018.

5) Lisa-Marie Niklas, "Wie viel Urlaub steht mir eigentlich zu? – Fallstricke bei der Berechnung des Urlaubsanspruchs," *Arbeitsrecht Aktuell*, 2018 (pp. 193–196), p. 193.

3. The Working time Regulations by German Employment Law

a. The Daily Working Time of the Working Time Act

Under German Law, the daily working hours are regulated in the Working Time Act (*Arbeitszeitgesetz, abbr. ArbZG*). Section 3, Sentence 1 Working Time Act states that the maximum working time is eight hours per day:

> Employees' daily working time may not exceed eight working hours. The working hours can be extended up to ten working hours only if within six calendar months or within 24 weeks an average of 8 working hours per day is not exceeded.

According to daily working hours, rest periods are also a relevant aspect of working time. Insofar, section 4 Working Time Act provides clear rest periods:

> The working time shall be interrupted by rest periods which shall be fixed in advance. These shall be of at least 30 minutes, if working hours last for between six and nine hours, and of 45 minutes, if working hours last for more than a total of nine hours. The rest periods regulated in the first sentence can be divided up into periods of at least 15 minutes each period. Employees may not be employed without a rest period for more than six consecutive working hours.

b. Working-free Sundays and Bank Holidays in Germany?

Under German law, Sundays and bank holidays are supposed to be a time that is completely free of work in order to give the employee some time for himself. This is due to the fact that the German culture is strongly influenced by Christianity, which finds its expression even in the German constitution, stating in article 140 Basic Law in connection with article 139 Weimar Constitution that Sundays and bank holidays recognised by the state shall remain protected by law as days of rest from work and of spiritual improvement. However, the legislation has made lots exceptions from this principle.

By law, section 9 of the Working Time Act first states the principle:

> Section 9 Rest on Sundays and bank holidays.
> (1) Employees may not be employed from midnight to midnight (0h to 24h) on Sundays and bank holidays.
> (2) In enterprises working in several regular shifts by day and night, the beginning or end of the rest on Sundays and bank holidays can be brought forward or postponed by up to 6 hours, if the enterprise closes

for the 24 hours following the beginning of the daily rest.
(3) For drivers and assistant drivers, the beginning of the 24-hour rest on Sundays and bank holidays can be brought forward by up to two hours.

The exceptions from the principle of section 9 follow in the subsequent section 10–13 Working Time Act. For example, in section 10 para. 1 there are exceptions for employees working in jobs that make working on Sundays and bank holidays necessary, e.g. on emergency and rescue services and in the fire service (section 10 para. 1 number 1), in hospitals and other institutions for the treatment, nursing and care of persons (section 10 para. 1 number 3) or in restaurants and other institutions for entertainment and lodging, and in household work (section 10 para. 1 number four).

In section 12, the law states that exceptions from section 9 can also be made by collective agreement between the employer and a trade union or an works council. Finally, in section 13 para. 5, the law even states that the regulating authority can, under certain circumstances, permit the occupation of employees on Sundays and bank holidays for the case that the competiveness of the firm is affected unacceptably. In practice, this competiveness can be already affected unacceptably by another firm of the same company in another country, where working on sundays is commonly accepted. This opens plenty of opportunity for introducing work on Sundays and bank holidays to German medium-sized and major enterprises because of their international network.

However, even if the principle of the working-free Sunday became very permeable over the years, section 11 para. 1 Working Time Act provides the legal guarantee of 15 working-free Sundays per year for the employees.

4. The Employees' Representation Act

a. Introduction

A very particular legal division in the German Collective Employment Law is the labour relations law (*Betriebsverfassungsrecht*), which is mostly regulated in the Employees Representative Act (*Betriebsverfassungsgesetz, abbr. BetrVG*). By sections 1 and 7 Employees Representative Act, in every firm[6] (*Betrieb*) with more than 5 employees of the age of 18 years and older,

6) The legal term *Betrieb*, over here translated with "firm," is not defined by the law. It is not identical with what the term "enterprise" describes. A *Betrieb* in the meaning of the Employees' Representatives Law is moreover an organisational unit, where an entrepreneur and his/her co-workers pursue certain procedural purposes by means of material or immaterial work equipment (continuous case law definition by the Federal Labour Court e.g. in *Neue Juristische Online Zeitschrift* 2005, p. 3725; Nicolai Besgen, 1 para. 14, in: Christian Rolfs, Richard Giesen, Ralf Kreikebohm, Peter

an works council (*Betriebsrat*) should be elected. This council, formed by the employees, is an organ of employees' participation in a firm aside the trade unions. The usual unlimited power of the employer is supposed to be limited by the democratic rights the Employees Representative Act grants to these representatives of the firm's employees. The existence of this unique legal concept in Germany is on the one hand an achievement of the workers movement. On the other hand, it is also the result of the policy of the western allies after World War 2; especially the US-Americans aimed at democratising the post-fascist German society and also at preventing sympathies of the working class for communism by conceding them a more powerful position in economic decisions. Therefore, the western allies came to the opinion that also a policy of industrial democracy should be set into practice by the Allied Control Council Act No. 22 (*Kontrollratsgesetz Nr. 22*), from 1946 which led to today's Employees' Representative Act.

b. The Works Council

An works council has to come to existence by the initiative of the employees, which means that this internal institution in a firm does not come to existence solely by law. Moreover, employees have to organize an election for an works council by the regulations of the sections 7-20 Employees Representative Act as also by the First Ordinance Implementing the Employees Representative Act - Election Regulations (*Erste Verordnung zur Durchführung des Betriebsverfassungsgesetzes – Wahlordnung (WO)*). The first election in a firm can be conducted at any time, but the regular elections are hold all four years between 1st March and 31st May, under section 13 para. 1 Employees Representative Act. Following a four years-term in all firms all-over Germany, the next regular elections will be in 2022.

The number of members of an works council depends on the number of employees in the firm, due to section 9 Employees Representative Act. The more employees a firm has hired, the more council members can be elected: If a firm got 20 employees or less, there will be merely one representative. For between 21-50 employees, there will be three representatives. Then, between a number of 51-100 employees, there will be five representatives. From a number of 200 employees on, one member of the works council has to be indemnified from work. This means that the work-indemnified council member receives the ordinary salary by the employer, but instead of working he or she takes only care about the duties of the council within the firm.

Udsching (Editors), *Becker'scher Online Kommentar Arbeitsrecht*, 48th edition, München 2018, 1 BetrVG para. 14). Hence, an enterprise can exist by many *Betriebe* (firms), but a firm can solely be part of one enterprise.

c. The Rights and Duties of the Works Council

Even when under section 2 Employees Representative Act the works council and the employer are supposed to work together to the advantage of the firm, the works council's first duty is to represent the interests of the firm's employees. The council conducts this legal duty independently by its own discretion, which means that the council is not fixed to the directives of the employees in the firm. However, not every interest of the firm's employees is represented by the council, but only the interests, which are stated by the Employees' Representative Act. Those interests appear mainly in matter of decisions, which are concerning the individual employed person as e.g. employment, relocation or dismissal, or in social matters as e.g. safety at work. In opposition the regular salary of the employees is not an interest by the Employees' Representative Act and thereby not an issue of the works council. Moreover, the struggle for higher wages is in the business of the trade unions.

The means of the representation of the employees' interests are also stated by the Employees' Representative Act, in the fourth part of the act, sections 74-113. The council got several democratic rights to the employer for participating in the firm's organisation. Those rights differ in their intensity depending on the field of interest the council is acting on.

The lowest right the works council has, but also the basic of all of its acting, is the *right to be informed* by the employer about issues that matter to the employees. The right for controlling the adherence of laws is already a little stronger; accident prevention regulations and also collective wage agreements, under section 80 no. 1 Employees Representative Act. In cases in which the employer does not stick to laws or contract, the council can inform the supervisory state authority.

In some cases of employer decisions, the law states that the employer has the duty to *hear the opinion of the works council before acting*. This duty of the employer exists for example in the cases of the dismissal of another employee, section 102 para. 1 Employees Representative Act. However, this does not mean that the employer has to follow the opinion of the council. In fact, the employer only has to listen to the council's opinion. If the employer does not inform and consult the works council before the dismissal, the dismissal is legally ineffective.

More than a right to be heard is the *council's right for a consultation with the employer*, which describes an exchange of opinions and arguments, hence a discussion about the issue. This right exists, for example, in cases when the employer plans to reorganise the existing working method in a firm, section 90 para. 1 Employees Representative Act.

A higher level of rights of the works council exists in the cases of decisions of the employer, which concern the individual person of the employee, e.g. when the employer of a firm of 20 employees or more wants employing a person, or grouping, redeploying or relocating an employee within the firm. Under section 99 para. 1 Employees Representative Act the employer can not conduct his decision before the *works council agreed on the decision* within one week. If the works council does not react to the case within one week, the agreement is considered to be given, section 99 para. 3 Employees Representative Act. But under the conditions of section 99 para. 2 the council can deny a consent, which leads to the situation that the employer can not conduct his decision before a labour court substitutes the decision of the council by decree on demand of the employer, section 99 para. 4 Employees Representative Act. Thereby, the works council has a kind of a veto right against the decision of the employer.[7]

The strongest legal position exists for an works council in the field of social matters within the firm, under sections 87-89 Employees Representative Act, which is also the most important field within the duties of the works council. Social matters contain cases of working security, the health of the employee affected by work in common or even the right of privacy of the employee, namely e.g. the order within the firm and the behaviour and performance of the employees, section 87 no. 2 Employees Representative Act, the commence and end of the daily working time, section 87 no. 2 Employees Representative Act, or regulations for the prevention of work accidents and occupational diseases, section 87 no. 7 Employees Representative Act. In this context, the works council can *propose own matters to the employer*, and if the employer does not agree on it, the works council got the right to *convoke an arbitration committee* by section 87 para. 2 Employees' Representative Act, which will search for a common solution then.

Finally, the costs for all activities of the works council have to be paid by the employer, under section 40 para. 1 Employees Representative Act.

III. Current Employment Law Conflicts in Germany

1. Working Time and the Right to Disconnect under the Working Time Act

The new standards of digital communication offer the possibility to the employer to contact the employee in off-working time. In the first, doing so appears to be in the interest of the employer because reacting quickly on suddenly appearing situations seems to be efficiently to his enterprise. However, the German Working Time Act (*Arbeitszeitgesetz, ArbZG*) sets clear regulations in section 5 para. 1 Working Time Act, stating, that after finishing

7) For further information about the participation rights of employees' council, *see* Wolfgang Däubler, *Arbeitsrecht: Ratgeber für Beruf-Praxis-Studium*, 2017, para. 265–268.

the daily work shift, the employee must have an uninterrupted period of rest for at least eleven hours. Exceptions are made for employees working in the sector of medical treatment, nursing and care as also for employees working in the sector of lodging or food, transport, broadcast, agriculture and animal husbandry by section 5 para. 2 Working Time Act. An uninterrupted period of rest in the sense of section 5 para 1 means that no intervention by the employee will happen in between, even when it is "only one mail" or "only one short question by phone." Thereby it would be unlawful for the employer to contact his employee during this eleven-hour period. The same is valid for an interruption of the vacation of the employee. So on the one hand, the German Working Time Act seems quite inflexible in respect to the new standards of digital communication and the several possibilities to connect. On the other hand, the law contains the advantage of setting clear regulations, which have positive effects to both sides, employer and employee.[8]

Hence, the law provides employees' protection in an aspect that can be called a *right to disconnect* since it provides employees the opportunities not to be available for the employer in their leisure time. But in fact, this right to disconnect is taken seriously by many employers in their own interest. The protection aim of the Working Time Act often corresponds with the fact that many German employers, especially the big companies, assume that employees need to rest and feel satisfied with their work in order to achieve best performance. In German culture, high performance and efficiency of labour is a strong value as we can see from the international success of German companies like Mercedes, Porsche, Audi, Lufthansa, Bosch, Siemens and others. Respecting the strict regulations of working time comprises to respect that leisure of employees is supposed to be free of work. Consequently, this also requires that employees do not have to be available for the employer by modern media, like e-mail, mobile or other social media. Therefore, many big companies, firms or institutions use an innovative system which replies to the sender during the absence of the employee when he or she is e.g. on vacation. If a client or college sends an e-mail to the employee on vacation he or she will promptly receive an automatic mail reply saying "I am on vacation until (*date*). In urgent cases please contact my college (*name*) under this address (*address*). Thank you for your understanding."

2. Flexible or Reduced Working Hours in Times of Demographic Change

The right to choose flexible working hours such as the option of choice of a reduction of working hours in the times of demographic change is a contro-

8) Hans Hanau, "Schöne digitale Arbeitswelt?" *NJW*, 2016, p. 2613.

versial discussed issue in Germany. Basically, the majority of the employees are very critical toward the term of "flexible working hours" since it was mostly used by the employers in the meaning of working overtime or reduction of rest periods between working days. A different meaning of the term "flexible working hours" was introduced by the German metal and electrical industry trade union *Industriegewerkschaft Metall* (*IG Metall*, engl. Industrial Union of Metalworkers) during the campaign for an collective wage agreement in January 2018.

In Germany, trade unions (labour unions) are an accepted part of society. The *IG Metall* with its 2.27 million members is the biggest trade union in Germany as in the world. Every few years, the *IG Metall* and the employer federation of the steel and electrical industry *Gesamtmetall* (*Gesamtverband der Arbeitgeberverbände der Metall- und Elektro-Industrie e. V.*; *Federation of German Employers' Associations in the Metal and Electrical Engineering Industries*) conclude an agreement about wages and other working conditions in the metal and electric industry. This collective agreement is a mandatory rule as long as it contains better working conditions for the employee as his individual employment agreement (*Günstigkeitsprinzip*; "favourability principle"). For the employer the advantage of a collective agreement is the *Friedenspflicht* ("peace duty," the duty not to engage in industrial actions) during its period of validity, which means that all actions of the trade unions against articles of the agreement are illegal.

The time period of validity of a collective agreement depends on the agreement of the bargaining partners, which is in most cases around two years. After expiry employers and trade unions are bargaining about a new collective agreement. Possibly then it can come to industrial actions as strikes. In the round of collective bargaining in 2018 the *IG Metall* came up with a new demand. Aside of a wage rise of 6%, the industrial trade union demanded for their members an option of choice in working hours, concretely the option on reducing the weekly working hours down to 28 hours per week for a period of up to two years. The *IG Metall* explained on this demand:

> Working hours are an important part of the working conditions. They determine on physical stress, on compatibility of work and life, on quality of life. (...) In the last years the working hours became more and more flexible but mostly to the advantage of the employers. Almost two-thirds of the employees are working overtime. One third of the employees work shift-times, day and night, also on the weekends. One quarter is working on Sundays. The IG Metall wants to re-establish the balance of work and life. (...) Therefore, the IG Metall demands for its members an option of choice for reducing their weekly working hours down to 28 hours per week. This can be made by shorter working days, an additional free day

> per week, more free shifts or longer downtimes at a stretch. After two years maximum it is supposed to get back to usual full-time work. (...) Thus, the employees are healthier, got the possibility to care about their children or family members in need of care, and are able to combine life and work much better.[9]

Gesamtmetall rejected this demand in the first. However, after 1.5 million employees in the metal and electric industry went on a warning strike for 24 hours in January 2018, *Gesamtmetall* and *IG Metall* made a collective agreement in February 2018. Aside of a wage rise of 4,3% the *IG Metall* and *Gesamtmetall* agreed:

- Introduction of an agreed yearly additional payment of 27.5% of a monthly salary (...)
- Employees having increased private or professional stress (children up to 8 years old, home care for family members (...), being in shift work from a certain period of shift work on including a certain length of employment in the company) can choose instead of the agreed additional payment eight free days; for parents and carers only two times per child and per nursing case.
- the right for all employees for a limited part-time including the right to return into full-time; limited from 6 to 24 months and lowering down to 28 working hours per week; the rejection for internal reasons remains possible (e.g. lost of key qualifications, overload rate of 10% of all employees in "reduced full-time" or 18% in part-time overall).[10]

This result was remarkable especially because in advance some observers questioned the working time-demand of the *IG Metall*, suspecting this demand being dropped for a higher wage rise.[11] But it seems that the *IG Metall's* working-hours demand was inspired by the true wish of their members, which was again a result of the demographic change in Germany with more seniors in need of care at home. Thereby the agreement was really appreciated by the members of the *IG Metall*.[12] However, it was also remarkable that *Gesamtmetall* agreed in this point because it demonstrates that a flexible working-time model as favoured by the employees and also challenged by the demographic change is manageable for the employer's side.

9) https://www.igmetall.de/metall-tarifrunde-2018-26283.htm (12.09.2020).

10) https://www.gesamtmetall.de/tarifpolitik/tarifrunden/tarifabschluss-der-metall-und-elektro-industrie (02.03.2018).

11) Class Tatje, "Zeit ist Geld," in: *Die Zeit*, 1st Februar 2018, p. 1.

12) https://www.igmetall.de/metall-tarifrunde-2018-beschaeftigte-zum-abschluss-27062.htm (12.09.2020).

In conclusion the round of collective bargaining in the metal and electrical industry 2018 in Germany can be assessed as a new level of collective agreements between employees and trade unions.

Chapter 8

Law Procedure

I. Introduction to Law Procedure

As already explained, the different fields of law are all related to substantive law and to adjective law, which is actually the procedure law (*Verfahrensrecht).* Adjective law or procedural law can be described as the way and manner in which these rights and duties are enforced within the legal system. In fact, adjective law comprises the rules by which the jurisprudence hears and determines what happens in civil lawsuits, criminal or administrative proceedings and other proceedings before courts including the constitutional courts.

II. Civil Law Procedure

1. Overview on Civil Law Proceeding

In German Law, the procedure in civil litigation is basically codified in the Civil Procedure Code (*Zivilprozessordnung, ZPO*). This law provides detailed regulations on the conduct of contentious proceedings before German courts such as provisions regarding the execution (*Vollstreckung*) after a decision was made. Another relevant statute is the abovementioned Court Constitutional Act (*Gerichtsverfassungsgesetz, GVG*), which complements the Civil Procedure Act in order to provide comprehensive procedural regulations.

Most important are the regulations on the Civil Law proceedings in a whole. To sum up, the regulations of the Civil Procedure Code govern how a case may be commenced and regulates the types of pleadings, motions or applications and orders allowed in civil cases. The code also regulates the timing and manner of depositions and discovery or disclosure such as the conduct of trials. Moreover, it states details on the processing regarding the trial and its judgement such as the matters of how the courts and clerks must function.

2. Principles on Civil Law Procedure

To begin with, there are some very relevant principles in German civil procedure law which determine the happening before and during a trail before a court. Firstly, there is a principle of litigation that the decision to bring a matter to court is entirely at the discretion on the individual involved (*Dispositionsmaxime*).[1] Secondly, the parties are responsible for providing the factual basis for decision due to the adversary system of German Civil Law Procedure (*Verhandlungsmaxime*).[2] Thirdly, it will be an oral trial (*Grundsatz der Mündlichkeit*). This principle ensures the parties to have the chance to present the facts, evidence and arguments orally in court.[3] However, several exemptions are possible, for example under 128 para. 2 Civil Procedure Act, if the parties agree upon the reception of a court decision without a public hearing. Today, written presentation is quite common practice by lawyers in civil law cases (*schriftliches Verfahren*).[4]

Apart from this, section 169 Court Constitutional Act states the principle of the public hearing (*Öffentlichkeitsgrundsatz*):

> The hearing before the adjudicating court, including the pronouncement of judgments and rulings, is public. Audio and television or radio recordings and also audio and film recordings intended for public presentation or for publication of their content shall be inadmissible.

Exemptions of a public hearing can be made if one party can maintain a proper interest for example under section 170 Court Constitutional Act in discussions and hearings in family matters and in non-contentious matters or under section 171b Court Constitutional Act for the protection of privacy in sensitive cases.

Then, in Civil Law procedure Article 103 para. 1 Basic Law (*Recht auf rechtliches Gehör*), it is also stated that in the courts every person shall be entitled to a hearing in accordance with law which also corresponds with the guarantee to a fair trail under Article 6 European Convention of Human

---

1) Wolfgang Grunsky/Florian Jacoby, *Zivilprozessrecht*, 2014, p. 27.
2) Gerhard Robbers, *German Law*, 2017, p. 242.
3) Nigel Foster/Satish Sule, *German Legal System and Laws*, 2010, p. 140.
4) Wolfgang Grunsky/Florian Jacoby, *Zivilprozessrecht*, 2014, p. 39.

Rights.

Finally, the taking of evidence has to be done directly before the court which is recognized under the principle of directness (*Unmittelbarkeitsgrundsatz*) under section 355 Civil Law Procedure Code. Each party bears the burden of proof (*Beweislast*) of facts that support its legal position. Basically, evidence in Civil Law Procedure could be any kind of evidence providing proof of the fact. This is due to the principle of free assessment of evidence under section 286 para. 1 Civil Law Procedure Code (*Freie Beweiswürdigung*). Under this principle, the court has to evaluate the results of the evidences provided by the parties at the end of the hearing and subsequently draws a conclusion from it. The result depends exclusively on the fact whether the court is convinced or not.[5] Under Section 286 para. 2 Civil Law Procedure Code the court can be limited in taking its free assessment of evidence but only in a few exemptions which are explicitly stated by law.

III. Criminal Law Procedure

1. Principles of Criminal Law Procedure

The criminal law procedure is basically controlled by the Criminal Procedure Act (*Strafprozessordnung, StPO*) by providing regulations on investigation and prosecution of crimes which are codified in the German Criminal Code.

To begin with, the principle of official duty (*Offizialprinzip*) imposed on the state attorneys by section 151, 152 and 160 Criminal Procedure Act, is to investigate whenever information is obtained about circumstances that might suggest an offence has been committed.[6] Then, the principle of accusation (*Akkusationsprinzip*) describes the system that gives the state the monopoly (*Anklagemonopol*) to prosecute criminal offences while investigations can merely done by the prosecution service.[7] Another main principle is that the State Prosecution Service (*Staatsanwaltschaft*) is bound to uphold the rule of law (*Legalitätsprinzip*) under section 152 para. 2 Criminal Procedure Act.[8] This principle seeks to ensure that prosecutions are put into effect while all participants in the criminal process are subject equally to the law and no arbitrary decisions should be reached either in the case or in the decision to prosecute.[9] In contrast, under the principle of opportunity (*Opportunitätsprinzip*)

5) Reichhold, in: Heinz Thomas/Hans Putzo (Editors) *ZPO*, 2014, Section 286 note 2.

6) Nigel Foster/Satish Sule, *German Legal System and Laws*, 2010, p. 383.

7) Nigel Foster/Satish Sule, *German Legal System and Laws*, 2010, p. 383; Schmitt, in: Meyer-Großner/Schmidt (Editors) *Strafprozessordnung*, 2017, p. 151, note 1.

8) Gerhard Robbers, *German Law*, 2017, p. 141.

9) Nigel Foster/Satish Sule, *German Legal System and Laws*, 2010, p. 384.

only a few crimes are, under the discretion of the State Prosecution Service, not to be accused if there is no public interest for investigation, for example regarding petty offences under Section 153 Criminal Procedure Act.[10] The decision whether to prosecute or not is on discretion of the prosecution service.

2. Investigation and Rights of Suspects

First of all, the State Prosecution Service plays a major role in the criminal law procedure since it initiates and controls investigation (*Ermittlung*) and then brings the case to trial in order to accuse the suspect (*Tatverdächtiger*). During the whole procedure the State Prosecution Service is assisted by the police. Since the State Prosecution Service is not party of the case it is recognized as a strictly neutral institution within the state. Therefore, under section 244 para. 2 Criminal Procedure Act the prosecution must investigate and review all relevant facts of the case including all details of the scenario, even those in favour of the suspect.[11] Secondly, the criminal investigation authorities have a series of precisely defined statutory powers for the purpose of investigation.[12] In fact, the German law puts a strong focus on the position of the suspect, especially on human rights including a fair trial under the European Convention on Human Rights.[13] One of the central issues of legal policy is how to reach a reasonable balance between the public interest in the investigation and prosecution of the crime on the one hand and the rights of the persons who are affected by the investigations, especially the suspect, on the other hand.[14] For those reasons, the limitations of investigations are always related on the concrete circumstances of the single case (*Einzelfallbetrachtung*).

A suspect has to be brought in front of a judge no later than the day following the arrest, and the judge is obliged to issue a warrant of arrest (*Haftbefehl*) specifying reasons for detention or else release the suspect. In addition, a relative or another familiar person selected by the person affected has to be notified immediately of any detention lasting beyond the day after arrest. Due to section 140 Criminal Procedure Act, accused individuals have the right of free access to legal counsel (*notwendige Vertretung*).[15]

10) *See* Diethelm Klesczewski, *Strafprozessrecht*, 2013, pp. 101–103.

11) *See* Meyer-Großner, in: Meyer-Großner/Schmidt (Editors) *Strafprozessordnung*, 2017, p. 244, notes 2–11.

12) Gerhard Robbers, *German Law*, 2017, p. 141.

13) Diethelm Klesczewski, *Strafprozessrecht*, 2013, p. 2.

14) Gerhard Robbers, *German Law*, 2017, p. 141.

15) *See* Egon Müller/Jens Schmidt, "Aus der Rechtsprechung zum Recht der Strafverteidigung," *NStZ*, 2016, p. 568.

Within the process of investigation, the interrogation (*Vernehmnung*) of the suspect is an important element. Regarding the interrogation of the suspect and the witnesses, there are many regulations provided in the Criminal Procedure Act. Moreover, Article 102 German basic law and the European Convention of Human Rights provide further regulations to secure the interests of the suspect. Article 6 European Convention of Human Rights, for example, provides the right to have a fair hearing which means that the suspect has a fully accepted right to defend himself. Relating to that, the suspect is not obliged to make any admission or a confession at no stage of the proceeding due to the rule that a suspect does not have to assist the authorities in establishing his or her guilt ("Nemo tenetur se ipsum accusare[16]).[17] In fact, the German Criminal Procedure Act provides precise regulations on the first examination in order to guarantee the suspect's rights on the level of basic rights and human rights. Section 136 Criminal Procedure Act [First Examination] states that:

> (1) At the commencement of the first examination, the accused shall be informed of the offence with which he is charged and of the applicable criminal law provisions. He shall be advised that the law grants him the right to respond to the charges, or not to make any statement on the charges, and the right, at any stage, even prior to his examination, to consult with defence counsel of his choice. He shall further be advised that he may request evidence to be taken in his defence and (...) request the appointment of defence counsel (...). In appropriate cases the accused shall also be informed that he may make a written statement, and of the possibility of perpetrator-victim mediation.
> (2) The examination shall give the accused an opportunity to dispel the grounds for suspecting him and to assert the facts which speak in his favour.
> (3) At the first examination of the accused, consideration shall also be given to ascertaining his personal situation.

During examination, certain methods of interrogation are banned under Section 136a Criminal Procedure Act (Prohibited Methods of Examination):

> (1) The freedom of the accused to make up his mind and to express his will shall not be impaired by ill-treatment, induced fatigue, physical interference, administration of drugs, torment, deception or hypnosis. Coercion may be used only as far as this is permitted by criminal procedure law. Threatening the accused with measures not permitted

16) Diethelm Klesczewski, *Strafprozessrecht*, 2013, p. 12.
17) Gerhard Robbers, *German Law*, 2017, p. 141.

under its provisions or holding out the prospect of an advantage not envisaged by statute is not allowed.
(2) Measures that impair the accused's memory or his ability to understand are not allowed.
(3) The prohibition under subsections (1) and (2) shall apply irrespective of the accused's consent. Statements which were obtained in breach of this prohibition shall not be used, even if the accused consents to their use.

Concerning the law of evidence, the forms of proof (*Beweismittel*) are relevant. First of all, evidence by the suspect (*Beschuldigter*) or accused (*Angeklagter*) maybe heard, then follows those by witnesses (*Zeugen*), by experts (*Sachverständige*) or those taken from physical evidence (*Augenschein*) or documents (*Urkunden*).[18] However, in some constellations certain kinds of evidence are prohibited (*Beweisverwertungsverbote*).[19] First of all, there are some codified examples of prohibitions. The most relevant example would be the aforementioned section 136a Criminal Procedure Act. Due to its wording, any evidence obtained contrary to this provision, is inadmissible. Secondly, there are non-codified rules which prohibit certain kind of evidence. Generally, such prohibitions can follow either from a breach of criminal procedural law provisions or from breach of certain constitutional rights.[20] Both types of prohibitions of evidence were recognized by the legal scholars and developed by the jurisprudence.

The first example is the violation of a procedural provision: When a procedural provision has been violated, the general opinion will examine the 'purpose of protection' intended by this provision (*Schutzzweck der Norm*[21]).[22] Section 52 Criminal Procedure Act [Right to Refuse Testimony on Personal Grounds] gives the most relevant example:

(1) The following persons may refuse to testify:
1. the fiancé of the accused
2. the spouse of the accused, even if the marriage no longer exists;
2a. the civil partner of the accused, even if the civil partnership no longer exists;

18) *See* Richard Haase/Rolf Keller, *Grundlagen und Grundformen des Rechts*, 2003, p. 473.
19) *See also* Tobias Paul, "Unselbstständige Beweisverwertungsverbote in der Rechtsprechung," *BGH, NStZ*, 2013, p. 489.
20) Nigel Foster/Satish Sule, *German Legal System and Laws*, 2010, p. 400.
21) The Schutzzwecklehre was developed by the German Federal Court of Justice, *see BGHSt* 42, p. 73 (77), in earlier days the German Federal Court of Justice referred to the Rechtskreistheorie, *see BGHSt* 1, p. 39 (40).
22) Nigel Foster/Satish Sule, *German Legal System and Laws*, 2010, 401; Hans Meyer-Mews, "Beweisverwertungsverbote im Strafverfahren," *JuS*, 2004, p. 126.

3. a person who is or was lineally related or related by marriage, collaterally related to the third degree or related by marriage to the second degree to the accused.

(2) If minors for want of intellectual maturity, or minors or persons placed in care due to mental illness or mental or emotional deficiency have no sufficient understanding of the meaning of their right of refusal to testify, testimony may be taken from such persons only if they are willing to testify and if their statutory representative also agrees to their examination. If the statutory representative is accused himself, he cannot decide on the exercise of the right of refusal to testify; if both parents are entitled to act as statutory representative, the same shall apply to the parent who is not accused.

(3) Persons who are entitled to refuse to testify, and in the cases referred to in subsection (2) also their representatives authorized to decide on the exercise of the right of refusal to testify, shall be instructed concerning their right prior to each examination. They may revoke the waiver of this right during the examination.

Due to this section, a witness can have a right to refuse testimony on personal grounds.[23] Thus, if a witness has not been informed of these rights before interrogation by the police, then a subsequent use of the statement in court is inadmissible because the infringed provision which is section 52 Criminal Procedure Act, was designed to protect the witness' rights, in this case to respect family ties with the accused.[24]

The second example causing a prohibition of evidence could be a breach of constitutional rights, especially certain basic rights. When stated such violation a comprehensive balancing of both interests – the public interest on investigation one the one side and the basic rights of the suspect on the other side – will develop a solution and decide whether the violation is justified and therefore legal or not.[25]

The Federal Constitutional Court has developed three 'spheres' of privacy to provide legal grounds on which the courts can assess whether an intervention by the law enforcement authorities violated the citizen's right rendering the evidence and thus gained inadmissibility in court.[26] Interventions in the social sphere such as business contacts are generally admissible in the first sphere while interventions in the private sphere such as private talks held in public places can be justified. However, here the interests at stake including

23) Richard Haase/Rolf Keller, *Grundlagen und Grundformen des Rechts*, 2003, p. 473.

24) Nigel Foster/Satish Sule, *German Legal System and Laws*, 2010, p. 401; Hans Meyer-Mews, "Beweisverwertungsverbote im Strafverfahren," *JuS*, 2004, p. 126 (127).

25) *See* Andreas Mosbacher, "Aktuelles Strafrecht," *JuS*, 2016, p. 706 (707).

26) Nigel Foster/Satish Sule, *German Legal System and Laws*, 2010, p. 401.

gravity of charge have to be balanced.[27] Interventions in the intimate sphere such as bedroom conversation between spouses cannot be justified.[28] The protection of this sphere is generally strong and cannot be justified.[29]

Section 52 Criminal Procedure Act is considerably relevant in combination with section 252 Criminal Procedure Act [Prohibition of Reading Out of Statement Following Refusal to Testify].[30] This section prohibits any introduction of evidence given by a witness during pretrial proceedings, who in the main trail exercises his right to refuse to give evidence according to sections 52 – 53 Criminal Procedure Act.[31] Referring to the jurisprudence, this rule applies exclusively to interrogations previously made by the police or the prosecution service itself but not by a judge since judges are of the highest rank within the system of criminal law procedure and therefore interrogations made by them are of special significance.[32]

The question whether the proof by certain evidence is prohibited or not is always decided on the grounds of the individual case and the concrete violation of basic rights in question. Therefore, all circumstances have to be taken in account. Compared to other legal systems worldwide, German Criminal Law Procedure is recognized as a liberal law system taking the suspects rights into account by a comprehensive framework of regulations, including the individual's right to a fair trial under Article 6 ECHR.

IV. Administrative Law Procedure

Administrative Law Procedure (*Verwaltungsprozessrecht*) is the procedure law of administration law as a part of public law. Although there is no focus of administrative law within the field of public law in this book, the basic function and construction of public administration is provided in Chapter 3 and administrative law in Chapter 4.

Administrative Law Procedure concerns the procedural law which is relevant for cases at general administrative courts (*Verwaltungsgerichte*). There, citizens or artificial legal persons can seek compensation from the state for any harm caused by incorrect administrative actions by officials or even have administrative acts to be overturned. All regulations concerning the

27) Nigel Foster/Satish Sule, *German Legal System and Laws*, 2010, p. 401.

28) Nigel Foster/Satish Sule, *German Legal System and Laws*, 2010, p. 401.

29) *BVerfGE* 109, p. 279 (313).

30) Mohamad El-Ghazi/Andreas Merold, "Die Reichweite des Beweisverwertungsverbotes nach §252 StPO," *JA*, 2012, p. 44.

31) Nigel Foster/Satish Sule, *German Legal System and Laws*, 2010, p. 401; *see also* Mohamad Al-Gazi/Andreas Merold, "Die Reichweite des Beweisverwertungsverbotes nach §252 StPO," *JA*, 2012, p. 44 (46).

32) *BGHSt* 2, p. 99.

legal procedure are codified in the Administrative Courts Act (*Verwaltungsgerichtsordnung – VWGO*).

1. Principle of Official Investigation

In contrast to Civil Law Procedure, for example, the principle of official investigation (*Amtsermittlungsgrundsatz*) applies for cases before the administrative courts.[33] Under this inquisitorial maxim the court is responsible for investigating the factual background of the case within the bounds set by the relief sought which means that whether a fact has been alleged by one of the parties or whether there has been a formal motion to take evidence is not decisive.[34] In this respect, administrative law procedure is rather assimilable to criminal law procedure were the public interest is playing a centre role in several aspects.

2. Forms of Actions Before Administrative Courts

Despite the principle of official investigation, the citizens as individuals with subjective rights have the possibility to bring personal claims to court. In fact, there are several forms of actions (*Klagearten*) before Administrative Courts in Germany.[35] One elementary prerequisite to bring an action to court (*Zulässigkeitsvoraussetzung*) is that the individual must allege that he or she has already experienced a violation of subjective rights or that, at least, such a violation is possible by an action of state power (*Klagebefugnis*).[36] If that is the case, there is a variety of different claims adequate for various scenarios.

The correct form of action if the claimant wants an administrative act (*Verwaltungsakt*) declared invalid is the action to set aside (*Anfechtungsklage*).[37] This kind of action is actually one of the most relevant legal actions in administrative law procedure as it always concerns restrictive state actions.[38] If the aim is to compel a public authority to issue an administrative act then the correct remedy is the action for the issue of an administrative act (*Verpflichtungsklage*).[39] Both types of legal action are regulated in section 42 Administra-

33) *See* Herrmann Pünder, "Grundlagen des Verwaltungsverfahrensrecht," *JuS*, 2011, p. 289.
34) Gerhard Robbers, *German Law*, 2017, p. 107.
35) For critical discussion on the forms of action *see* Wolfgang Durner, "Reformbedarf in der Verwaltungsgerichtsordnung," *NVwZ*, 2015, p. 841.
36) Richard Haase/Rolf Keller, *Grundlagen und Grundformen des Rechts*, 2003, p. 489.
37) Gerhard Robbers, *German Law*, 2017, p.108.
38) *See* Walter Frenz, "Die Anfechtungsklage," *JA*, 2011, p. 433.
39) Gerhard Robbers, *German Law*, 2017, p. 108.

tive Courts Act. Before either of these types of action can be brought to the court, the so-called objection procedure (*Widerspruchsverfahren*[40]) must usually be complied with due to the regulation of section 68 Administrative Courts Act within the time limitation of one month.[41] This procedure aims to give the authorities the possibility to correct their own action *(Selbstkontrolle der Verwaltung*), to provide more legal security to the citizen (*Rechtsschutz des Bürgers*) and to relieve the administrative courts from having to take too many cases (*Entlastung der Gerichte*)[42] and thereby contributing the courts effectiveness and their capacity for complex cases. Only if the objection procedure fails, can the case be brought to court with the time limitation of one month under section 70 Administrative Courts Act.

For the remaining forms of action in German administrative procedure law, it is not necessary to follow this objection procedure before bringing the matter before a court and also, there is no limitation period in which the action must be brought, referring to section 43 Administrative Courts Act which are namely the general action for relief (*allgemeine Leistungsklage*) and the action for a declaratory order (*Feststellungsklage*).[43] Moreover, interim injunctions (*einstweiliger Rechtsschutz*) are also recognized in administrative law procedure under section 80 para. 1 Administrative Law Procedure for an administrative act to set aside and section 123 Administrative Law Procedure for all other scenarios. In these urgent cases, the courts can usually make short-term decisions.

V. Constitutional Law Procedure

1. Remedies and Features of Constitutional Law Procedure

Constitutional Law Procedure (*Verfassungsgerichtsbarkeit*) is a special discipline since it is separate from the law of the other branches as explained above. Constitutional jurisprudence is neither a part of ordinary law nor of specialized law jurisprudence like labour law or administrative law. Legal Remedies before the Constitutional Court (*verfassungsrechtliche Rechtsbehelfe*) are explicitly stated in Article 93 para. 1 Basic Law. The most relevant one is the interpretation of Basic Law in the event of disputes concerning the extent of the rights and duties of a supreme federal body or of other parties vested with rights of their own by the Basic Law or by the rules of procedure

40) For examples and detailed information *see* Max-Emanuel Geis/Sven Hinterseh, "Grundfälle zum Widerspruchsverfahren," *JuS*, 2001, p. 1047; Richard Haase/Rolf Keller, *Grundlagen und Grundformen des Rechts*, 2003, pp. 490–491.

41) Gerhard Robbers, *German Law*, 2017, p. 108.

42) Richard Haase/Rolf Keller, *Grundlagen und Grundformen des Rechts*, 2003, p. 490.

43) Gerhard Robbers, *German Law*, 2017, p. 108.

of a supreme federal body under No. 1 (*Organstreitverfahren*). Then, under No. 2 the Constitutional Court shall rule in the event of disagreements or doubts concerning the formal or substantive compatibility of federal law or state law with the Basic Law, or the compatibility of state law with other federal law, on application of the Federal Government, of a state government, or of one fourth of the Members of the Federal Parliament (*abstrakte Normenkontrolle*). Finally, the constitutional complaint under No. 4a is very important since it is the most relevant remedy for citizens claiming a violation of their Basic Rights by the German state. Under this regulation, a constitutional complaint may be filed by any person alleging that one of his basic rights or one of his rights under paragraph (4) of Article 20 or under Article 33, 38, 101, 103 or 104 has been infringed by public authority (*Verfassungsbeschwerde*). All remedies refer to further regulations regarding the legal procedure under Federal Constitutional Court Act (*Bundesverfassungsgerichtgesetz; BVerfGG*).

Basically, a German citizen can impose a constitutional complaint quite easily if the standards of the basic requirements are met. Even a representation by a lawyer (*Anwaltszwang*) is not necessary. However, the complainant must be represented by a lawyer if an oral hearing takes place.

Unlike proceedings before ordinary and specialized German courts, under section 34 para. 1 Federal Constitutional Court Act proceedings before the Federal Constitutional Court shall be free of charge which is important to provide access to the courts' justice for all citizens. However, under para. 2 the court may charge a fee of up to EUR 2,600 if, for example, the lodging of a constitutional complaint or the application for a preliminary injunction constitutes an abuse of rights (*Missbrauchsgebühr*).[44]

2. The Constitutional Court

a. The Court as a Constitutional Organ

The German Federal Constitutional Court, located in Karlsruhe in the state of Baden-Württemberg in the South of Germany, is intentionally distanced from the other federal institutions in the capitol. The Federal Constitutional Court is a federal court of justice that is autonomous and independent of all other constitutional organs. These formal conditions on the courts structure are actually codified in section 1 Act on the Federal Constitutional Court, which regulates the organisation and jurisdiction of the court. In fact, it is both a court and a constitutional organ at the same time.

The main task of the court is judicial review. The court is able to declare

44) Hans Lechner/Rüdiger Zuck (Editors), *Bundesverfassungsgerichtsgesetz*, 2011, Section 34, note 3.

legislation as unconstitutional (*verfassungswidrig*) and hence rendering them ineffective. In this respect, it is similar to other supreme courts with judicial review authority. Moreover, the German Constitutional Court possesses a number of additional powers, like interpreting the German Constitution and setting constitutional values such as making law. The latter power roots from the legal principle that the Constitutional Courts jurisprudence is considered as legislation at the level of proper statute law. Under section 31 para. 3 Federal Constitutional Court Act decisions of the Federal Constitutional Court are strictly binding for all constitutional organs of the Federal Government and the various states as well as all courts of law and administrative structures.[45]

b. Structure and Organization of the Court

The German Constitutional Court consists of two Senates, each of them with eight Justices. Three Justices of each Senate shall be elected among the judges of the supreme federal courts. Under section 1 para. 3 Act on the Federal Constitutional Court, there is a general rule that only judges who have served for at least three years at one of the supreme federal courts shall be elected to one of the senates.

The President and the Vice-President are the chairpersons of their respective Senates. Under section 15 para. 2 Act on the Federal Constitutional Court each Senate shall have a quorum if at least six Justices are present. If a Senate does not have a quorum in a particularly urgent case, the presiding Justice shall order the drawing of lots to designate Justices of the other Senate as substitutes until the quorum is reached. Each Senate has its own precisely defined competences, but always decides as "the Federal Constitutional Court."[46] This is an important aspect since it is in contrast to those Supreme Courts or Constitutional Courts worldwide which indicate the Justices opinion. Basically, the judges of the German Constitutional Court act as a court on a whole that causes the argumentation of the separate judges to be not transparent. However, if a Justice completely disagrees with the decision he or she can give a dissenting opinion (*Sondervotum*), which is also part of the decision.[47]

The precisely defined competences are specified in section 14 para. 1 and para. 2 Act on the Federal Constitutional Court. Basically, under this regulation the First Senate shall be competent for judicial review proceedings in which the main issue is the alleged incompatibility of a legal provision with

---

45) *See* Gerhard Robbers, *German Law*, 2017, p. 19.

46) https://www.bundesverfassungsgericht.de/EN/Das-Gericht/Gericht-und-Verfassungsorgan/gericht-und-verfassungsorgan_node.html, (12.09.2020).

47) Klaus Schlaich/Stefan Korioth, *Das Bundesverfassungsgericht*, 2015, p. 31.

fundamental rights or equivalent rights[48] as well as for constitutional complaints (*Verfassungsbeschwerde*). The same shall apply if a state government files an application for judicial review (*Normenkontrollantrag*) pursuant to the first sentence together with an application pursuant to these rights. The second Senate shall be competent to all other cases, as well as for judicial review proceedings and constitutional complaints not assigned to the First Senate.

Therefore, the competence of the two Senates is decided by the Federal Constitutional Court Act. Then, it has to be decided which of the several judges in a Senate is in charge of a single case. Usually, this is decided by some internal rules of the court. In rare cases, the Plenary decides a case itself; this is mandated if one Senate intends to deviate from the other Senate's interpretation of a specific legal matter.[49]

As a constitutional organ – and unlike the regular courts – the Federal Constitutional Court is not subject to the administrative supervision of a ministry. The Plenary decides on basic organisational issues; the Committee on Budgetary and Personnel Matters, which is appointed by the Plenary, prepares the draft budget of approximately EUR 28 million per year. The president heads the administration of the Court and represents it externally.[50]

Each Justice is basically assisted by four judicial clerks (*Wissenschaftliche Mitarbeiter am Bundesverfassungsgericht*) who have prior work experience in regular courts, public authorities, law firms or universities. These persons are completely involved in the work of the chambers and prepare the cases for the judges. Their importance is recognized and therefore the term "third senate" ("*Dritter Senat*"[51]) in the Federal Constitutional Court is used. The "third senate" is also needed since the workload of the Court is massive. In particular, it receives more than 6,000 constitutional complaints every year. In order to deal with this high number of new proceedings, both Senates form three-member Chambers. These usually decide cases that have no general constitutional significance – approximately 99 per cent of proceedings.[52]

c. Justices

As already explained, the Court consists of two Senates, each of them with eight members which are the Justices. Both Senates maintain several Cham-

---

48) These right are Law Procedure Rights under Articles 33, 101, 103 and 104 of the *Basic Law*.

49) *See also* https://www.bundesverfassungsgericht.de/EN/Verfahren/Der-Weg-zur-Entscheidung/der-weg-zur-entscheidung_node.html, (12.09.2020).

50) https://www.bundesverfassungsgericht.de/EN/Das-Gericht/Gericht-und-Verfassungsorgan/gericht-und-verfassungsorgan_node.html, (12.09.2020).

51) Martin Pagenkopf, "Fachkompetenz und Legitimation der Richter des BVerfG," *ZRP*, 2011, p. 229 (232).

52) http://www.bundesverfassungsgericht.de/EN/Homepage/home_node.html, (10.10.2018).

bers, each of them with three members.[53] Under section 3 para. 1 Act on the Federal Constitutional Court the Justices must be the age of forty or older and must declare naturally in writing that they are willing to become a member of the Federal Constitutional Court. Half of the 16 members of the Federal Constitutional Court are elected by the *Bundestag*, and half by the *Bundesrat*. Candidates are proposed by the political parties acting on the federal level of reign.[54] Due to section 6 Act Federal Constitutional Court the Justices shall be elected if they obtain two-thirds majority of the votes by the electoral bodies.[55] This requirement is due to the intension to ensure that the composition of the Senates is well-balanced. Moreover, *Bundestag* and *Bundesrat* also take turns in determining the President and Vice-President of the Court.[56] Usually, the Vice-President of the court can become President of the court later which means that his or her nomination is an enduring decision. Insofar, this decision actually made by politicians is discussed to be one of the significant political decisions.[57] However, before the election, the candidates are not disclosed for the general public[58] which effects that the whole procedure does not get much attention and also lacks of transparency.

At least three members of each Senate must be elected from the Supreme Federal Courts (Federal Court of Justice, Federal Administrative Court, Federal Finance Court, Federal Labour Court and Federal Social Court) in order to allow the Federal Constitutional Court's decisions to benefit from their particular judicial experience.[59]

Moreover, the Act on the Federal Constitutional Court provides regulations on the conditions to act as a Justice of the German Federal Constitutional Court. Basically, anyone who is at least 40 years old and qualified to hold judicial office pursuant to the German Judiciary Act is eligible for election. The Justices are elected to serve a twelve-year term and the retirement age is 68.[60] A re-election (*Wiederwahl*) is not recognized.[61] This rule is practiced strictly in order to ensure the independence of the judges. Insofar, the term of office is terminated by law for this time-period. This is also an important aspect since in other states Justices obtain their status lifelong, like the Law-

---

53) *See also* Martin Pagenkopf, "Fachkompetenz und Legitimation der Richter des BVerfG," *ZRP*, 2011, p. 229.

54) *See* Heinrich Wefing, "Auf der Suche nach Mr. Right," *DIE ZEIT*, No 39/September2018, p. 2.

55) Klaus Schlaich/Stefan Korioth, *Das Bundesverfassungsgericht*, 2015, p. 30.

56) https://www.bundesverfassungsgericht.de/EN/Das-Gericht/Organisation/organisation_node.html, (12.09.2020).

57) *See* Karlsruher Republik, Heinrich Wefing, "Gewand der Macht," *DIE ZEIT*, No 10/March 2018, p. 2.

58) *See* Heinrich Wefing, "Auf der Suche nach Mr. Right," *DIE ZEIT*, No 39/September 2018, p. 2.

59) https://www.bundesverfassungsgericht.de/EN/Das-Gericht/Organisation/organisation_node.html, (12.09.2020).

60) *See* Heinrich Wefing, "Auf der Suche nach Mr. Right," *DIE ZEIT*, No 39/September 2018, p. 2.

61) Hans Lechner/Rüdiger Zuck (Editors), *Bundesverfassungsgerichtsgesetz*, 2011, Section 4, note 3.

Lords in the United Kingdom which are today the Justices of the Supreme Court and the former judicial House of Lords.

d. Power of the Court

The reputation of the German Federal Constitutional Court is very highly acclaimed. It is regarded as one of the most interventional and powerful national courts worldwide without any opportunist or corruptive tendency. In fact, the power of the judges of the German Constitutional is so strong that some US-American lawyers once spoke of the "Karlsruher Republic."[62] That is because it interprets the German Constitution and sets values in terms of a modern society.

Unlike other Supreme Courts, the Constitutional Court is not an integral stage of the judicial or appeals process (aside from cases concerning constitutional or public international law). It does not serve as a regular appellate Court from lower courts or the Federal Supreme Court on any violation of federal laws.

The courts' practice of enormous constitutional control frequency on the one hand, and the continuity in judicial restraint and political revision on the other hand, have created a unique defender of the Basic Law since World War II and given it a significant role in Germany's modern democracy.

3. Constitutional Complaint

Constitutional Complaint (*Verfassungsbeschwerde*) is the most relevant remedy for German citizens. As stated above, it derives from Article 93 para. 1 No. 4a Basic Law. The constitutional complaint is an extraordinary remedy for the protection of constitutional rights. These are the basic rights (Articles 1 – 19 Basic Law) and certain related rights (Article 20 para. 4, Article 33, Article 38, Article 101, Article 103 and Article 104 Basic Law). The constitutional complaint is a very special action since everybody ("*jedermann*") can refer to it (*Bürgerrechtsbehelf*). Although everyone can take this action, the appellant must meet certain requirements. The appellant must allege that their above-mentioned constitutional rights have been violated by an act of German public authorities. In fact, the appellant needs to be affected firstly oneself, secondly currently and thirdly immediately.[63] The latter requirement will usually be merely met by constitutional complaints against judgements by courts and acts of the executive (*Verwaltungsakte*). Laws are not self-executing. As an extraordinary remedy the constitutional complaint is subsidiary

62) *See* Karlsruher Republik, Heinrich Wefing, "Gewand der Macht," *DIE ZEIT*, No 10/March 2018, p. 2.

63) Christian Hillgruber/Christoph Goos, *Verfassungsprozessrecht*, 2015, pp. 86–90.

to other regular remedies. This principle of subsidiary (*Subsidiaritätsprinzip*) means that in the first place the appellant may only be lodged after all remedies have been exhausted, including the remedy in case of infringement of the claim for hearing (*Anhörungsrüge*) as well. This is why practically constitutional complaints are mostly directed against judicial acts instead of acts of the executive which can still be contested at the administrative court. Basically, the principle of subsidiary applies to the constitutional complaint due to capacity reasons, and it is also to relieve the Constitutional Court from too many applications. Moreover, the appellant must claim the violation of the abovementioned rights already while making use of the regular remedies at courts of all instances (*Rechtswegerschöpfung*).[64] The negligence of this is the reason why many complaints are dismissed as inadmissible.

Finally, under Section 23 para. 1 Federal Constitutional Court Act applications to initiate proceedings shall be submitted to the Federal Constitutional Court in writing and must state reasons (*Schriftformerfordernis*). It may be submitted by telefax but not by email.[65] The constitutional complaint shall be lodged, and reasons shall be stated within one month, under Section 93 para. 1 Federal Constitutional Court Act. Para. 3 states if the constitutional complaint challenges a law or another sovereign act against which legal recourse is not possible, the constitutional complaint may only be lodged within one year of the law entering into force or of the sovereign act being issued.

64) Christian Hillgruber/Christoph Goos, *Verfassungsprozessrecht*, 2015, pp. 92–96.
65) Hans Lechner/Rüdiger Zuck (Editors), *Bundesverfassungsgerichtsgesetz*, 2011, Section 23, note 3.

Chapter 9

The European Union and European Human Rights

I. Introduction — Europe, EU and ECtHR

The terms *Europe*, the *European Union (EU)* and the *European Convention of Human Rights* (ECHR) have to be distinguished from each other. While Europe is considered as a continent like America, Oceania, Asia or Africa in geographical terms, EU and ECHR are used as technical terms of political and legal constructions within Europe.

The European Union is an organisation of European countries that have joint policies on matters such as trade, agriculture and finance. In fact, the EU is an economic and political union of twenty-eight members at the moment, which was established by the *Treaty of Maastricht* in the year 1993 upon the foundations of the European Communities. Under Article 47 *Treaty of Lisbon* the EU has a legal personality now which enables to conclude treaties with countries. The development shows that the European Union was established as an economic, political and social unit and became more powerful during the decades. In fact, the European Union consists of various institutions such as the European Parliament, the Commission and its own Jurisprudence in accordance with EU Law, which is the European Court of Justice. Over the years, the EU grew and still grows not only as an economic, political and social unit, but also as a legal unit which changes and unifies the laws of its member states. Nowadays, there exists a huge and comprehensive system of laws made by the EU which are either *direct* or at least *indirect binding* for the national legislation, executive and courts.[1] Many political areas are partly or completely transferred from national sovereigns to the EU and therefore, many decisions are made in Brussels instead by national authorities. There is hardly an area of law in the member states which is not at least touched or in-

1) Robert Schütze, *Introduction to European Law*, 2012, pp. 107, 128.

directly influenced by the EU law. However, the law of the European Union is seen as an independent legal system.

The European Convention of Human Rights (ECHR) is another important aspect of Europe and of the European Union as well. In fact, the ECHR is an international treaty in order to protect human rights and fundamental freedoms in Europe. The treaty of this convention was drafted in 1950 after the end of the second World War by the then newly formed Council of Europe. In order to give these human rights and freedoms a practical effect, the Convention established the European Court of Human Rights (ECtHR), which is located in Strasbourg (France).

II. The Historical Development of the EU

The history of the European Union is not identical with the history of Europe. However, it is connected and sometimes overlapping. Of course, the European history is much older and draws a broader picture of the history of the continent. But already in the 17th century the idea of an union of European states came up as e.g. by the "Grand Plan" by Maxmilien de Béthune, Duke of Sully, who developed a concept of 15 European states under the direction of a common council, or by William Penn, who presented in his "Essay towards the Present and Future Peace of Europe" the vision of a united Europe in form of a confederation with common institutions. Immanuel Kant also wrote in 1795 in his book *Perpetual Peace: A Philosophical Sketch* (*Zum Ewigen Frieden. Ein philosophischer Entwurf*) about the idea of a federal association of European republics for securing peace in Europe. However, the history of the European Union actually begins in the middle of the 20th century. After the end of the Second World War, the development towards an European integration were seen by many as an escape from the extreme political forms of nationalism, which had devastated the continent. It was a common goal to unite the European states in order to keep the peace in Europe[2] as e.g. it was expressed clearly by *Winston Churchill* in his famous speech at Zurich in 1946.

In Germany, it was mainly the German chancellor *Konrad Adenauer* who advocated the idea of an European Union as a part of his plans of a west-integration of the Federal Republic of Germany.[3] But the architect of the European Union was the French entrepreneur and consultant *Jean Monnet*, who could convince the French foreign minister *Robert Schumann* in the early 1950s for a concept of cooperation between France, Germany and other European states in the fields of coal and steel industry, later known as

2) Christian Calliess, "Bausteine einer erneuerten Europäischen Union," *NVwZ*, 2018, p. 1.
3) *See* Chapter 2.

Schumann-Plan.

The result of this plan became the *European Coal and Steel Community*, which had been founded to integrate one industrial sector in Europe.[4] Although it just had the modest aim of centralised control of the previously national coal and steel industries of its member states, it was declared to be a first step in the federation of Europe, not only for economic but also for peace-keeping reasons, as the materials of coal and steel were strategic materials. Besides Germany and France, Italy, the Netherlands, Belgium and Luxemburg joined the project.

In 1957, those six countries signed the *Treaties of Rome*, which extended the earlier cooperation within the *European Coal and Steel Community (ECSC)* and the *European Atomic Energy Community (EAEC)* and it created the new organization named *European Economic Community (EEC)*. It was signed on 25 March 1957 and applied from 1 January 1958. As a result, there were three establishing treaties (*Europäische Wirtschaftsgemeinschaft* (*EWG*), which had later established *European Communities (Europäische Gemeinschaften)*.[5] *The Treaty establishing the European Coal and Steel Community* contained provisions on competition, prices, free movement of coal and steel workers and subsidies for the coal, iron and steel industry. Its objective was to set up a common market for heavy-industry products. The Treaty was of declining importance since it proved to be unable to solve the structural crisis within the industry. The *ECSC Treaty* had been concluded for a period of 50 years and expired at the end of 2002.

Then, the French government promoted the European Atomic Energy Community in order to provide for a common and peaceful utilisation of atomic energy. The Treaty contains detailed provisions on atomic energy research and on the development and the diffusion of atomic energy technologies. It also provides for subsidies and for the creation of a European Atomic Energy Commission, the purpose of which is to control the acquisition and diffusion of nuclear fuels.

The Treaty establishing the European Economic Community is the most important Treaty of all. Actually, the aim of the EEC was to establish a common market in Europe and to work towards integration and economic growth through trade. The final objective of the treaty is to realize one large and uniform economic region for all positive impacts such region has on the development and the stability of the economy and on the common wealth of its citizens. Then, the aim of the EEC and the common market was firstly to transform the conditions of trade and production on the territory of its six members and secondly to serve as a step towards the closer political unification of Europe. Most relevant, the EEC created a common market based on

4) Rudolf Streinz, *Europarecht*, 2019, p. 9.

5) Richard Haase/Rolf Keller, *Grundlagen und Grundformen des Rechts*, 2003, p. 236.

the free movement of goods, persons, services and capital.[6] In fact, the EEC did not only create a common market in Europe but it actually established a customs union. The customs union means that certain quotas (i.e. ceilings on imports) and customs duties between the member states were abolished. Moreover, it established a common external tariff on imports from outside the EEC, replacing the previous tariffs of the different states. Afterwards, the customs union was accompanied by a common trade policy. This policy, managed at EEC level and no longer at national level, distinguishes the customs union from a mere free-trade association. While the basic idea of the EU was to keep the peace in Europe in the beginning, it later developed into a complex union in which trade and economics play a great role, even in international free trade. A good example for the dimension of the EU Trade policies would be the *European Union-South Korea Free Trade Agreement* which entered into force in 2015.

III. Overview of the Treaties

The EU was developed through the decades by several treaties. In the beginning of EU history, the *Treaty of Maastricht* was signed on the 7th of February in 1992 by twelve European states such as Belgium, Denmark, France, Germany, Greece, Ireland, Italy, Luxembourg, Netherlands, Portugal, Spain and the United Kingdom. Before ratifying the treaty, some of the national parliaments held referendums. The *Maastricht Treaty* came into force on the 1st of November in 1993 and the European Union was officially established. Since then, additional 16 countries have joined the EU and adopted the rules set out in the *Maastricht Treaty* or in the treaties that followed later. The *Maastricht Treaty* was an important step within the development of the European Union since it integrated the different communities into the European Union. It was made for establishing the European Union based on an enlarged Community pillar.[7] So, it created the economic and monetary union and set two new pillars: the *common foreign and security policy* (CFSP) and the *cooperation in the fields of justice and home affairs* (JHA). Moreover, the *Maastricht Treaty* started the move towards the creation of the *Euro*, the current currency. The idea of a single currency for Europe was first proposed in the early 1960s by the European Commission. However, an unstable economic landscape in the 1970s was the reason that the project was brought to a halt. Then, the *Maastricht Treaty* also established the *European Central Bank (ECB)* and the European System of Central Banks and described their objectives. The main

6) Robert Schütze, *Introduction to European Law*, 2012, p. 207; *see also* Stephen, Weatherill, *Cases and Materials on EU Law*, 2012, pp. 359–409.

7) Richard Haase/Rolf Keller, *Grundlagen und Grundformen des Rechts*, 2003, note 733.

objective for the *ECB* is to maintain price stability, i.e. to safeguard the value of the *Euro*. So, besides a political union, an economic and monetary union was created (*Wirtschafts- und Währungsunion*).[8] An internal market with a strong economy and a common currency became more important through the decades. On the 1st of January in 2002, the Euro began to circulate as banknotes and coins, replacing national currencies. In Germany, the Deutsche Mark was replaced by the Euro for example. In fact, eighteen members have adopted the common currency, constituting the Euro zone.

In 1999, the *Amsterdam Treaty* established an area of freedom, security and justice, and integrated the Schengen Agreement into EU law. The treaty modifies the role of Secretary-General of the Council, who also becomes High Representative for Common Foreign Security Policy.[9] Later, in 2003, the *Treaty of Nice* introduced the reform of the EU institutions, in preparation for a future enlarged Union of twenty-seven members. The Council was reformed to extend the use of qualified majority voting and to introduce the principle of enhanced cooperation between member states. In 2004, the European Union experienced an enlargement as ten more states joined such as the Czech Republic, Estonia, Cyprus, Latvia, Lithuania, Hungary, Malta, Poland, Slovakia and Slovenia. The following years were shaped by the attempt to create a European Convention. Actually, a European Convention was charged to draft a *Constitutional Treaty (Europäischer Verfassungsvertrag)*. But this treaty failed since this idea was rejected by French and Dutch voters in referendums in 2005.[10] In 2007, however, the *Treaty of Lisbon* was initially drafted to reform the idea of the constitutional basis of the EU and as a replacement for the *Constitutional Treaty*. The *Treaty of Lisbon* came into force on the 1st of December in 2009.[11] It intended to reform the functioning of the European Union by giving it a new structure. In this respect, the *Treaty of Lisbon* amends former treaties which are known in updated forms as the *Treaty on European Union (TEU)* and *Treaty on the Functioning of the European Union (TFEU)*. The *Treaty of Lisbon* provided several changes since it established the "High Representative of the Union for Foreign Affairs and Security Policy."[12] Through that changes, the European Council became a fully-fledged institution with its own president while before the head of the European Council was merely an unofficial position. Moreover, the *Treaty of Lisbon* included other changes, for example regarding the election system of the European Parliament and the weighting of votes by Member States such

8) Richard Haase/Rolf Keller, *Grundlagen und Grundformen des Rechts*, 2003, note 733.

9) Rudolf Streinz, *Europarecht*, 2019, p. 17.

10) Albrecht Weber, "Vom Verfassungsvertrag zum Vertrag von Lissabon," *EuZW*, 2008, p. 7.

11) *See* Franz C. Meyer, "Die Rückkehr der Europäischen Verfassung? Ein Leitfaden zum Vertrag von Lissabon," *ZaöRV*, 2007, p. 1141 (1149).

12) Vanessa Hellmann, *Der Vertrag von Lissabon*, 2009, p. 37.

as extending the scope of qualified majority voting to new areas.[13]

IV. Overview of the EU-Institutions

Due to the fact that the creation of governmental institutions is the central task of all constitutions worldwide, the EU also consists of various institutions. In fact, there is no separation of powers in a classical sense on the EU level. The roles of the government are shared by several institutions rather than being clearly divided from each other. The most relevant institutions are: The European Parliament, the European Council, the Council of Ministers, the European Commission, the Court of Justice of the European Union, the European Central Bank and the Court of Auditors. Although, the European treaties established a number of European institutions to make, execute, and arbitrate European Union Law and politics, the focus lies on the following institutions which are the European Council, the Council, the European Parliament, the European Commission and the Court of Justice of the EU.

The *European Council* (*europäischer Rat*), which was not an European Union's regular body before the *Treaty of Lisbon* but a genuine organ of the European Union, became a regular organ. It consists of the heads of state of the twenty-eight Member States, the President of the European Council and the President of the Commission. The European Council convenes two times within a half-year and gives direction and the genuine political guidelines to the EU. For that reason, it is an institution with extraordinary powers and of great political significance.

The *Council* (*Rat*) of the European Union or Council of Ministers is the legislative body of the EU together with the European Parliament. Alongside the European Parliament, it decides on political matters and exercises the budgetary function of the EU.[14] It consists of representatives of all Member States which delegate each one member of their national government. The presence in the Council changes according to the issues discussed. National governments usually send the ministers responsible for the particular political field in question. Although legally there is just one Council, its composition and name depend on the subject matter of its configurations as it is evident in the names of councils such as General Affairs, Foreign Affairs, Economic and Financial Affairs, Justice and Home Affairs, Employment, Social Policy, Health and Consumer Affairs, Competitiveness (Internal Market, Industry and Research), Transport, Telecommunications and Energy, Agriculture and Fisheries, Environment and Education, Youth and Culture.[15] The chairman-

---

13) Vanessa Hellmann, *Der Vertrag von Lissabon*, 2009, p. 35.
14) Rudolf Streinz, *Europarecht*, 2019, p. 108.
15) Robert Schütze, *Introduction to European Law*, 2012, p. 20.

ship in the Council (*EU-Ratspräsidentschaft*) rotated on a six-months-basis according to a firm schedule.

As already mentioned, the *European Parliament* (*Europäisches Parlament*), located in Brussels, shares the function of the EU legislator with the Council. Moreover, it has budgetary powers and supervisory powers of holding the executive to account which involves the rights to debate, question and investigate.[16] The Parliament constitutes the democratic element within the Union since its members are elected in a general and free election by the citizens of the member states for a five-year term. The European Parliament has a total of 751 members (750 seats plus the president).[17]

The *Commission* (*Kommission*) is the executive body within the governmental structure of the EU. Article 17 TEU states the functions of the Commission as the initiative right on legislation which is the right to put forward legislative proposals. Actually, the Commission acts like an animator or manager to promote the general interests of the Union and therefore functions as a so-called motor for European integration.[18] Besides the right to initiate legislation, the Commission possesses some executive competences granted by the treaties itself.[19] In political terms it is probably the most powerful institution of the European Union.

Finally, the *Court of Justice of the European Union* (CJEU; *Europäischer Gerichtshof*) located in Luxembourg is one of the core institutions and the judicial branch within the EU. Moreover, regarding its jurisprudence it has high importance for the member states. The CJEU consists of the European Court of Justice (ECJ) which is the highest court in the EU legal system and of the European General Court (EGC).[21] Under Article 19 para. 1 TEU the CJEU has to ensure that the law of the treaty is observed in its interpretation and application. The various kinds of judicial procedures are enumerated by this regulation.

V. The Supranational Law System of the EU

1. Supranationality

The European Union is a very good example for a supranational law system.

---

16) Albrecht Weber, "Vom Verfassungsvertrag zum Vertrag von Lissabon," *EuZW*, 2008, p. 7 (9); Robert Schütze, *Introduction to European Law*, 2012, p. 15.

17) Vanessa Hellmann, *Der Vertrag von Lissabon*, 2009, p. 35.

18) *See* Rudolf Streinz, *Europarecht*, 2019, pp. 139-144.

19) Robert Schütze, *Introduction to European Law*, 2012, p. 31.

20) *See* Richard Haase/Rolf Keller, *Grundlagen und Grundformen des Rechts*, 2003, note 790; Richard K. Gardiner, *International Law*, 2003, p. 25.

Actually, supranationality (*Überstaatlichkeit*) is the main feature of the legal construction of the EU. In the EU, the sovereign member states merge their authorities within a complex system of institutions and courts. Actually, the EU law system consists of a framework of legal sources. The supranational law of the EU is made by the EU legislator. The nature of EU law is predetermined by the nature and structure of the Union itself. When signing the founding treaties, the Member States agreed to transfer some of their sovereign powers in defined and limited areas onto the European Communities. By shifting powers to another – common – level, the signatories created a *supranational* (international) organisation which has got autonomous public power and the right to adopt rules binding on its members. So, within the EU system legal competences and political power are transferred from the national level to the level of the Union which means that member states gave up their national sovereignty in many aspects. This had the consequence that the contractors were no longer allowed to exercise these powers due to their national traditions and politics. Therefore, this aspect has always been criticized by some parts of society.

While the prefix "inter" indicates that *intergovernmental* acts are acts between governments, or rather between states which confront each other on the *same level* (co- ordination), the prefix "supra" hints at a relation of subordination between the Union and the Member States. A *supranational* organisation overlooks its members; it exists *above* them and not merely between them. But at the same time, the notion of subordination must be handled with great caution because the Member States are and remain as the "Masters of the Treaties." That also means that the Member States hold the ultimate authority to develop and amend treaties.

It was for the autonomous decision of each Member State that they subordinated themselves voluntarily to the legislative power of the European Union. At any point in time a Member State can decide to resign its participation in the European Union and to withdraw (and insofar elude) from its contractual obligations at the European level. Although this power could not be found in any of the founding treaties from the past, it always existed as a factual right. Now, the *Lisbon Treaty* contains the first formal statement of the right to leave the EU. The only – and probably unenforceable – condition is a two years' notice. The so-called Brexit (United Kingdom is leaving the EU) is the first case of a member state leaving the EU.

Some parallels can be drawn between *supranationality* and *federalism*, although there are many differences. In a federalist state, e.g. Germany, the sovereign power is divided up between different levels of power – in Germany between the "Bund" (the federation) and the "Länder" (federal states). Similarly, in the European Union, the power to legislate or to act in the different policy fields is divided up in Union competences and competences remaining at the national level. In both cases problems arise when it comes to the definition and clear allocation of competences.

2. EU Legislation

As explained above, governmental powers on the EU level are shared by the institutions. That is why it is not possible to declare any single institution as the legislator of the EU. While the Commission is able to bring up initiatives, the European Parliament and the Council make a law to undergo the legislative process.

The law of the EU exists as an independent legal system. EU primary law (*Primärrecht*) and secondary law (*Sekundärrecht*) form the legal source at this level. Basically, EU law takes precedence over national law, as it is the case in the German legal system. Primary law consists of founding and amending treaties.[21] It can be scrutinized by the Federal Constitutional Court for compatibility with the Basic Law. Secondary law consists, for example, of regulations and directives.[22] In many fields of law, the member states, as already mentioned, transferred their legislating competence to the EU and therefore, their sovereignty in those areas then no longer lies in the Member States but in the EU.

EU primary law consists of the establishing treaties of the Communities and the EU treaties, including amendments and supplementary provisions, customary law and the general principles of Union law.[23] Primary law may be characterised as some kind of constitutional law, which determines the basic structures of the European Union. The (amended) founding treaties regulate mainly the institutional system of the European Union. They spell out the general aims and basic principles of the Union. Furthermore, they establish rights and obligations of the Member States and the Union bodies.

EU secondary law comprises all legal acts passed by institutions of the Union. All secondary legal acts such as regulations, directives, decisions and legal acts sui generis are based on primary Union law. Secondary law forms the more voluminous set of rules and has major effects on the European citizens' rights and duties. In fact, regulations, directives and decisions are legally binding.

Decisions are immediately binding in their entirety to all of their addressees. Unlike regulations, decisions are addressed towards one or several particular legal entities or towards a determinable number of those. The addressee may be a Member State, an individual private or legal person. Other than

21) Rudolf Streinz, *Europarecht*, 2019, p. 157.

22) Robert Schütze, *Introduction to European Law*, 2012, notes 803–805.

23) Stephen Weatherill, *Cases and Materials on EU Law*, 2012, pp. 24–25.

a directive, a decision is binding in its completeness. Decisions have direct effect on their addressees. To give an example, the case *Google Spain SL, Google Inc. v Agencia Española de Protección de Datos, Mario Costeja González ruled by the ECJ*[24] in 2014 had to deal with a so-called right to be forgotten under Article 7 and Article 8 Charter of Fundamental Rights of the European Union, which was a relevant decision for all member states and the development on personality rights and data protection in constellations regarding the use of the internet, especially internet search engines like Google.

Regulations are generally and directly applicable throughout the Union. They are of a binding nature and become immediately effective in all Member States instantly when they are adopted. A regulation bears all characteristics of a statute. Its provisions take effect in all Member States without any further requirements, especially without any legislative transposition act of each Member State. Regulations have direct effect: a regulation carries direct effect by its very nature. One recent example would be the General Data Protection Regulation (GDPR)[25] which came into force in 2018. This legislation standardizes data protection law for all EU states by imposing strict regulations on controlling and processing personal data EU citizens.

Directives are addressed to the governments of the Member States but not to individuals. They are legally binding only upon the Member States. Therefore, they basically cannot have direct effect. A directive is an assignment to or obligation for the Member States to enact national measures which are required to implement the directive's content into national law. It is binding as to its contents but leaves to the particular state to choose means and modes for the materialisation of the directive's stipulations. Consumer Protection Law (*Verbraucherschutzrecht*) is strongly influenced by EU directives providing detailed regulation like Directive 2001/95/ EC on product safety.

Recommendations, statements and other legal acts have basically no legally binding force. They are directed towards an undetermined group of addressees and are not of direct effect. Recommendations and statements usually bear the character of declarations of intent and, as such, are first of all of political impact.

3. The Doctrine of Direct Effect

The most prominent feature of EU law is the so-called direct effect of provisions adopted at the Union level. This means that there are no further trans-

24) European Court of Justice, Decision from 13.05.2014 – C-131/12, *NJW*, 2014, p. 2257.

25) For more information, *see* Winfried Veil, "Die Datenschutz-Grundverordnung: Des Kaisers neue Kleider," *NJW*, 2018, p. 686.

formation acts necessary within the domestic laws in order to bring EU law to effect. This also applies to a regulation but basically not to a directive[26] which has to be transformed in domestic law.

The jurisdiction of the European Court of Justice (ECJ) has played an essential role in the development of the concept of the direct effect of EU law. In a number of very early judgements, the ECJ stated that not only the Member States themselves can be subject to legal acts of the Community/Union, but also ruled that individuals can derive rights and obligations directly from the Union provisions and can therefore – under certain circumstances – invoke Union rules in front of a national court or European court.[27] However, the principle relates only to certain European acts. Furthermore, it is subject to several conditions. It can apply in relation to regulations, directives, treaty provisions and decisions.

The significance of this legal invention of the ECJ as a major step in the history of international law should not be underestimated. The direct effect doctrine is the characteristic that differentiates EU law from the classic law of nations. Treaties, according to international law, only bind the contracting parties (states) and usually have to be implemented by the national parliaments in order to create applicable rules for private individuals under domestic law. But, as opposed to this two-step system, EU provisions can also affect a single person in a Member State immediately when they enter into force and give him or her the opportunity to enforce a Union rule before a domestic judge.

Article 288 [TFEU] provides that regulations and decisions shall be binding in all member states:

> To exercise the Union's competences, the institutions shall adopt regulations, directives, decisions, recommendations and opinions.
> A regulation shall have general application. It shall be binding in its entirety and directly applicable in all Member States.
> A directive shall be binding, as to the result to be achieved, upon each Member State to which it is addressed, but shall leave to the national authorities the choice of form and methods.
> A decision shall be binding in its entirety. A decision which specifies those to whom it is addressed shall be binding only on them.
> Recommendations and opinions shall have no binding force.

---

26) *See also* Stephen Weatherill, *Cases and Materials on EU Law*, 2012, p. 122.

27) *See also* European Court of Justice, Decision from 05.02.1963, case 26/62 – *Van Gend en Loos*.

VI. Transnational Jurisprudence and Human Rights in Europe

The European Union is a part of a broad structure on Human Rights protection. In fact, Human Rights protection within Europe occurs in a complex system of national and international courts such as different laws. While the domestic legal systems in Europe provide their own protection and jurisprudence under their national constitution and by national constitutional courts, the European level provides Human Rights jurisprudence in a parallel system that is interconnected with the national level of the states. Therefore, human rights protection in Europe these days is connected to a multilevel system. At a European level, the European Court of Justice in Luxemburg and the European Court of Human Rights in Strasbourg provide the jurisdiction. *Andreas Voßkuhle*, the president of the German Constitutional Court, even speaks of the triangle of jurisdiction between Karlsruhe, Luxemburg and Strasbourg.[28]

1. The Council of Europe and Human Rights Protection

The European Convention of Human Rights (ECHR) is an international treaty for the protection of human rights and fundamental freedoms in Europe. The treaty was drafted in 1950 by the then newly formed Council of Europe (*Europarat*). Today, all 47 states in Europe are members of this protection system. Although the following terms are quite similar, the Council of Europe has to be distinguished from the aforementioned Council and the European Council. In fact, it is important that the whole system of the Council of Europe and the ECHR has to be distinguished from the European Union. The membership is open to all countries of the European continent which share the same values and goals such as peace, cooperation, good governance and the protection of human rights, and such a common development is to improve democracy and the principle of the rule of law within the domestic legal systems.

The Council of Europe is an international organisation, which was founded in 1949, shortly after the end of World War II, in order to protect Human Rights and the democratic development in Europe. The Council of Europe consists of two statutory bodies, which are the *Committee of Ministers*, composed of each member per state, and the *Parliamentary Assembly*, comprising the members of the national parliaments of each member state. Unlike the European Union, however, the Council of Europe is not able to bring up binding legislation but is has the power to enforce international agreements

---

28) Andreas Voßkuhle, "Multilevel Cooperation of the European Constitutional Courts," *European Constitutional Law Review* 6, 2010, p. 175 (178).

like the ECHR, which is enforced by its own court, the European Court of Human Rights – ECtHR –, located in Strasbourg (France).

2. The General Scope of the European Convention of Human Rights

In order to define the European Convention of Human Rights in legal terms, this convention is an international treaty (*völkerrechtlicher Vertrag*). All member states of the Council of Europe are necessarily contractual party of the ECHR, and new members are expected to ratify the convention at the earliest opportunity. The convention provides a comprehensive catalogue of guarantees and freedoms that codify a parallel protection system to the constitutional systems of the national states. Moreover, the ECHR has several protocols which amend the framework of the convention.

The legal system of the ECtHR is completely separate from the national systems. However, the interconnectedness between the law levels gets more intensive. As an international court, the ECtHR offers merely an additional system to protect human rights. Under the principle of subsidiary (*Subsidiaritätsprinzip*), the Convention system has the task of ensuring respect for the fundamental rights and can intervene only where the domestic authorities fail in that task. Its jurisprudence and interpretation of the Convention provides orientation for the domestic judiciary. However, the court merely sets a minimum standard of protection and leaves a *margin of appreciation* to national authorities when it comes to the domestic level. The purpose of the margin of appreciation is to cope with national interests during the interpretation of convention rights. Its scope depends on whether there is a common core of interpretation of the concrete right already. If not, the ECtHR recognizes a wide margin of appreciation in order to respect different terms of interpretation and legal variety on the level of the member states.

3. The Articles of the European Convention of Human Rights

Article 1 ECHR [Obligation to respect Human Rights] clearly binds the signatory parties to secure the rights under the other Articles of the Convention "within their jurisdiction which means in domestic laws. Then, Article 2 ECHR [Right to Life] protects the right to life of every person and even of legal persons such as corporations. Under the scope of Article 2 ECHR the court provides a broad scope of interpretation. In *Evans v United Kingdom* from 2007 the court stated that the question of whether this right also extends to a human embryo falls within a state's own decision under the margin of appreciation.[29] In *Vo v France*, however, the ECtHR declined to extend the right to life to an unborn child, while ruling that it is neither desirable, nor even possible as matters stand, to answer in abstract the question whether the unborn child is a person for the purposes of Article 2 of the Convention.[30] Article 3 ECHR [Prohibition of Torture] says that "no one should be subject to torture or to inhuman or degrading treatment or punishment" which is important to state explicitly, especially due to the experiences of several dictatorships and abuse of state power in European history. This also refers to the guarantee under Article 4 ECHR [Prohibition of Slavery and forced Labour]. Under Article 5 ECHR [Right to Liberty and Security] liberty and security of the person are concerned as a coherent concept of Human Rights protection. However, in jurisprudence there is a strong focus on protecting the personal freedoms as security of the person has not been subject to separate interpretation by the ECtHR yet.

Article 6 ECHR [Right to a fair Trail] provides a comprehensive right to a fair trial. This refers to the right of a public hearing before an independent and impartial tribunal within reasonable time. Insofar, a legal proceeding must take no longer than usually one year per instance before national courts.[31] Then, the right includes the presumption of innocence (*Unschuldsvermutung*) such as a standard of rights for those persons charged with a criminal offence. This can again refer to adequate time and facilities for the preparation of the legal defence, the access to legal representation, the right to examine witnesses against them or have them examined and right to the free assistance of an interpreter.[32] Germany has quite a high standard in providing these kinds of rights due to its various regulations concerning these rights in the German Criminal Law Procedure and moreover the jurisprudence takes these rights seriously. Today, the majority of cases violating Article 6 ECHR grounds on excessive delays in civil and criminal proceedings before national courts and insofar breaches of the reasonable time requirement. Article 7 ECHR [No punishment without Law] also provides regulations securing the structure of the legal state. This provision states that no one shall be held guilty of any criminal offence on account of any act or omission, which did not constitute a criminal offence under national or international law at the time when it was committed. Nor shall a heavier penalty be imposed than the one that was applicable at the time the criminal offence was committed. This Article corresponds with the guarantee in the German constitution under Article 103 Basic Law.

29) ECtHR, Decision from 10.04.2007, App. No. 6339/05 – *Evans v United Kingdom.*

30) ECtHR, Decision from 08.07.2004, App. No. 6339/05 – *Vo v France.*

31) Jens Meyer-Ladewig/Martin Nettesheim/Stefan von Raumer (Editors), *EMRK*, 2017, Article 6, note 199.

32) Robin C A White/Claire Ovey, *The European Convention on Human Rights*, 2010, pp. 288–295.

Article 8 ECHR [Right to respect for private life and family life] provides protection for private life like as home, correspondence and several personality rights such as for family life. Due to the wording of the provision, these rights are subject to certain restrictions that are "in accordance with law," and "necessary in a democratic society," which means that certain limitations of Article 8 ECHR are foreseen. The ECtHR gives a broad interpretation of the protection of private life and family life and as an example, prohibitions of private consensual homosexual acts violate this article.[33] Regarding the protection of personality rights, the ECtHR accepted the right to privacy, defamation, self-determination and image rights more than a decade ago.[34] Actually, as an international court, the ECtHR is supposed to set a minimum standard of protection. But in some cases, the scope of Article 8 ECHR can comprise positive obligations (*positive Verpflichtungen*). In this case, national authorities are obliged to provide a minimal standard of protection under domestic law. In fact, the European states practice a different standard of the rights under Article 8 ECHR. There was a strong development in the last decade due to the influence of the Conventions legal system. An important example is the development of the protection of privacy as a person's private sphere (*Privatsphäre*) when some European states did not recognize a right to privacy either due to their early stage of development regarding democracy and human rights or due to their traditional legal interpretation like in the United Kingdom. Traditionally, the right to privacy was not accepted as a value requiring protection in the United Kingdom, especially not in collisions with freedom of speech as a fundamental freedom of highest rank in the British legal system. However, this situation changed when the Human Rights Act 1998 was enacted, and the European Convention of Human Rights was incorporated in the British Common Law. Under the influence of the ECtHR's jurisdiction, the British jurisprudence developed a comprehensive protection of privacy which is actually beyond the minimum standard as set by the ECtHR.

Article 9 ECHR [Freedom of thought, conscience and religion] provides a right to freedom of thought, conscience and religion (*Religionsfreiheit*). This includes the freedom to change a religion or belief, and to manifest a religion or belief in worship, teaching, practice and observance.[35] Like under

---

33) *See* Robin C A White/Claire Ovey, *The European Convention on Human Rights*, 2010, pp. 285–387.

34) ECtHR, Decision from 24.6.2004 – App. No. 59320/00 – *von Hannover v Germany*; ECtHR, decisions from 7.2.2012 – App. Nos. 40660/08 and 60641/08 – *von Hannover v Germany (No. 2)*; see also ECtHR, Decision from 7.2.2012 – App. No. 44585/10 – *Springer v Germany*; for more information, *see* Judith Janna Märten, *Die Vielfalt des Persönlichkeitsschutzes*, 2015, Chapters 4, 5 and 9.

35) Jens Meyer-Ladewig/Martin Nettesheim/Stefan von Raumer (Editors), *EMRK*, 2017, Article 9, notes 3–5.

Article 8 ECHR, para. 2 of this regulation states that this provision is subject to certain restrictions "in accordance with law" and if they are "necessary in a democratic society."

Article 10 ECHR [Freedom of expression] includes the freedom to hold opinions, and to receive and impart information and ideas. Critic can be expressed in private and in public. Opinions can be favoured or disfavoured. This right applies to everybody such as private persons, public figures and of course the media as the "public watchdog" in the state under the freedom of press.[36] Although the ECtHR provides a wide interpretation, again under Article 10 para. 2 ECHR, this provision is subject to certain restrictions that are "in accordance with law" and "necessary in a democratic society."[37] Restrictions can be justified especially for interests of national security and the protection of third party's rights, as mentioned as personality rights such as defamation and privacy protected under Article 8 ECHR. By balancing the conflicting interests, the ECtHR stresses on the importance of Article 10 ECHR regarding the meaning and importance for democracy. Next to freedom of expression, Article 11 ECHR [Freedom of assembly and association] is also one cornerstone for realising a democratic society. Under Article 11 ECHR everyone has the right to freedom of peaceful assembly and to freedom of association with others, including the right to form and to join trade unions for the protection of his or her interests.

Furthermore, Article 12 ECHR [Right to marry] provides the right to marry which is actually just relevant in a few cases. Then, Article 13 ECHR [Right to an effective remedy] provides an important procedural law (*Verfahrensrecht*) in order to give the Human Rights stronger practical effect. This provision states that everyone whose rights and freedoms as set forth in this Convention are violated shall have an effective remedy before a national authority notwithstanding the violation has been committed by persons acting in an official capacity.

Article 14 ECHR [Prohibition of discrimination] prohibits from discrimination on personal characteristics and corresponds to the idea of Article 3 para. 3 Basic Law in the German constitution (*Diskriminierungsverbot*). The wording of Article 14 ECHR expresses clearly that the enjoyment of the rights and freedoms set forth in this European Convention on Human Rights shall be secured without discrimination on any ground such as sex, race, colour, language, religion, political or other opinion, national or social origin, association with a national minority, property, birth or other status.

Finally, the convention provides some regulations regarding the application of the aforementioned Human Rights such as Article 15 ECHR [Deroga-

36) Robin C A White/Claire Ovey, *The European Convention on Human Rights*, 2010, pp. 432–436.

37) *See* ECtHR, Decision from 07.12.1976, No. 5493/72, Series A No. 24 – *Handyside v United Kingdom*.

tion in times of emergency], Article 16 ECHR [Restrictions on political activity of aliens], Article 17 ECHR [Prohibition of abuse of rights] and Article 18 ECHR [Limitations on use of restrictions on rights].

Any person who feels his or her rights have been violated under the Convention by a national states authority can take this case to the court with an individual complaint (*Individualbeschwerde*) under Article 34 ECHR. Individuals have full standing before court.[38] Judgments finding violations are legally binding on the states concerned, and they are obliged to execute them. If the ECtHR states a violation of the convention, compensation by the member state is granted to the applicant.

4. EU Fundamental Rights

To begin with, the European Union does not provide its own system to protect Human Rights. That is why, on a supranational level, the ECHR is more relevant than the framework of protection of EU Fundamental Rights. However, the missing charter of EU Fundamental Rights does not mean that there is no protection system of fundamental rights on this level at all. Originally, the EU legislator did not dispose of any set of fundamental rights comparable to that of the German Basic Law or the French Constitution which are actually shaped by the countries' historical developments. However, as already mentioned, the fact that there is no codified catalogue on fundamental rights does not necessarily mean that there are no fundamental rights on the European level. The situation can be compared to that in the United Kingdom, where an efficient protection of fundamental rights is granted despite the absence of any written catalogue. In this case it is due to common values and principles that have been developed over the time. Through numerous decisions in the last 30 years, the European Court of Justice has developed a system of fundamental rights comparable to the catalogue contained in the German Basic Law. Insofar, the case law of the European Court of Justice is a relevant legal source.

By the time, several provisions have been included in the EU treaties, which explicitly address the fundamental rights issue, the introduction of which can be seen as a reaction of the European political bodies to the jurisdiction of the Court. An attempt of a proclamation of the Charter of Fundamental Rights of the European Union (*EU Grundrechte Charter*) included in a European constitution with a draft from 2007 finally failed. With the *Treaty of Lisbon* the Charter of Fundamental Rights of the European Union is now legally binding. However, the protection that was developed and advanced

38) Robin C A White/Claire Ovey, *The European Convention on Human Rights*, 2010, p. 12.

by the ECJ used to exist before. Although the (former) EC Treaty did not dispose of a catalogue of fundamental rights in a strict sense before the *Treaty of Lisbon*, it contained clauses which could be employed as a basis to derive a protection of such rights (which was done by interpretation). Moreover, the provisions of the ECHR have always been relevant for the ECJ interpretation of EU law, even though it is not part of Union law in the strict sense. But nevertheless, the charter is now included in the TEU after *Treaty of Lisbon* and it is legally binding for all institutions and Member States.

Under Article 6 para. 1 TEU, the Union recognises the rights, freedoms and principles set out in this Charter, which shall have the same legal value as the Treaties. However, the Charter is not technically implemented in the text of the treaty but referred to in Article 6 para. 1 TEU. The Treaty of Lisbon also allowed the European Union to accede to the European Convention on Human Rights. Article 6 para. 2 TEU states: "The Union shall accede to the European Convention for the Protection of Human Rights and Fundamental Freedoms."

Now, EU law provides protection by the Charter of Fundamental Rights of the European Union. This Charta is conceptualized like any other charter of fundamental rights, for example the German constitution as it begins with the Human Dignity under Article 1. Then, basic individual rights are guaranteed like Article 2 [Right to life] and Article 3 [Right to the integrity of the person] such as democratic rights including especially Article 11 [Freedom of expression and information] and Article 12 [Freedom of assembly and association].

5. Jurisprudence in the Multilevel Court System

The Human Rights Protection System in Europe can be seen as an example for transnational law. The term transnational law is broadly used to include the idea that public, semi-public and private entities of one state may be involved in international cooperation with bodies in other states where governments are not the centre stage.[39] Courts play an important role in transnational law. Although national law systems are independent and separate from the European level, the national constitutional courts have been collaborated by both the European Court of Justice and the European Court of Human Rights. Due to the different levels of legislation and jurisprudence, the European system on protection of Human rights is recognized as a multilevel system (*Mehrebensystem*). The concept of this system refers to the cooperative, non-hierarchical handling of multilevel constitutional issues between con-

39) Richard K. Gardiner, *International Law*, 2003, p. 24.

stitutional and European courts.[40] As time passed, the German constitutional court became more open towards the European jurisprudence. This becomes evident by the adaption of the ECtHR's jurisprudence in many cases by the interpretation of the Basic Law in the light of the convention.[41] Moreover, a *judicial dialogue* between the European judges and domestic judges is recognized, which also describes the special relationship between the international and domestic courts in Europe.[42]

Basically, the member states of the ECHR apply the convention rights within their domestic laws and jurisprudences by referring to their own interpretation which can be different due to the states' specific legal traditions. In order to take the differences between the domestic laws of the contracting states into account, the ECtHR approves a wide scope of interpretation and expected state obligations under the *margin of appreciation doctrine*.[43] Under this doctrine, the court is able to reconcile the existing differences in implementing the articles of the Convention. By applying the *margin of appreciation doctrine* in its jurisdiction, the ECtHR focuses on a common European consensus for interpretation of the particular article of the Convention. The concept of a common European consensus in the ECtHR's case law may be defined as a general agreement among the majority of the contracting states on certain rules, values and principles identified through comparative research of national and international law and practice.[44] If a common consensus is not recognized, the ECtHR refers to a wide interpretation such as on the protection of private and family life under article 8(1) ECHR which is interpreted differently by the European states, especially on abortion rights, same-sex marriage and the scope of personality rights like the right to privacy.

40) Andreas Voßkuhle, "Multilevel Cooperation of the European Constitutional Courts," *European Constitutional Law Review* 6, 2010, p. 175 (184).

41) For a great example *see* the development of personality rights in *ECtHR*, Decision from 24.6.2004 – App. No. 59320/00 – *von Hannover v Germany*; *ECtHR*, Decisions from 7.2.2012 – App. Nos. 40660/08 and 60641/08 – *von Hannover v Germany* (No. 2).

42) *See* Lize R. Glas, *The Theory, Potential and Practice of Procedural Dialogue in the European Convention on Human Rights System*, 2016, p. 3.

43) Gerards, Janneke, "Pluralism, Deference and the Margin of Appreciation Doctrine," *European Law Journal*, (2011) Vol 17, No 1, 80.

44) *See* Dzehtsiarou, Kanstantsin, *European Consensus and the Legitimacy of the European Court of Human Rights*, 2016, Chapter 2.

Bibliography

Chapter 1 Selected Aspects on German Culture

References

Engelhardt, Hanns. 2017. "Die 'Ehe für alle' und ihre Kinder." *Neue Zeitschrift für Familienrecht(NZFam)* (p. 1042).

Esping-Andersen, Costa. 1998. *The three worlds of welfare capitalism*. Princeton.

Fischer-Lescano, Andreas. 2018. "Natur als Rechtsperson — Konstellation der Stellvertretung im Recht." *Zeitschrift für Umweltrecht(ZuR)* (p. 205).

Haase, Richard, and Rolf Keller. 2003. *Grundlagen und Grundformen des Rechts*(11th ed.). Stuttgart (p. 369).

Koch, Hans-Joachim. 2007. "Die Verbandsklage im Umweltrecht." *Neue Zeitschrift für Verwaltungsrecht(NVwZ)* (p. 369).

Marschall, Stefan. 2016. *Parlamentarismus – Eine Einführung*(2nd ed.), Baden-Baden.

Knoop, Martina. 2017. "Die Ehe für alle." *Neue Juristische Wochenschrift-Spezial(NJW-Spezial)* (p. 580).

Köck, Dilling. 2018. "Was bleibt? Deutsches Umweltrecht in vergleichender Perspektive." *Die Öffentliche Verwaltung(DÖV)* (p. 594).

Krüper, Julian(ed.). 2017. *Grundlagen des Rechts*(3rd ed.). Baden-Baden.

Laufer, Heinz and Ursula Münch. 2006. *Das föderative System der Bundesrepublik Deutschland*, Wiesbaden.

Märker, Klaus. 2018. "Drittes Geschlecht? — Quo vadis Bundesverfassungsgericht." *Neue Zeitschrift für Familienrecht(NZFam)* (p. 1).

Morlok, Martin. 2000. "Spenden – Rechenschaft – Sanktionen, Aktuelle Rechtsfragen der Parteienfinanzierung." *Neue Juristische Wochenschrift(NJW)* (p. 761).

Münch, von, Ingo. 1993. "Rechtskultur." *Neue Juristische Wochenschrift(NJW)* (p. 1673).

Schmidt, Manfred G. 2012. *Der Deutsche Sozialstaat — Geschichte und Gegenwart*.

München.

Voßkuhle, Andreas and Thomas Wischmeyer. 2015. "Grundwissen — Öffentliches Recht: Das Sozialstaatsprinzip." *Juristische Schulung(JuS)* (p. 693).

Cases

Bundesverfassungsgericht. Decision from 15.01.1958 *BVerfGE* 7, 198 – *Lüth*

Bundesverfassungsgericht. Decision from 27.6.2017 – 2 *BvR* 1333/17. *Neue Juristische Wochenschrift(NJW)* 2017, p. 2333 – *Kopftuchverbot für Rechtsreferendarinnen in Hessen*

Bundesverfassungsgericht. Decision 10.10.2017 – 1 *BvR* 2019/16. *Neue Juristische Wochenschrift(NJW)* 2017, p. 3643 – *Das dritte Geschlecht*

Online Sources

https://www.tatsachen-ueber-deutschland.de/de/rubriken/auf-einen-blick/geografie-klima (15.07.2018)

https://www.tatsachen-ueber-deutschland.de/de/rubriken/gesellschaft/bereichernde-vielfalt (15.07.2018).

https://de.statista.com/statistik/daten/studie/249925/umfrage/sonnenstunden-im-jahr-nach-bundeslaendern (15.07.2018)

https://www.umweltbundesamt.de/wasserqualitaet-in-badegewaessern (12.09.2020)

https://www.umweltbundesamt.de/themen/fakten-zur-nitratbelastung-in-grund-trinkwasser (15.07.2018)

https://www.bundeswaldinventur.de/index.php?id=665 (Bundesministerium für Ernährung und Landwirtschaft) (15.07.2018)

https://www.bundeswaldinventur.de/index.php?id=710 (Bundesministerium für Ernährung und Landwirtschaft) (15.07.2018)

https://www.bmel-statistik.de/fileadmin/user_upload/monatsberichte/FHB-0320126-2017.pdf, (Bundesministerium für Ernährung und Landwirtschaft) (21.08.2018)

https://www.bfn.de/fileadmin/BfN/presse/2015/Dokumente/Artenschutzreport_Download.pdf,Bundesamt für Naturschutz, Artenschutzreport 2015 – Tiere und Pflanzen in Deutschland, S. 13; URL (21.08.2018)

https://www.waldkulturerbe.de/fileadmin/Publikationen/UnserWald_WEB_doppelseitige_Ansicht.pdf Bundesministerium für Ernährung und Landwirtschaft, Unser Wald – Natur aus Försterhand, S. 45; URL (21.08.2018)

https://www.tatsachen-ueber-deutschland.de/de/jugend/offene-gesellschaft/offen-fuer-neue-buerger (12.09.2020)

https://www.bamf.de/DE/Service/Left/Glossary/_function/glossar.htm-

l?lv3=3198544 (27.10.2018)
https://www.deutschland.de/de/topic/leben/stadt-und-land-fakten-zu-urbanisierung-und-landflucht (12.09.2020)

Chapter 2 German History at a Glance

References

Althammer, Beate. 2009. *Das Bismarckreich 1871–1890*. Paderborn (pp. 11–21).

Bauer, Kurt. 2008. *Nationalsozialismus*. Wien/Köln/Weimar (pp. 419–488).

Becher, Matthias. 2007. "Von einer Randkultur zum Zentrum Europas: Das Frankenreich." in: Meinhardt, Matthias, Andreas Ranft and Stephan Selzer (ed.). *Mittelalter*. München (pp. 23–38).

Bedürftig, Friedemann. 1996. *Lexikon Deutschland nach 1945*, Hamburg (p. 11)

Benz, Wolfgang. "Die Bundesrepublik Deutschland 1949–1989." in: Weidenfeller, Werner and Hartmut Zimmermann (eds.). 1989. *Deutschland-Handbuch — Eine doppelte Bilanz 1949–1989*. Düsseldorf (pp. 50, 53).

Besch, Werner. *Wie groß war Luthers Einfluss auf unsere Sprache?* URL: https://www.uni-bonn.de/neues/228-2014 (2018-07-26)

Bilzer, Bert, Jürgen Eyssen and Otto Stelzer. 1958. *Das Grosse Buch der Kunst*, Braunschweig (p. 466).

Boden, Martina. 1998. *Chronik Handbuch Europa*. Gütersloh/Munich (pp. 50, 195).

Bollmann, Peter, Ulrich March and Traute Petersen. 1990. *Kleine Geschichte der Deutschen*. Stuttgart (pp. 21–22, 51–52, 55, 158, 179-182).

Both, Siegfried, Jürgen Engelhardt and Erwin Grusa. 1997. *Recht im Alltag der mittelalterlichen Bevölkerung*. 2nd Ed. Dessau (p. 15).

Brechtken, Magnus. 2004. *Die nationalsozialistische Herrschaft 1933–1939*. Darmstadt (pp. 77, 78).

Bruder, Wolfgang and Peter Hofelich. "Chronik der Ereignisse und Entwicklungen." in: Ellwein, Thomas and Wolfgang Bruder (eds.). 1985. *Ploetz: Die Bundesrepublik Deutschland*. 2nd Ed. Freiburg/Würzburg (pp. 155–156).

Bundesarchiv Koblenz. *Akten der Reichskanzlei, Nachlass Pünder, Nr. 154*, (pp. 48–49), Aktennotiz Herrmann Pünder vom 16. April 1932, available from (29.05.2010): http://www.bundesarchiv.de/aktenreichskanzlei/19191933/1021/bru/bru3p/kap1_1/para2_208.html.

Burleigh, Michael. 2000. *The Third Reich — A New History*. New York (p. 792).

Caplan, Jane. 1992. *The Rise of National Socialism*, in: Gordon Martel (ed.). *Modern Germany Reconsidered, 1870–1945*. London (pp. 117–139).

Cunliffe, Barry. 2000. *Die Kelten*. 7th Ed. Turin (pp. 146–159).

______. 2007. *Rom und sein Weltreich*, 2nd Ed. Turin (pp. 248–253).

Dahm, Felix. 1996. *Die Germanen*. Essen (p. 24).

Derks, Heidrun. 2009. "Die Varusschlacht." in: *2000 Jahre Varusschlacht – Konflikt.* ed. by Varusschlacht im Osnabrücker Land GmbH. Stuttgart (pp. 36–55).

Dietmar, Carl and Werner Jung. 1996. *Geschichte der Stadt Köln.* 8th Ed. Cologne (p. 58, 62, 76, 179).

Donat, Peter, Achim Leube and Günter Behm-Blancke. 1988. "Grundzüge der materiellen und geistigen Kultur." in: Bruno Krüger (LdA-edit.). *Die Germanen — Geschichte und Kultur der germanischen Stämme in Mitteleuropa Bd. 1.* Berlin (pp. 321–385).

Drollinger, Kuno. 1998. "Deutscher Orden." in: Gerhard Taddey. *Lexikon der deutschen Geschichte.* Stuttgart (p. 259).

Eberling, Hans and Wolfgang Birkenfeld. 1971. *Die Reise in die Vergangenheit, Band 2 – Aus Mittelalter und Neuzeit.* Braunschweig (pp. 65, 80, 81, 93, 148–150, 153–158).

______. 1981. *Die Reise in die Vergangenheit Band 3, Ausgabe N.* Braunschweig (pp. 36, 66, 69, 81, 109, 110, 119, 126–128, 129, 138, 139, 140–141, 148, 152, 153, 155).

Eckert, Jörn. 2008. "Allgemeines Landrecht (Preußen)." in: Albrecht Cordes, Dieter Werkmüller (ed). *Handwörterbuch zur deutschen Rechtsgeschichte Bd. 1.* 2nd Ed. Berlin (pp. 155–162).

Evans, Richard J. 2005. *The Third Reich in Power.* London (pp. 81–118).

______. 2008. *The Third Reich at War.* London (p. 726).

Geisthövel, Alexa. 2008. *Restauration und Vormärz.* Paderborn (pp. 13, 38, 45–46).

Gilcher-Holtey. Ingrid. 2001. *Die 68er-Bewegung — Deutschland, Westeuropa, USA.* München (pp. 115–116, 123).

Gmür, Rudolf and Andreas Roth. 2014. *Grundriss der deutschen Rechtsgeschichte.* 14th Ed. München (pp. 108, 119, 120, 124-125).

Goetz, Hans-Werner. 1986. *Leben im Mittelalter – vom 7. bis zum 13. Jahrhundert.* Munich (pp. 115, 116–128, 178–179).

Gorys, Andrea. 2004. *Wörterbuch Archäologie.* Wiesbaden (p. 258).

Gotthard, Axel. 2009. *Das Alte Reich 1495–1806.* 4th Ed. Darmstadt (pp. 162–163).

Grebing, Helga. 1979. *Geschichte der deutschen Arbeiterbewegung.* 9th Ed. München (pp. 22–26, 38–44, 48–49, 70–72).

Gruchmann, Lothar. 1994. "Georg Elser." in: Hermann Graml, Hermmann. *Widerstand im Dritten Reich — Probleme, Ereignisse, Gestalten.* Frankfurt a. M. (pp. 183–189).

Gruner, Erich and Eduard Sieber. 1961. *Weltgeschichte des 20. Jahrhunderts – Fünfter Band.* Erlenbach-Zürich und Stuttgart (p. 15, p. 288).

Hähnchen, Susanne. 2012. *Rechtsgeschichte – Von der römischen Antike bis zur Neuzeit.* Heidelberg/München/Landsberg/Frechen/Hamburg (pp. 316–320, 343).

Halder, Winfried. 2006. *Innenpolitik im Kaiserreich 1871–1914*, 2nd Ed., Darmstadt (pp. 38–45, 58–59, 64–66).

Hammel-Kieslow, Rolf. 2000. *Die Hanse*. Munich (pp. 10, 11).

Hartmann, Wilfried. 2010. *Karl der Große*. Stuttgart (pp. 103, 198, 203).

Hein, Dieter. 1998. *Die Revolution von 1848/1849*. München (p. 11).

Hitler, Adolf. 1933. *Mein Kampf*, 40th Ed. München (pp. 702–703).

Hobsbawn, Eric. 1995. *Das Zeitalter der Extreme*. Wien (p. 161).

Hortzschansky, Günter, Roland Grau, Werner Imig, Siegfried Ittershagen, Ingo Materna, Horst Naum, Walter Nimtz and Kurt Wrobel. 1978. *Illustrierte Geschichte der Novemberrevolution*, Berlin (pp. 251–255).

Jenal, Georg. 2007. "Mönchtum." in: Meinhardt, Matthias, Andreas Ranft and Stephan Selzer (eds.). *Mittelalter*. München (pp. 185–192).

Jooß, Rainer. 1998. "Friedrich II." in: Gerhard Taddey (ed.). *Lexikon der deutschen Geschichte*. Stuttgart (pp. 410–411).

Kant, Immanuel. 1963. "What is Enlightenment?" in: Immanuel Kant. *On History*. edited with an introduction by Lewis White Beck. trans. by Lewis White Beck, Robert E. Anchor and Emil L. Feckenhein. Indianapolis (p. 3).

Kleinschmidt, Harald. 2011. *Die Angelsachsen*. Munich (pp. 9–10).

Klueting, Harm. 1989. *Das konfessionelle Zeitalter 1525–1648*. Stuttgart (p. 145).

Köbler, Gerhard. 1996. *Deutsche Rechtsgeschichte — Ein systematischer Grundriss der geschichtlichen Grundlagen des deutschen Rechts von den Indogermanen bis zur Gegenwart*. Munich (pp. 66–69).

Kolb, Eberhard und Schumann, Dirk. 2013. Die Weimarer Republik. München (pp. 115-116, 124-125, 151).

König, Werner. 2007. *dtv-Atlas Deutsche Sprache*. 16th Ed. Munich (p. 18).

Kroeschell, Karl. 1980. *Deutsche Rechtsgeschichte 1 (bis 1250)*. 7th Ed. Opladen (pp. 220–221).

______. 1989. *Dt. Rechtsgeschichte 3 (seit 1650)*. Opladen (p. 118).

______. 1991. "Die gesellschaftlichen und politischen Veränderungen in Deutschland bis 1848." in: Wolfgang W. Mickel. (ed.) *Geschichte, Politik und Gesellschaft 1 – Von der französischen Revolution bis zum Ende des 2. Weltkrieges*. Frankfurt a.M. (pp. 55–104).

Lieberwirth, Rolf. 2008. "Constitutio Criminalis Carolina." in: Albrecht Cordes, Dieter Werkmüller (eds.). *Handwörterbuch zur deutschen Rechtsgeschichte Bd. 1*. 2nd Ed. Berlin (pp. 886–890).

Zu Löwenstein, Hubertus. 1951. *Deutsche Geschichte – Der Weg des Reiches in zwei Jahrtausenden*. Frankfurt/M. (pp. 90, 96–97, 101).

Mann, Golo. 1961. *Deutsche Geschichte des neunzehnten und zwanzigsten Jahrhunderts*. Frankfurt a. M. (p. 204).

Margedant, Udo. 1991. "Die Weimarer Republik." in Wolfgang W. Mickel. (ed.) *Geschichte, Politik und Gesellschaft 1 – Von der französischen Revolution bis zum Ende des 2. Weltkrieges*. Frankfurt a.M. (pp. 258–318).

Marx, Karl. 1978. *Manifest der Kommunistischen Partei*. München (p. 89).

Meder, Stephan. 2017. *Rechtsgeschichte*. 6th Ed. Cologne (p. 125).

Mickel, Wolfgang W. 1991. "Die Entstehung und Entwicklung des Deutschen Reiches im Spannungsfeld liberaler, nationaler und konservativer Kräfte des 19. Jahrhunderts." in: Wolfgang W. Mickel. (ed.) *Geschichte, Politik und Gesellschaft 1 – Von der französischen Revolution bis zum Ende des 2. Weltkrieges*. Frankfurt a.M. (pp. 105–162).

______. 1991. "Die soziale Frage und die Kritik an der bürgerlichen Gesellschaft." in: Wolfgang W. Mickel. (ed.) *Geschichte, Politik und Gesellschaft 1 – Von der französischen Revolution bis zum Ende des 2. Weltkrieges*. Frankfurt a.M. (pp. 206–318).

______. 1991. "Entstehung und Entwicklung." in: Wolfgang W. Mickel. (ed.) *Geschichte, Politik und Gesellschaft 1 – Von der französischen Revolution bis zum Ende des 2. Weltkrieges*. Frankfurt a.M. (pp. 105–162, 138).

Mickel, Wolfgang W. and Frieder Mutschler. 1991. "Die Revolution des Bürgertums 1789: Der Kampf um den demokratischen Verfassungsstaat." in: Wolfgang W. Mickel. (ed.) *Geschichte, Politik und Gesellschaft 1 – Von der französischen Revolution bis zum Ende des 2. Weltkrieges*. Frankfurt a.M. (pp 5–54).

Mickel, Wolfgang W. and Petra Rentschler. 1991. "Wirtschaft und Gesellschaft im Zeitalter der Industrialisierung: Von der Agrar- zur Industriegesellschaft." in: Wolfgang W. Mickel. (ed.) *Geschichte, Politik und Gesellschaft 1 – Von der französischen Revolution bis zum Ende des 2. Weltkrieges*. Frankfurt a.M. (pp. 163–205).

Mieck, Ilja. 1992. "Preußen von 1807–1850 — Reformen, Restauration und Revolution." in: Otto Büsch. (ed.) *Handbuch der preußischen Geschichte, Bd. II – Das 19. Jahrhundert und Große Themen der Geschichte Preußens*. Berlin/New York (pp. 3–292).

Moosbauer, Günther. 2009. *Die Varusschlacht*. 2nd Ed. Munich (pp. 62–69).

______. 2009. "Die Römer in Germanien." in: Varusschlacht im Osnabrücker Land GmbH(ed.). *Varusschlacht im Osnabrücker Land – Museum und Park Kalkriese*. Mainz (pp. 32–43).

Müller, Frank-Lorenz. 2009. *Die Revolution von 1848/1849*. 3rd Ed. Darmstadt.

Neebe, Reinhard. 1981. *Großindustrie, Staat und NSDAP, 1930–1933* Göttingen (p. 119).

Orthbandt, Eberhard. 1963. *Illustrierte Deutsche Geschichte*. Munich (pp. 60, 147, 415).

Peukert, Detlev J.K. 1987. *The Weimar Republic – The Crisis of Classical Modernity*. trans. Richard Deveson. London (p. 249, 255).

Pesch, Otto-Hermman. 2002. "Luther." in: Klaus Ganzer and Bruno Steimer (eds.). *Lexikon der Reformationszeit*. 3rd Ed. Freiburg (pp. 452–475).

Pohl, Dieter. 2011. *Verfolgung und Massenmord in der NS-Zeit*. 3rd Ed. Darmstadt (p. 16)

Pohl, Walter. 2002. *Die Völkerwanderung*. Stuttgart-Berlin-Cologne (pp. 106–107, 126, 157, 157).

Probst, Gabi. *Zahl der Toten an der innerdeutschen Grenze vermutlich falsch*. available from (2018-11-13): https://www.rbb24.de/politik/beitrag/2018/11/grenztote-berlin-mauer-innerdeutsche-grenze-studie.html?fbclid=IwAR1OM-kiLc-T2yR33vSF-6yuJIO8a9iuFk0pmlk-2H774Db4V-6H0MfNuzTE

Recker, Marie-Luise. 2005. *Geschichte der Bundesrepublik Deutschland*. 2nd Ed. München (p. 52).

Rosenberg, Arthur. 1984. *Entstehung und Geschichte der Weimarer Republik*. Frankfurt a.M. (p. 197)

Schindling, Anton. 2002. "Bauernkrieg" in: Klaus Ganzer and Bruno Steimer (eds.). *Lexikon der Reformationszeit*. 3rd Ed. Freiburg (pp. 61–63).

Schüddekopf, Otto-Ernst. 1966. "Die erste deutsche Republik." in: Golo Mann, Paul Kluke, Werner Conze, Otto-Ernst Schüddekopf, Dietrich Bracher, Hans-Adolf Jacobsen and Hans Herzfeld (eds.). *Unser Jahrhundert im Bild*, Gütersloh (pp. 213–396).

Schulz, Ursula (Hrsg.). 1978. *Die deutsche Arbeiterbewegung 1848–1849 in Augenzeugenberichten*. 2nd Ed. Munich.

Staritz, Dietrich. 1985. *Geschichte der DDR, 1949–1985*. Frankfurt a. M. (pp. 24–33, 138).

Steinacher, Roland. 2009. "Gebrauchsweisen! Der römische Germanen- und Germanienbegriff." in: *2000 Jahre Varusschlacht – Konflikt*. ed. by Varusschlacht im Osnabrücker Land GmbH. Stuttgart (pp. 78–82).

Steininger, Rolf. 1985. *Deutsche Geschichte 1945–1961 — Darstellung und Dokumentation in zwei Bänden, Bd. 2*. Frankfurt a. M. (pp. 376–378, 453–458, 498).

Taddey, Georg. 1998. "Fugger, Jabob II." in: Gerhard Taddey (ed.). *Lexikon der deutschen Geschichte*. Stuttgart (p. 422).

______. 1998. "Judenverfolgungen." in: Gerhard Taddey (ed.). *Lexikon der deutschen Geschichte*. Stuttgart (p. 61).

______. 1998. "Zwei-Schwerter-Lehre." in: Gerhard Taddey (ed.). *Lexikon der deutschen Geschichte*. Stuttgart (p. 1408).

Timmermann, Manfred. "Vom Wirtschaftswunder zur Wachstumsindustrie." in: Ellwein, Thomas and Wolfgang Bruder (eds.). 1985. *Ploetz: Die Bundesrepublik Deutschland*. 2nd Ed. Freiburg/Würzburg (pp. 41–45).

Ulrich, Gerhard. 1972. *Schätze deutscher Kunst*. Gütersloh (pp. 305–306).

Valentin, Veit and Erhard Klöss. 1991. *Geschichte der Deutschen*. Cologne (pp. 152, 158).

Weber, Hermann. 1991. *DDR – Grundriss der Geschichte*. Hannover (pp. 21, 34, 38, 146, 200–205, 212).

Weitz, Eric D. 2007. *Weimar Germany: promise and tragedy*. Princeton/Oxford (p. 91).

Wesel, Uwe. 1997. *Geschichte des Rechts*. Munich (p. 259).

Wilharm, Irmgard. 1985. *Deutsche Geschichte 1962–1983 — Dokumente in zwei Bänden, Bd. 2*. Frankfurt a. M. (p. 22).

Zimmerling, Dieter. 1993. *Die Hanse – Handelsmacht im Zeichen der Kogge*. Bindlach (pp. 21, 245–247).

Chapter 3 The German Legal System

References

Alder, John. 2011. *Constitutional Law and Administrative Law*. 8th Ed. New York.

Blumenwitz, Dieter. 2003. *Einführung in das anglo-amerikanische Recht*. 7th Ed. München.

Calmes-Brunet, Sylvia. 2014. "Rechtssicherheit und Vertrauensschutz im Verwaltungsrecht." *Juristische Schulung (JuS)* p. 1077.

Foster, Nigel and Satish Sule. 2010. *German Legal System and Laws*. 4th Ed. Oxford.

Haase, Richard and Rolf Keller. 2003. *Grundlagen und Grundformen des Rechts*. 11st Ed. Stuttgart.

Haase, Florian. 2005. "Einführung in die Methodik der Rechtsvergleichung." *Juristische Arbeitsblätter (JA)* p. 232.

Keller, Robert and Mara Hellstern. 2018. "Das öffentliche Interesse und Wettbewerb in der Daseinsvorsorge." *Neue Zeitschrift für Baurecht und Vergaberecht* p. 323.

Köbler, Gerhard. 2012. *Juristisches Wörterbuch — Für Studium und Ausbildung*. 15th Ed. Vahlen.

Krüper, Julian (ed.). 2017. *Grundlagen des Rechts*. 3rd edition. Baden-Baden.

Robbers, Gerhard. 2017. *An Introduction to German Law*. 6th Ed. Baden-Baden.

Schön, Walter and Rainer Holtschneider. 2007. *Die Reform des Bundesstaates*. Baden-Baden.

Tegethoff, Carsten. 2018. "Die Entwicklung des Verwaltungsverfahrensrechts in der Rechtsprechung." *Neue Zeitschrift für Verwaltungsrecht (NVwZ)* p. 1081.

Voßkuhle, Andreas and Ann-Katrin Kaufhold. 2012. "Grundwissen: Öffentliches Recht – Der Grundsatz der Gewaltenteilung." *Juristische Schulung* (*JuS*) p. 314.

Cases

Federal Administrative Court (Bundesverwaltungsgericht). Decision from 13.02.2013. *Neue Zeitschrift für Verwaltungsrecht (NVwZ)* 2013, p. 1082.

Chapter 4 Public Law

References

Augsburg, Ino and Sebastian Unger (eds.). 2012. *Basistexte: Grundrechtstheorie*. Baden-Baden.

Alder, John. 2011. *Constitutional Law and Administrative Law*. New York.

Badura, Peter. 2018. *Staatsrecht – Systematische Erläuterung des Grundgesetzes*. 7th Ed. Munich.

Foster, Nigel and Satish Sule. 2010. *German Legal System and Laws*. 4th Ed. Oxford.

Grimm, Dieter. 2007. "Proportionality in Canadian and German Constitutional Jurisprudence." 57 *University of Toronto Law Journal* 383.

Haase, Richard and Rolf Keller. 2003. *Grundlagen und Grundformen des Rechts*. 11th Ed. Stuttgart.

Hufen, Friedhelm. 2010. "Die Menschenwürde, Art. 1 I GG." *Juristische Schulung (JuS)* p. 1.

Isensee, Josef. 1994. "Braucht die Republik einen Präsidenten?" *Neue Juristische Wochenschrift (NJW)* p. 1329.

Jarass, Hans D. and Bodo Pieroth (eds.). 2018. *Grundgesetz für die Bundesrepublik Deutschland*. Kommentar. 15th Ed. Munich.

Kaufhold, Ann Kathrin. 2013. "Grundwissen – Öffentliches Recht: Die Wahlgrundsätze." *Juristische Schulung (JuS)* p. 1078.

Klöpfer, Michael. 2016. "Über erlaubte, unerwünschte und verbotene Parteien." *Neue Juristische Wochenschrift (NJW)* p. 3003.

______. 2017. "Parteienfinanzierung und NPD-Urteil – Zum Ausschluss der staatlichen Teilfinanzierung für verfassungsfeindliche Parteien." *Neue Zeitschrift für Verwaltungsrecht (NVwZ)* p. 913.

Kriele, Martin. 2003. *Einführung in die Staatslehre — Die geschichtlichen Legitimitätsgrundlagen des demokratischen Verfassungsstaates*. 6th Ed. Stuttgart.

Marschall, Stefan. 2016. *Parlamentarismus – Eine Einführung*. 2nd Ed. Baden-Baden.

Maunz, Theodor and Gunter Düring (eds). 2018. *Grundgesetzkommentar*. München.

Möllers, Christoph. 2014. "Scope and Legitimacy of Judicial Review in German Constitutional Law — the Court versus the Political Process." in: Hermann Pünder and Christian Waldhoff (eds.). *Debates in German Public Law*. Oxford p. 9.

Morlok, Martin and Lothar Michael. 2019. *Staatsorganisationsrecht*. 4th Ed. Baden-Baden.

Peters, Wilfried and Norbert Janz. 2016. "Aktuelle Fragen des Versammlungsrechts — Rechtsprechungsübersicht." *LKV (Verwaltungsrechts-Zeitschrift für die Länder Berlin, Brandenburg, Sachsen, Sachsen-Anhalt und Thüringen)* p. 193.

Robbers, Gerhard. 2017. *An Introduction to German Law*. 6th Ed. Baden-Baden.

Schwarz, Kyrill-A. 2017. “Der Ausschluss verfassungsfeindlicher Parteien von der staatlichen Parteienfinanzierung.” *Neue Zeitschrift für Verwaltungsrecht (NVwZ)*-Beilage p. 39.

Sodan, Helge and Jan Ziekow. 2016. *Grundkurs Öffentliches Recht.* München.

Stelkens, Paul, Heinz Joachim Bonk and Michael Sachs (eds.). 2018. *Verwaltungsverfahrensgesetz (VwVfG)*. 9th Ed. Munich.

Stiehr, Friderike. 2015. “Das Parteiverbotsverfahren.” *Juristische Schulung (JuS)* p. 994.

Thiele, Alexander. 2017. “Neugestaltung des Wahlrechts zur Wiederbelebung der Demokratie.” *Zeitschrift für Rechtspolitik (ZRP)* p. 105.

Tschentscher, Axel. 2014. “Interpreting Fundamental Rights — Freedom versus Optimization.” in: Hermann Pünder and Christian Waldhoff (eds.). *Debates in German Public Law.* Oxford.

Voßkuhle, Andreas, Ann Katrin Kaufhold and Öffentliches Recht. 2010. “Das Rechtstaatsgebiet.” *Juristische Schulung (JuS)* p. 116.

Voßkuhle, Andreas. 2018. “Rechtsstaat unter Druck.” *DIE ZEIT*, no. 40.

Zippelius, Reinhold and Thomas Würtenberger. 2008. *Deutsches Staatsrecht*. 32nd Ed. Munich.

Cases

Bundesverfassungsgericht. Decision from 23.01.1957. - 2 BvE 2/56, *Neue Juristische Wochenschrift (NJW)* 1957, p. 377.

Bundesverfassungsgericht. Decision from 12.07.2001. - 1 BvQ 28/01 and 1 BvQ 30/01 – *Love Parade*

Bundesverfassungsgericht. Decision from 23.10.1952. BVerfGE 2, p. 1.

Bundesverfassungsgericht. Decision from 17.08.1956. BVerfGE 5, p. 85 – *KPD-Verbot*

Bundesverfassungsgericht. Decision from 15.01.1958. BVerfGE 7, p. 198 – *Lüth*

Bundesverfassungsgericht. Decision from 06.06.1981. BVerfGE 80, p. 137 – *Reiten im Walde*

Bundesverfassungsgericht. Decision from 14.05.1985. BVerfGE 69, p. 315 – *Brokdorf*

Bundesverfassungsgericht. Decision from 15.02.2006. BVerfGE 115, p. 118 – *Luftsicherheitsgesetz*

Chapter 5 Private Law

References

Brox, Hans Brox and Wolf-Dietrich Walker. 2015. *Besonderes Schuldrecht*. München.

Foster, Nigel and Satish Sule. 2010. *German Legal System and Laws*. 4th Ed. Oxford.

Haase, Richard and Rolf Keller. 2003. *Grundlagen und Grundformen des Rechts*. 11st Ed. Stuttgart.

Klode, Michael. 2009. "Punitive Damages - Ein aktueller Beitrag zum US-amerikanischen Strafschadensersatz." *Neue Juristische Online Zeitschrift* (NJOZ) p. 1762.

Märten, Judith Janna. 2012. "Personality Rights and Freedom of Expression – A Journey through the Development of German Jurispridence under the Influence of the European Court of Human Rights." *Journal of Media Law* (2) pp. 333–349.

Medicus, Dieter and Jens Petersen. 2017. *Bürgerliches Recht*. 26th Ed. Vahlen.

Neuner, Jörg. 2007. "Was ist eine Willenserklärung?" *Juristische Schulung* (*JuS*) p. 881.

Stürner, Rolf, in: *Jauernig* (ed.), *Bürgerliches Gesetzbuch*, 17th Ed. München 2018

Palandt. 2018. *Bürgerliches Gesetzbuch mit Nebengesetzen*. Kommentar. 77th Ed. München.

Picker, Eduard. 2015. "Das Deliktsrecht im Zivilrechtssystem." *Zeitschrift für die gesamte Privatrechtswissenschaft* (*ZfPW*) p. 385.

Robbers, Gerhard. 2017. *An Introduction to German Law*. 6th Ed. Baden-Baden.

Staudinger, Ansgar and Björn Steinrötter. 2007. "Minderjährige im Zivilrecht." *Juristische Schulung* (*JuS*) p. 97.

Weller, Frank. 2005. "Der Zugang von Willenserklärungen." *Juristische Schulung* (*JuS*) p. 788.

Cases

Bundesverfassungsgericht. Decision from 15.01.1958. *BVerfGE* 7, p. 198 – *Lüth*

Bundesgerichtshof. Decision from 21.12.1970. – II ZR 133/68, BGHZ 55, p. 1 153 – *Fleet Fall*

Bundesgerichtshof. Decision from 19.12.1995. – VI ZR 15/95, BGHZ 131, p.1 332 – *Caroline von Hannover*

Bundesgerichtshof. Decision from 14.05.2002. – XI ZR 50/51, BGHZ 151, p. 34

Bundesgerichtshof. Decision from 30.11.2004. – VI ZR 335/03 BGHZ 161, p. 180

Bundesgerichtshof. Decision from 27.03.2009. – V ZR 30/08, *Neue Juristische Wochenschrift* (*NJW*) 2009, p. 2120

Bundesgerichtshof. Decision from 17.02.2010. – VIII ZR 70/07, *Neue Juristische Wochenschrift Rechtsprechungsreport Zivilrecht* (*NJW-RR*) 2017, p. 1289

Bundesgerichtshof. Decision from 18.10.2017. – VIII ZR 32/16, *Neue Juristische Wochenschrift* (*NJW*) 2018, p. 150

Chapter 6 Criminal Law

References

Bandura, Albert. 1976. *Lernen am Modell. Ansätze zu einer sozial-kognitiven Lerntheorie*. Stuttgart.

Brugger, Winfried. 2006. "Hassrede, Beleidigung, Volksverhetzung." *Juristische Arbeitsblätter (JA)* p. 687.

Cohen, Albert K. 1951. *Delinquent Boys. The culture of the gang*. New York.

Dubber, Markus Dirk. 2005. "Theories of Crimes and Punishment in German Criminal Law." *The American Journal of Comparative Law*. Vol. 53, No. 3 (Summer, 2005), pp. 679–707.

Eppner, Dirk and Antje Hahn. 2006. "Die Tatbestände der Beleidigungsdelikte." *Juristische Schulung (JuS) p.* 860.

Eser, Albin and Detlev Sternberg-Lieben. 2014. in: Adolf Schönke and Horst Schröder (eds.). *Strafgesetzbuch Kommentar*. 29th Ed. Munich.

Fischer, Thomas (ed.). 2018. *Strafgesetzgesetzbuch mit Nebengesetzen, Kommentar.* 65th Ed. Munich.

Glaser, Daniel (ed.). 1974. *Handbook of Criminology*. Chicago.

Gentz, Werner. 1931/1932. "The Problem of Punishment in Germany." *22 Journal of Criminal Law and Criminology* (Am. Inst. Crim. L. & Criminology).

Haase, Richard and Rolf Keller. 2003. *Grundlagen und Grundformen des Rechts*, 11th Ed. Stuttgart.

Herren, Rüdiger. 1973. *Freud und die Kriminologie. Einführung in die psychoanalytische Kriminologie.* Stuttgart.

Hinderer, Patrick A. 2009. "Tatbestandsirrtum oder Verbotsirrtum?" *Juristische Schulung (JuS)* p. 864.

Hoffmann-Holland, Klaus. 2017. in: *Münchener Kommentar Strafgesetzbuch (MüKoStGB)*. 3rd Ed. Munich.

Joecks, Wolfgang. 2017. in: *Münchener Kommentar Strafgesetzbuch (MüKoStGB)*. 3rd Ed. Munich.

Krey, Volker and Robert Esser. 2012. *Deutsches Strafrecht — Allgemeiner Teil, Studienbuch in systematischer-induktiver Darstellung*. 5th Ed. Stuttgart.

Köhne, Michael. 2003. "Resozialisierungsunfähige Strafgefangene." *Zeitschrift für Rechtspolitik (ZRP) p.* 207.

Kühl, Kristian. 2014. "Das Unterlassungsdelikt." *Juristische Arbeitsblätter (JA)* p. 507.

Kunz, Karl-Ludwig. 1998. *Kriminologie*. 2nd Ed. Bern/Stuttgart/Wien.

Kunz, Karl-Ludwig and Tobias Singelnstein. 2016. *Kriminologie — Eine Grundlegung*. 7th Ed. Bern.

Mergen, Armand. 1968. *Der geborene Verbrecher*. Hamburg.

Mösl, Albert. 1981. "Zum Strafzumessungsrecht." *Neue Zeitschrift für Strafrecht (NStZ)* p. 425.

Murmann, Uwe. 2017. *Grundkurs Strafrecht — Allgemeiner Teil, Tötungsdelikte, Körperverletzungsdelikte*. 4th Ed. München.

Putzke, Holm. 2009. "Der strafbare Versuch." *Juristische Schulung (JuS)* p. 985.

Ransiek, Andreas. 2010. "Das unechte Unterlassungsdelikt." *Juristische Schulung (JuS)* p. 490.

Robbers, Gerhard. 2017. *An Introduction to German Law*. 6th Ed. Baden-Baden.

Schaffenstein, Friedrich, Werner Beulke and Sabine Swoboda. 2014. *Jugendstrafrecht – Eine systematische Darstellung*. 15th Ed. Stuttgart.

Cases

Bundesgerichtshof. *Neue Juristische Wochenschrift* (*NJW*) 1973, p. 255 – *Brusttaschenfall*

Bundesgerichtshof. Decision from 25.10.2012. – 4 StR 346/12, *Neue Zeitschrift für Strafrecht (NStZ)* 2013, p. 156

Bundesgerichtshof. Decision from 29.06.2016. – 2 StR 588/15, *Neue Zeitschrift für Strafrecht (NStZ)* 2016, p. 664

Bundegerichtshof. Decision from 8.12.2016. – I ZB 118/15, *Gewerblicher Rechtsschutz und Urheberrecht (GRUR)* 2017, p. 318 – *Dügida*

Bundesverfassungsgericht. Decision from 15.01.1958. – BVerfGE 7, p. 198 – *Lüth*

Bundesverfassungsgericht. Decision from 17.05.2016. – 1 BvR 257/14 – "ACAB," *Juristische Schulung (JuS)* 2016, p. 751

Bundesverfassungsgericht. Decision from 17.07.1984. – 1 BvR 816/82 *Neue Zeitschrift für Strafrecht (NStZ)* 2016, p. 313 – *Anachronistischer Zug*

Bundesverfassungsgericht. Decision from 4.02.2010. – 1 BvR 369/04, *Neue Juristische Wochenschrift (NJW)* 2010, p. 2193 – *Ausländerrückführung*

Chapter 7 Employment Law

References

Besgen, Nicolai. 2018. "1 para. 14." in: Christian Rolfs, Richard Giesen, Ralf Kreikebohm, Peter Udsching (eds.). *Becker'scher Online Kommentar Arbeits-*

recht. 48th Ed. Munich.

Däubler, Wolfgang. 2017. *Arbeitsrecht: Ratgeber für Beruf-Praxis-Studium*. 12th Ed. Frankfurt a. M.

Hanau, Hans. 2016. "Schöne digitale Arbeitswelt?" *Neue Juristische Wochenschrift (NJW)* p. 2613.

Niklas, Lisa-Marie. 2018. "Wie viel Urlaub steht mir eigentlich zu? – Fallstricke bei der Berechnung des Urlaubsanspruchs." *Arbeitsrecht Aktuell (ArbR)* pp. 193–196.

Oetker, Hartmut. 2018. "Kündigungsschutzgesetz (KSchG)." Section 1–2 KSchG. in: Rudi Müller-Glöge, Ulrich Preis, Ingrid Schmidt (eds.). *Erfurter Kommentar zum Arbeitsrecht*. 18th Ed. Munich.

Robbers, Gerhard. 2017. *An Introduction to German Law*. 6th Ed. Baden-Baden.

Tatje, Class. 2018. "Zeit ist Geld." *Die ZEIT*. 1st Februar. p. 1.

Online Sources

https://www.igmetall.de/metall-tarifrunde-2018-26283.htm (02.03.2018)

https://www.gesamtmetall.de/tarifpolitik/tarifrunden/tarifabschluss-der-metall-und-elektro-industrie (02.03.2018)

https://www.igmetall.de/metall-tarifrunde-2018-beschaeftigte-zum-abschluss-27062.htm (02.03.2018)

Chapter 8 Law Procedure

References

Al-Gazi, Mohamad and Andreas Merold. 2012. "Die Reichweite des Beweisverwertungsverbotes nach § 252 StPO." *Juristische Arbeitsblätter (JA)* p. 44.

Durner, Wolfgang. 2015. "Reformbedarf in der Verwaltungsgerichtsordnung." *Neue Zeitschrift für Verwaltungsrecht (NVwZ)* p. 841.

Frenz, Walter. 2011. "Die Anfechtungsklage." *Juristische Arbeitsblätter (JA)* p. 433.

Foster, Nigel and Satish Sule. 2010. *German Legal System and Laws*. 4th Ed. Oxford.

Geis, Max-Emanuel Geis and Sven Hinterseh. 2001. "Grundfälle zum Widerspruchsverfahren." *Juristische Schulung (JuS)* p. 1047.

Grunsky, Wolfgang and Florian Jacoby. 2014. *Zivilprozessrecht*. 14th Ed. München.

Haase, Richard and Rolf Keller. 2003. *Grundlagen und Grundformen des Rechts*. 11th Ed. Stuttgart.

Hillgruber, Christian and Christoph Goos. 2015. *Verfassungsprozessrecht*. 4th Ed. Heidelberg.

Klesczewski, Diethelm. 2013. *Strafprozessrecht*. 2nd Ed. Munich.

Lechner, Hans and Rüdiger Zuck (eds.). 2011. *Bundesverfassungsgerichtsgesetz Kommentar*. 6th Ed. Munich.

Meyer-Großner, Lutz and Bertram Schmidt (eds.). 2017. *Strafprozessordnung*. 60th Ed. Munich.

Meyer-Mews, Hans. 2004. "Beweisverwertungsverbote im Strafverfahren." *Juristische Schulung (JuS) p*. 126.

Mosbacher, Andreas. 2016. "Aktuelles Strafrecht." *Juristische Schulung (JuS)* 706.

Müller, Egon and Schmidt, Jens. 2016. "Aus der Rechtsprechung zum Recht der Strafverteidigung," *Neue Zeitschrift für Strafrecht (NStZ)*, p. 568

Pagenkopf, Martin. 2011. "Fachkompetenz und Legitimation der Richter des BVerfG." *Zeitschrift für Rechtspolitik (ZRP) p*. 229.

Paul, Tobias. 2013. "Unselbstständige Beweisverwertungsverbote in der Rechtsprechung." *Neue Zeitschrift für Strafrecht (NStZ) p*. 489.

Pünder, Herrmann. 2011. "Grundlagen des Verwaltungsverfahrensrecht." *Juristische Schulung (JuS)* p. 289.

Thomas, Heinz and Hans Putzo (eds.). 2014. *Zivilprozessrecht Kommentar*. 35th Ed. Munich.

Robbers, Gerhard. 2017. *An Introduction to German Law*. 6th Ed. Baden-Baden.

Schlaich, Klaus and Stefan Korioth. 2015. *Das Bundesverfassungsgericht — Stellung, Verfahren, Entscheidungen — Ein Studienbuch*. 10th Ed. Munich.

Wefing, Heinrich. 2018. "Gewand der Macht." *DIE ZEIT*. No 10/March. p. 2.

Wefing, Heinrich. 2018. "Auf der Suche nach Mr. Right." *DIE ZEIT*. No 39/September, p. 2.

Cases

Bundesgerichtshof. Decision from 27.02.1951. BGHSt 1, p. 39

Bundesgerichtshof. Decision from 15.01.1952. BGHSt 2, p. 99

Bundesgerichtshof. BGH, *Neue Zeitschrift für Strafrecht (NStZ)* 2013, p. 489

Bundesgerichtshof. Decision from 07.03.1996. BGHSt 42, p. 73

Bundesverfassungsgericht. Decision from 03.03.2004. BVerfGE 109, p. 279

Online Sources

https://www.bundesverfassungsgericht.de/EN/Das-Gericht/Gericht-und-Verfassungsorgan/gericht-und-verfassungsorgan_node.html, (12.09.2020).

https://www.bundesverfassungsgericht.de/EN/Verfahren/Der-Weg-zur-Entscheidung/der-weg-zur-entscheidung_node.html, (12.09.2020)

https://www.bundesverfassungsgericht.de/EN/Das-Gericht/Organisation/organisation_node.html, (12.09.2020)

References

Calliess, Christian. 2018. "Bausteine einer erneuerten Europäischen Union – Auf der Suche nach einem europäischen Weg: Überlegungen im Lichte eines Weißbuchs zur Europäischen Kommission zur Zukunft Europas." *Neue Zeitschrift für Verwaltungsrecht (NVwZ)* p. 1.

Dzehtsiarou, Kanstantsin. 2016. *European Consensus and the Legitimacy of the European Court of Human Rights*. Cambridge.

Gardiner, Richard K. 2003. *International Law*. Harlow.

Glas, Lize R. 2016. *The Theory, Potential and Practice of Procedural Dialogue in the European Convention on Human Rights System*. Cambridge.

Gerards, Janneke. 2011. "Pluralism, Deference and the Margin of Appreciation Doctrine." *European Law Journal*. Vol 17, No 1, p. 80.

Haase, Richard and Rolf Keller. 2003. *Grundlagen und Grundformen des Rechts*. 11th Ed. Stuttgart.

Hellmann, Vanessa. 2009. *Der Vertrag von Lissabon*. Heidelberg and Berlin.

Märten, Judith Janna. 2015. *Die Vielfalt des Persönlichkeitsschutzes – Pressefreiheit und Privatsphärenschutz in der Rechtsprechung des Europäischen Gerichtshofs für Menschenrechte, in Deutschland und im Vereinigten Königreich*, Baden-Baden.

Meyer, Franz C. 2007. "Die Rückkehr der Europäischen Verfassung? Ein Leitfaden zum Vertrag von Lissabon." *Zeitschrift für ausländisches öffentliches Recht und Völkerrecht (ZaöRV)* p. 1141.

Meyer-Ladewig, Jens, Martin Nettesheim and Stefan von Raumer (eds.). 2017. *EMRK, Europäische Menschenrechtskonvention, Handkommentar*. 4th Ed. Baden-Baden.

Schütze, Robert. 2012. *Introduction to European Law*. Cambridge.

Streinz, Rudolf, 2019, *Europarecht*, 11th Ed. München.

Veil, Winfried. 2018. "Die Datenschutz-Grundverordnung: Des Kaisers neue Kleider." *Neue Juristische Wochenschrift (NJW)* p. 686.

Voßkuhle, Andreas. 2010. "Multilevel Cooperation of the European Constitutional Courts." *European Constitutional Law Review* 6. p. 175.

Weber, Albrecht. 2008. "Vom Verfassungsvertrag zum Vertrag von Lissabon." *Europäische Zeitschrift für Wirtschaftsrecht (EuZW)* p. 7.

White, Robin C A and Claire Ovey. 2010. *The European Convention on Human Rights*. Oxford.

Weatherill, Stephen. 2012. *Cases and Materials on EU Law*. 10th Ed. Oxford.

Cases

European Court of Justice. Decision from 05.02.1963. case 26/62 – *Van Gend en Loos*

ECtHR. Decision from 07.12.1976. – No. 5493/72, Series A No. 24 – *Handyside v United Kingdom*

ECtHR. Decision from 08.07.2004. – App. No. 6339/05 – *Vo v France*

ECtHR. Decision from 24.06.2004. – App. No. 59320/00 – *von Hannover v Germany*

ECtHR. Decision from 10.04.2007. – App. No. 6339/05 – *Evans v United Kingdom*

ECtHR. Decision from 07.02.2012. – App. Nos. 40660/08 and 60641/08 – *von Hannover v Germany (No. 2)*

ECtHR. Decision from 07.02.2012. – App. No. 44585/10 – *Springer v Germany*

European Court of Justice. Decision from 13.05.2014. – C-131/12, NJW 2014, 2257 – *Inc. v Agencia Española de Protección de Datos, Mario Costeja González ruled by the ECJ*

Index